Chicken

Indian Single's Soul®

Chicken Soup for the Indian Single's Soul®

101 Stories of Love and Inspiration

Jack Canfield,
Mark Victor Hansen,
Shalini Saran

westland

We would like to acknowledge the following publishers and individuals for permission to reprint the following material. (Note: the stories that were penned anonymously or that are public domain are not included in this listing.)

Staying Single. Reprinted by permission of Tanya Mendonsa. © 2011 Tanya Mendonsa.

The Solitary Reaper. Reprinted by permission of Averil Gomes. © 2011 Averil Gomes.

Butterflies for My Soul. Reprinted by permission of Ambika Pillai. © 2011 Ambika Pillai.

(continued on page 413)

westland ltd
Venkat Towers, 165, P.H. Road, Maduravoyal, Chennai 600 095
No. 38/10 (New No.5), Raghava Nagar, New Timber Yard Layout, Bangalore 560 026
Survey No. A - 9, II Floor, Moula Ali Industrial Area, Moula Ali, Hyderabad 500 040
23/181, Anand Nagar, Nehru Road, Santacruz East, Mumbai 400 055
4322/3, Ansari Road, Daryaganj, New Delhi 110 002

Copyright © 2011 Chicken Soup for the Soul Publishing LLC

All rights reserved

10 9 8 7 6 5 4 3 2 1

ISBN: 978-93-80283-86-9

This edition is published under arrangement with Chicken Soup for the Soul Publishing LLC, its logos and marks are trademarks of Chicken Soup for the Soul Publishing LLC

This edition is for sale in India, Pakistan, Bangladesh, Nepal and Sri Lanka only

Cover photograph courtesy Corbis Images

Inside book formatting and typesetting by Ram Das Lal

Printed at Aegean Offset Printers, Greater Noida

This book is sold subject to the condition that it shall not by way of trade or otherwise, be lent, resold, hired out, circulated, and no reproduction in any form, in whole or in part (except for brief quotations in critical articles or reviews) may be made without written permission of the publishers.

Contents

Introduction ix

1. BEING SINGLE

Staying Single *Tanya Mendonsa* 2
The Solitary Reaper *Averil Gomes*..5
Butterflies for My Soul *Ambika Pillai* 10
A Perfect Life *Arjun K. Bose*..13
Mother, Not Martyr *Ingrid Albuquerque-Solomon* 18
Vermilion at Amber Light *Anuradha Nalapat*............................23
God, Why Me? *Ambika Pillai*..27
Shaped by Nature *O.V. Usha*..31
A Dream and a Mojo *Vaishali Shroff*...35
The Little Girl's Town *Shifa Maitra* 40
Amma *Radhika Singh*..44
How I Found My Inner Dog *Tanya Mendonsa* 50
Holding Out for an Elusive Hero *Namratha A. Kumar*.............55
Strange and Lovely Things Happen *Radhika Chandiramani*....58
Awaiting a Wedding *As told to Bharati Mirchandani* 61
Married, Yet Single! *Roma Kapadia* 65
Status? Umm ... Single *Mumukshu Mohanty* 68
Till Death Do Us Part *Anuradha Gupta* 73

Escapade   *Joie Bose Chatterjee* 76
Find Yourself   *Ritika Chawla* 80
Single at Forty   *Reema Moudgil* 83
Window to the Soul   *Saadiya Kochar* 87
It's Only Fair   *Shifa Maitra* 91
The Single Soul   *Bhawana Somayya* 95
Parallel Best   *Anonymous* 99

2. SINGLE AND HAPPY

Following the Tambourine Man   *Tanya Mendonsa* 104
The Singles' Club   *Shifa Maitra* 106
Love in Licatuc   *Srinath Girish* 109
Alone is Not Lonely   *Anonymous* 114
Single in India   *Iona Lou Leriou (As told to Sandhya Mendonca)* 119
One Last Sip of Sap   *Tanya Mendonsa* 122
Single Belle, Single Belle,
Single All the Way   *Ingrid Albuquerque-Solomon* 128
Twice Married   *Khursheed Dinshaw* 133
My Story   *Varun Todi* 135
Free as a Bird   *Sarita Varma* 140
Culinary Adventures   *Hemant Patil* 145
My Nomadic Daughter   *Nina Irani* 148
Sister Lavinia   *Eva Bell* 151
Ann's Date-o-logy   *Khursheed Dinshaw* 155
Rocking K   *Hemant Patil* 157

3. SINGLE PARENTING

Family in Court   *Ingrid Albuquerque-Solomon* 162
Jacob's Joy   *Nina Irani* 167
Sisters-in-Arms   *Nandita D'Souza* 170
Remembering My Father   *Ranjan Pal* 174
A Debt for Life   *Roma Kapadia* 178
An Army Couple   *Anuradha Gupta* 181

My Dad, Superman *Sanaea Patel*	186
Oh, Alisha! *Preetha Nair*	189
Pop Tate, Take a Bow *Aditya Sondhi*	192
Thunder of a Blunder *Anonymous*	196
No Child's Play *Preetha Nair*	201

4. INSPIRATIONAL SINGLES

Dreams are Forever *Sruti Mohapatra*	206
A Turn of Events *Uma Praman (As told to O.V. Usha)*	211
Arunchandra, My Teacher *Khursheed Dinshaw*	215
The Caregiver *As told to Bharati Mirchandani*	218
Against All Odds *As told to Roma Kapadia*	222
A Count of Blessings *Shaphali Jain*	225
Amazing Grace *Shalini Saran*	229
Nobody's Single in a Community *Anuradha Gupta*	234
Cooking and Singing *Nina Irani*	239
In Quiet Confidence *Eva Bell*	243
A Giver to the End *Monika Pant*	246
Vikram, My Inspiration *Sanaea Patel*	249
Radha Bai *Gargi Chopra (As told to Anita Jaswal)*	253
Sheela Bua *Archana Pant*	256
OSCAR-Worthy *As told to Roma Kapadia*	261
The Bigger Picture *Preetha Nair*	265
Standing on My Feet *Elizabeth Koshy (As told to O.V. Usha)*	268

5. MATCHMAKING

St. Joseph and the Spirit-Filled Husband *Averil Nunes*	274
Being Single *Shoumik De*	276
The Perfect Match *Sarita Varma*	282
Women, Journalism and Matrimony *Sharada Balasubramaniam*	287
Oh! Are You Still Single? *Parul Gupta*	291
Dog-Sense *Anonymous*	295
Single Warriors *Xerses Irani*	297

So Not Ready to Mingle!   *Shifa Maitra* 300
Single and Fancy-Free   *Nonda Chatterjee* 303
That Someone Special   *Abhilasha Agarwal* 308

6. STARTING AFRESH
The Single Marathon Runner   *Samir Soni*
(As told to Roma Kapadia) 312
Suddenly Single   *Sandhya Mendonca* 316
Towards the Sky   *Jael Silliman* 320
Bless this Mess!   *Amisha Shah* 324
A New Sunrise   *Vishakha Rana* 328
Rainbow in Your Heart   *Amisha Shah* 332
Fruit Plate   *Raamesh Gowri Raghavan* 336
Life is Beautiful   *Asha Francis* 340
Gini   *Rajyashree Dutt* 344
A Second Chance   *Asha Francis* 347
The Woman with Two Birthdays   *Shikha Aleya* 350
Single by Choice   *Nonda Chatterjee* 355
The Gift of Life   *As told to Sarita Varma* 359
Resurrected   *Monika Pant* 362
I Look Forward   *Anushree Karnani* 365
Mamma's Boy   *Hemant Patil* 368
The Chanting Room   *Sarita Varma* 371
Single and Sane   *Shifa Maitra* 375
Starting Anew   *Sarita Varma* 379
Bait of Hate   *Ingrid Albuquerque-Solomon* 384
Awakening   *Preetha Nair* 388
Who's Listening?   *Ingrid Albuquerque-Solomon* 392
The Divine Touch   *Vanaja (As told to O.V. Usha)* 396

More Chicken Soup? 401
Contributors 403
Permissions 413

Introduction

As I look back over the past year, I am pleased to say that putting together this book about single people has been a most interesting experience.

Considering I know only a handful of the fifty-six contributors personally, I am amazed how these stories eventually landed in my mailbox. I guess it is the magic of cyberspace, which facilitated the process of garnering potential authors.

Only a very few of these are creatively engaged with the written word. Some are journalists and editors. But we also have contributions from architects, lawyers, counsellors, teachers, a gallerist, homemakers, a hair-stylist, a graphic designer, social workers, management professionals, photographers and entrepreneurs. The viewpoints are accordingly varied.

The contributors have all taken time out to share their own experiences or those of others well known to them. For these are true stories. The end result is a collection of stories about single people who are single by choice, single because they just go with the flow or single because of circumstances. They are stories about people of all ages and whose experiences range from the light-hearted and happy to the most deeply inspiring. It's a bit like looking through a kaleidoscope into the world of single persons.

The first story I received was from a woman I did not know, a woman who had attempted suicide, and then was able to get a hold on herself. She is not a professional writer and at first, the telling of the story was awkward. But I remember reading it again and again and being very moved by the reality she was sharing.

That's what this book is about — sharing. And offering hope and inspiration.

There are young adults who share stories of heartbreak and survival, or funny anecdotes about a traditional society's attitude to single persons and the joyous comfort zone in which a group of singles hang out. There are poets and writers who dwell upon the state of being single. And then there are stories that reveal the transformation of an ordinary person into an extraordinary one, because he or she had the courage to hope, the determination to think positively, the ability to see the beauty in life, the strength to pick up the pieces and move on and the faith that life is nurturing, if one allows it to be so.

The word limit may have curtailed somewhat the intensity or complexity of the experiences, but if you read between the lines, the truth surfaces stronger and the stories become even more inspiring.

I had prepared just a few guidelines, nothing too specific, because I wanted the contributors to feel free to choose their subject. So the six categories into which the stories are grouped emerged closer to the finishing point.

The first section, 'Being Single', could well (with apologies to Jung) be called Dreams, Memories and Reflections. For it's what these stories are: reflections upon the state of being single, memories of fleeting moments which could only be part of a single person's life and cherished dreams.

The next category, 'Single and Happy', gives a taste of the joys of being single and proves that contrary to popular imagination, single people can and do find happiness, and that there are people who are single by choice and content in their decision.

In the 'Single Parenting' category there are stories by contributors who as adults can now recall with gratitude and mature understanding, what it meant to be raised by a single parent. There are stories about persons who are forced by circumstances to take on the responsibility of a child, others about persons coping with child rearing after the loss of a partner and stories that tell of the brave and loving choice of adoption.

The 'Inspirational Singles' category has stories about men and women who have surmounted the most difficult of situations, who have chosen to see the goodness in life, found meaning in what they do and a purpose in living. The 'Matchmaking' category has a collection of funny stories about conventional attitudes to marriage and traditional ways of matchmaking.

What emerges from the stories in the last section, 'Starting Afresh', is the importance and empowering quality of self-worth. It is the realisation of this, which can change the course of a person's life. Self-worth can give rise to the desire and the strength to rise above negative circumstance, to forge a new path, to move ahead, to say, 'I owe it to myself,' to say, 'I deserve better.'

In these hundred and one stories, there is something for every single soul — young, middle-aged or old; divorced or widowed; or simply single and happy-go-lucky by choice. Something that will warm your heart, make you smile, comfort you, or force you to pause and think.

At a personal level, I have to share an unexpected and utterly pleasant outcome of this editorial exercise. As I read the stories of some of the contributors, I recognised the energy and gaze of a potential writer. When I conveyed this to the concerned persons they confessed they had always wanted to write, but ….

So, through the exchange of many emails and some urging, some encouragement and some feedback, their talent has started taking shape. It is a fine thing to observe.

I have made new friends. And I have been touched by this sharing.

I hope that you, too, will be touched and inspired.

Shalini Saran

1

BEING SINGLE

I don't need a man to rectify my existence. The most profound relationship we'll ever have is the one with ourselves.

–Shirley MacLaine

Staying Single

I love being single. It's almost like being rich.
 — Sue Grafton (D is for Deadbeat)

To live alone
is like sitting in a warm garden
full
of ripe strawberries;

eating them slowly.

To sleep till noon
and, summoned by the
moon through an open window,
go out to dig and plant
in her company.

Letting the dishes pile up in the sink;
to stand, elbows on a wall,
in the cool wind,

eating a sandwich
of hot boiled egg and salt
at 3 a.m.

Not to answer the phone for days;
to sing the blues,
at top volume,
with Billie Holiday.

– A holiday!

It never stales,
nor loses its freshness.
To watch *Pretty Woman*
uninterrupted
by questions:
socks

screwdrivers

nails

all lost.

To live alone
the mind uncluttered
or crammed
with as much furniture
as you wish.

To flow like water,
only meeting natural obstacles,
which can be dealt with
naturally:
to avoid;
to work your way through;
or to carry them with you to a mutual
conclusion.

To live alone
so that the days assume
the rhythm of water:
a river that meets other rivers;
or becomes a waterfall;
or joins the sea;
or simply carries on,
in its particular way —

carries the light and the shadow,
the shallow and the deep,
the gravel and the lilies,
the wind and the rain —

to sing its own,

particular

song.

Tanya Mendonsa

The Solitary Reaper

My cheeks are flushed and I've broken into a sweat. It's a wintry evening in Dharamsala. I know I'm not feverish so I sit with my eyes firmly shut not moving an inch but inside I'm scrambling up and down a sheer cliff, knees scraped, hands sore and bloodied, pulse racing. I wonder if I should remove my pullover. A voice in my head yells back, 'You're supposed to be sitting in Adhishtan (to sit with firm determination), don't move!' Meditation is hard work and I am in love with the mendicant in me, with my bhikshu-bowl (monk's begging bowl) and shaven head, walking the path to salvation. A salvation I have not yet experienced but yearn for.

'I am not lonely, I'm fine,' I tell my anxious parents who fret that I have not 'settled down'. I never played 'house-house' as a little girl, had no make-belief husband or children. I love being alone and never perceived myself as 'single' in the disparaging way people often look at those who choose not to tie themselves in the bonds of matrimony. I didn't like tags even though my friends often called me the hermit, 'Ma, Guru-

Ma'; we laughed, wondering if we could buy ourselves villas in France out of the spoils.

Growing up I would often take the harbour line from Bandra to V.T. and walk up and down the rows of bookshops that dotted the Fort area. I didn't have much money then but the shopkeepers were kind to the girl who loved books and let her browse through them for hours, reading the whole book at times. It didn't bother me that I wasn't hanging around with friends, playing games or just chatting. I had me and it was enough.

The madness of adulthood came with equal nonchalance. My first job and my own money, books I could buy, dinners at expensive restaurants, shoes, clothes, random boyfriends, all the appendages of an up-and-coming woman on the go and I immersed myself into it with abandon. Life was frenetic, working late hours, partying, drinking, and hurtling down the fast track to nowhere. I accepted it as though it was natural but through it all I searched, for me …

Meditation, the word sounds gloriously blissful until you dare to step on the path. It is 4.30 a.m., I'm in my cell at Igatpuri wondering why it's so hot when it's quite cold outside. The sound of cascading sand and pebbles hits my ears and jolts me to the present. I curse the truck that's 'distracting me' while it disgorges its contents. Being in the moment is such hard work; the frailty of my mind never ceases to amaze me. I scramble to pull myself together, failing; I observe my breath and allow myself to be. The cool air enters my nostrils, a heavier and hotter air exits … cool … hot … cool … hot … cool … warm … cool.

How fickle the mind can be! It's so easy to accept when you

read it in books, someone else's experience, so hard when you experience it and realise it's true for you. Me, I was a 'superwoman', I could do anything, I was disciplined, I had control, I didn't have vices unless I wanted to have them and I never made anything into a habit ... I? Who was I kidding and what the hell was this 'I' worth when it could not even observe its own breathing for a minute. No ... not even a second ... even that seemed too long at first. Who was 'I'?

Sitting in unmoving silence I watch my fortress of ego take its first hits of reality realising this is just the beginning. My body aches, my mind jumping around like a marionette on speed, it dawns on me that the path ahead is so full of centuries of self-created bramble. I know 'nibbana' (liberation) lies somewhere out there but for now it remains a mirage, a distant dream but my ultimate goal and I'm not a quitter, at least not without having done my mile, so I sit and perspire and try to watch my mind free-wheeling, trying to rein it in, lasso, corral, just get it under control. Damn! 'How hard can it be?' It is.

It's 2 p.m. and my left leg goes into uncontrollable spasms, my arm twitches. I want to open my eyes and see if everyone in the room can see me shake but my eyes refuse to cooperate. I'm five years old, in vivid colour un-muted by time I watch myself abused. I'm thirteen, almost a woman but not quite: naïve, afraid, a child in a woman's body and trust that is violated, again. I'm too afraid to tell my parents or anyone so I hide myself the only way I can, in clothes that are 'three sizes too big'. It's not easy to share the truth when you're too ashamed to admit it yourself, so you hide what you think is the problem. I want to open my eyes but I'm transfixed as wave upon wave of raw emotion buried deep within comes crashing onto the shore of my consciousness — the years of hidden trauma, shame, pain, anger, guilt, it rises and keeps rising steadily and continuously till it dissolves. I'm no longer a victim. As realisation dawns the spasms abate, tears roll down my cheeks; I sit still and silent undoing my bonds. I am free.

I am a nomad, I live and I have never wanted, more or less. For years I chose celibacy of myriad sorts, the mind over raw desire, of the flesh, of money, of things I once craved. It's not easy; it comes up during the oddest moments of sitting in deep meditation, a wave of heat, a wildfire seeking to claim everything in its path and me standing alone clothed only by this sense of discipline that I had chosen daring it to consume me. I don't try to fight, I know I wouldn't last to the end so I stand my ground as stoic as the moment permits, watching it come closer and as I watch it begins to consume itself; one little victory.

My thoughts drift to the hands of Fate that brought me here. The universe which reaches out to me in so many ways, my God who has no religion but who I worship in the only way I know, the 'Mother' who gave me a glimpse into the sea of nibbana years ago in Pondicherry. I am blessed by providence and by the friends who stand by me whenever I need them, my parents who raised me the best way they could, my mother who inspires me with her desire to keep learning and growing, wonderful strangers who flit in and out of my karmic circle helping me walk the walk in strange unseeing ways, some becoming friends, some moving on ... and my little four-legged friends: Scamp, who helped me get over my fear of dogs; Meow, who in her all too brief existence helped me through a difficult time in my life and the old dog outside the Himalayan Trout House whose name I don't know, with whom I shared a long lovely 'chat' and who followed me for over two miles snapping at anyone who tried to take him back home. I believe I am blessed and as I sit in this hall full of other seeking souls I know I can never be lonely because there is so much to fill life with.

Averil Gomes

Butterflies for My Soul

Everything out of the ordinary fascinates me. As a child studying and living in the mountains made my imagination run wild. I believed in fairies, angels, ghosts, goblins, pixies, elves and all the little beings that kept the other side busy. Many a time you would catch me in the woods peering under the pristine white folds of a white spotted red mushroom looking for the little winged fairies, my ears plastered to the mossy ground listening to the goblins and prodding under the uprooted eucalyptus tree for a big fat white talking worm. Life was beautiful and a constant treat to the imagination.

Growing up, my fairytale thought process went into hibernation and life after death fascinated me as much as it scared me. I wondered about the passage from one life to another. I was convinced souls used other beings when they found themselves hanging between two worlds. I constantly wondered if I was getting into a morbid space. I do believe that God works in mysterious ways and He chose to do just that to me one disastrous day.

Soul mate comes to mind when I think of my best friend Alka. Her thirty-seventh birthday had just gone by. She had a wild party with so many of her friends that were unknown to me. I could not recognise a single soul there. I left early feeling uneasy and to make up for it I visited her the next day to spend quality time. That was the last I saw of her. She was murdered that night and to this day, eleven years later, no one knows who did it.

I was lost in the depths of depression. My friends Joey and Sunil decided to drag me out. Sitting on their terrace at 11p.m., feeling utterly miserable I told them that every time I thought about Alka, I envisioned beautiful butterflies. We sipped wine late into the night and at some point and to our utter astonishment — out of nowhere a big beautiful butterfly with magical wings settled on the brim of my wine glass, took a sip and flew away. I treasured the incident but curbed my emotions lest my childhood fantasies surfaced and I got lost in another world.

My emotions stayed in check till I lost the one man I always looked up to, modelled myself on and loved with all my heart ... my dad. We lost him to cancer and it broke our hearts. I found myself experiencing that strongest and deepest sense of loss that follows the death of a much-loved parent. Wondering if I would ever emerge from that dark despair, I asked the universe for a sign that he really did love me, what with all the heartache I had given him through my growing-up years. Two divorces (unheard of down South) and then leaving home to head miles away from family must not have been the easiest thing for him to deal with. I looked skyward and asked for a sign. That night, with my loving family gathered around, talking about the times he kept us in splits with his funny crazy ways, out of the blue in full view of everyone, a big beautiful butterfly flew into the room and kissed me on the corner of my mouth. I will never forget the relief and the tears that went around that day. My mother instantly leaned towards me and said, 'Ambu, when I am gone and a colourful butterfly settles on your left shoulder, it's me.'

Magical is the word I think of when I let my thoughts backtrack to my past. I, of course, have two beautiful butterflies etched for life on my chest just below my left shoulder close to my heart, two tattoos in remembrance.

It does not matter how old or wise you get, life is about believing and listening to your inner voice. I still believe in angels, fairies and butterflies and that keeps me smiling.

Ambika Pillai

A Perfect Life

'Today is the day I take on the world,' I said to my reflection staring sharply back at me from the mirror, the red tilak (auspicious mark on the forehead) assuring that it will protect me. I did not mind that my thumb was stained red from the vermilion paste I had made for the tilak. In fact, I had woken up earlier than usual to pay homage to the gods and goddesses I had grown up worshipping. I was up till late the previous night, cleaning the pictures and idols with soap. I was acting as pious as possible; after all, that was all I had.

Though I had left home making my new job an alibi, I missed home. But frankly, the home I yearned for was never to be. When my parents died I was left in my maternal uncle's house. Abandoned, I had often wished for siblings to share my sorrow, my happiness, my anger and hatred but time had taught me to live alone. Although I am mature, at times I still wish I had siblings (if not my parents) like now, when I'm going to buy a car. Or, in the words of the salesman at Motilaal Motors: 'a brand new, second-hand car!'

In the absence of all who I could have made proud, I turn to the heavens and pray. I pray as earnestly as possible, sharing with God my innermost desires and fears. I prayed all morning asking for divine intervention to help me decide which car should I finally decide on — the sleek silver car or the more affordable red one. 'Help me make the correct decision,' I had said, concentrating on the collection of deities displayed in the corner I had reserved for worship. 'Next, I'll buy an apartment. Get married. Live the perfect life,' I had told my gods, before I left for the showroom.

Though in the final race, the pocket had prevailed, the euphoria that ran though my veins as I settled for the small red car was inexplicable. As my hands became accustomed to the grip of the steering wheel and my skin to the chill of the air-conditioning, my usual modesty took a backseat and was replaced by pride. A part of me sniggered at all the people rushing past me in their two-wheelers. 'Don't let your filthy fingers touch the car and ruin it!' I yelled at the little magazine seller who had made the mistake of leaning on the car to grab my attention. This happened at the traffic signal near my locality. He was trying his luck at selling me a magazine. With a dejected look on his face, he had backed off. But at that moment, my glee seemed far more important than that little boy's smile — after all I had spent all my life's savings on this car.

As I reached closer home I slowed down, hoping to make my entry in the new car rather prominent. Even a jealous nod from a neighbour would have made my day but unfortunately summer afternoons are times when people generally don't venture out. The spirit that had been bubbling in me suddenly fell flat. Approaching home, it suddenly occurred to me that a part of me was driven by social approval. But whose approval was I yearning for? Who was I saving all that money for? Incidentally, buying the car had also made me happy but that was not all, was it? I pushed the brakes of the car and decided not to go home.

I attempted a mental list of all the things I would have ideally liked to do but never got around doing. Getting married was the first thought that came to my head. It's what everyone keeps on telling me to do. But why couldn't I be happy as I was? Was marriage the only solution? Then, suddenly, it crossed my mind that I had never taken a holiday. I could drive down the highway to wherever the road would take me to. Thoughts of marriage disappeared. A road trip would be great! In the reckless mood that I was in, I immediately turned the car around and turned towards the highway without packing a single thing. What has become of me, I thought with a smile pasted on my face as the latest hit blasted from the radio.

The traffic was slow that day. I was stuck for a long time, or so it seemed. The magazine seller didn't leave the pavement this time, but kept giving me dirty looks. As I zoomed away, leaving the boy standing on the pavement, I began to feel uncomfortable. There was something about the way he looked that made me feel guilty. So I turned around and went back to the signal. The boy was still standing on the pavement, watching cars go by ... he seemed to have lost the zeal to sell his magazines. I called out to him. He ignored me. I called again. As if wanting to make it known that he was offended, he turned his face away. I found that touching. I was affecting someone. For the second time that day, I was filled with a new strange elation I had not experienced earlier. I pulled over, got out of the car and went to him.

'What is your name?'

'Chandu.'

'Are you angry with me?'

'Yes!'

'Will you forgive me if I say sorry?'

'No.'

'Will you forgive me if I take you for a drive?'

'In your car?'

'Yes.'

'Can I bring my friends Bittu and Madhubala? They have never been inside a car either.'

The gleam in his eyes said that he had forgiven me as I nodded. But when I made the mistake of asking him and his two friends (who had miraculously appeared in a jiffy) to take permission from their parents, the joy in their eyes disappeared. 'We don't have parents,' said Bittu, who appeared to be the eldest of the trio.

I tried to lighten the mood while getting into the car and said, 'Very good! You can come along with me. By the way, who named her Madhubala? It's such a beautiful name.'

The little girl giggled as Chandu replied, 'She was found under a poster of the actress Madhubala!' I laughed along with the kids and joined them in singing popular songs. I was singing after a long time.

After some time, I pulled over to buy food. Boiled eggs and fruitcake was all the kids yearned for. It reminded me of the tiffin my mother used to give me. The car was riding like a dream and even the potholes seemed fewer. Bittu was fiddling with the knobs on the dashboard. Chandu was dropping bits of egg-yolk on the seat-cover. Madhubala was drooling on the windows, as she stuck her head out to feel the wind.

Me? I was still alone, without any real family. But it didn't matter, for suddenly life seemed so perfect.

Arjun K. Bose

Mother, Not Martyr

I was greeted by such shocked incredulity that if I had not been processing this suggestion for many weeks before I put it forth, I might have quickly withdrawn it and run from the room.

The suggestion: would two of my three adult children consider moving out of the house and into a two-bedroom apartment that had miraculously come our way? The third adult child was also present but the suggestion did not apply to her since she was getting married in a few weeks.

In fact, that was one of the two events that had precipitated this discussion. The second event was that a comfortable rental apartment had come our way. At the nth hour the landlord decided he did not want to rent out the apartment to a company, as he would have to pay commercial tax.

That was when the idea was born; before surrendering it to the landlord, why not check with Johann (my eldest, a son, who was twenty-six) and Janet (the youngest, my darling twenty-two-year-old daughter) whether they wanted to move in there to live independently?

So here we are now, in shock zone.

'You are throwing us out!' said Janet in a voice that trembled.

'You are joking, aren't you Mom?' This came from Jackie, the bride-to-be.

Johann did not speak at once, just looked at me with that steady, unnerving gaze. Then he said, 'Why?'

I measured my words as I spoke: 'I love you guys dearly and I will remain a mother all my life. But darlings, I am tired of being a parent. I, too, have personal desires and things I want to do before I turn old and unable.'

'Like what?' said three voices in conjunction.

I could understand their consternation. This kind of thing simply does not happen in the Indian context. It's the mother who is supposed to cry and try to stop her unmarried children from leaving the house when they want to, not the other way around.

Was I being different? Not at all! As a single parent family, my children and I had had wonderful innings ... we had set up cute traditions and stored up memories of fun times, none of us had turned to drugs, alcohol or promiscuity; we had developed spiritual strength and maturity and I could not thank the Lord enough for using the situation to build us up and not tear us down as human beings.

However, in solitary moments during the months before this particular day, I had begun to notice jagged stones appearing in the Shangri-La that our home had been. I sensed these could cause potholes in the onward journey. I could never get to see a TV program I liked; even if I was watching one, the remote was pulled out of my hand for no one expects a mom to have a favourite programme. I like cats but my son hates them,

I'm crazy about animals, bonsai plants, Bible study, tailoring, joining a church choir. When on earth was I going to start if not now?

Above all, as they grow into complete adulthood, children turn, well, not exactly disrespectful, but they are preoccupied, impatient, their words are not always kind. Fact is, as they are growing up, you are growing older, so you turn ultra-sensitive (change of life and all that).

For the first time, I realised exactly why, in the West, children are barely out of their teens when they are encouraged to move out of their parents' home. I think it saves the beauty in a relationship and prevents thorns from popping out.

However, I did not mention all of these things when I answered their question with careful words: 'Please children, I am not throwing anyone out, don't even think such a thing. We have had such a great time so far that I just do not want it to turn into a downhill trip. You need to have the opportunity to make independent decisions. Budget, plan and run your own home. I believe I have done not just my duty, but 'double duty' as a parent, since your father went away. Now, I want to do other things with my life otherwise I may spend the rest of my life getting clothes washed and seeing that meals are prepared. I want to have regular Bible studies for friends, keeps cats, dogs and such things.'

Seeing a very fine mist in Janet's eyes, I finally said: 'Look children, I would not even have thought of such a thing if this apartment had not come our way at this price. It is close by. Moreover, we meet every day because of the family business. I want you to think about it seriously for a day or two. If you like the idea, we'll go for it. Otherwise, we will forget we even had this conversation, okay?'

They agreed, wearing their best Good Friday faces.

I am sure they must have discussed it threadbare for in a few days they came back and quietly announced (no smiles) they wanted to try out the living alone process.

So before the startled eyes of neighbours and relatives, my two adult but unmarried children moved into their own digs and began the process of living on their own. The night they left, I cried myself to sleep. I felt I was a few rungs lower on the ladder of kindness than Cinderella's stepmother had been and I had to resist the urge to run to them and call them back.

Somehow I held on, believing it was the right thing for all of us.

It took two or three months for raw feelings to subside and then suddenly, there was joy in the situation — one more house (apart from mine and my married daughter's) to gather together and have fun in, birthday parties, Christmas decorations, lots of sharing of experiences with neighbours, vendors, stuff like that. What delighted my heart the most was that their relationship with God grew in leaps and bounds. They got more involved in church activity and their friends' lists became longer and longer. We also developed boundaries of mutual consideration so that no one really gate crashed into another's life or home. We called before dropping in, to find out if it were convenient to drop in. We met in our office every single day. The taking-for-granted element went out of our relationship and we abided in mutual respect, treasuring the time we had together before parting each evening.

A few years down the line, Janet made the decision to go to Australia to do a course in Creative Arts; later, my son allowed God to lead him to the right life partner.

It was not selfishness but tough love that had prompted the unusual decision to let go of my children, and whip up a life for myself. I now have a dog, two cats and forty birds from six different species, and the family is growing all the time. Friday is set aside for family time when we all meet, usually in my house.

Sometimes it calls for shock to make life rock, doesn't it?

Ingrid Albuquerque-Solomon

Vermilion at Amber Light

Come to think of it, she was the one who had browsed the net and chanced upon Little Stars, the ideal kindergarten for Arush. No long queues behind an unapologetic half-open window for admission forms and no interviews. Whew! What a relief that was. What if he just didn't give his name when asked? What if, in that sudden inspiring moment Arush decided to answer a question with another question or throw back the same question? What is your name, baby? Answer: Whatees your name, babeee? How old are you? Answer: Ow old are youuu? Or what if he answered, 'My name ees nimbooo paaniii,' like he always did and rolled into a bout of laughter? Would she then have to apologise, pinch him and prod him to give the right answer, or could she just laugh it off as a childish prank. Would the teachers understand?

Therefore, she, Kavitha Sudarsan, daughter of Mrs and Mr Venugopal, wife of Tarun Sudarsan, and mother of Arush, had decided to put their child in Little Stars, a normal school with normal windows.

When Tarun came home with those pock marks and when his mother applied Neem paste and predicted recovery in two days, she was the one who, against everyone's wishes, insisted that he be hospitalised. What if it were chicken pox? What if it were small pox or measles? What if little Arush contacted it?

When her husband had died of chicken pox in a private hospital in Assam and no one could come to terms with the tragedy, the guilt, the anger and the helplessness, she was the one who had decided to look for a job in Bangalore. She lived alone and was a survivor in her own right, but she never did feel alone because friends and family were always there. All this was more than ten years ago and Kavita was thirty-six now and Arush had just turned ten last September.

After all these years, as she drove past the familiar high-rise buildings and up the highway and saw the loop of the adjacent flyover, an urge to straighten the loop rose defiantly within her. She automatically shifted to a lower gear, as the traffic began to crawl and darkness descended. Kavita noticed the setting sun and as always, her heart skipped a beat. Instinctively, she reached out to switch on the music. In quick response to nightfall, the lights came on, one by one. Her lights were now one amongst a million lights moving into the night. Suddenly, she felt alone.

'A very good evening to you. This is Rahoul on Radio City 91.1, your favourite FM channel.' She was grateful for the familiar voice. Rahoul was good for Kavita's wound up nerves. She slowed down at the red light and as her car came to a halt, she wiped her sweaty palms on her pants and in an effort to calm her nerves, took a deep breath. She stared blankly at the Ganesha figurine hanging from the rear view mirror, seeing it, but looking through the deity who was worshipped as the remover of all obstacles.

Her mind was focused elsewhere, reliving one of the memories that triggered panic attacks in her ... she saw herself walking in alone for a party hosted by her friend. She heard the sudden hush as she entered, a silence that reminded her that she didn't have a man by her side, that she was single. She suddenly felt the need to fill in that silence, to mask it with a random question or a forced, hollow laughter or by raising the bitter beer to her lips. Sometimes a frivolous comment on someone's attire helped.

Now, as the rear view mirror caught a flash of light, she thought, for a split second, that she saw bright red kumkum (vermilion, the mark of a married woman) aflame in the parting of her hair. Hope surged within her. Hope for the security that symbol bestowed. People would respect her, at least would leave her alone. And why? All because she was some man's property! Does a woman possess no inherent quality worthy of respect?

But there was no kumkum on her forehead and she felt dangerously alone, alone with her racing heart at the still traffic lights. Alone with her two breasts — symbols of her womanhood and definitely not desirable allies in the psychological battle she was waging. Oh! That kumkum box! What a perfect ally. If only she hadn't forgotten to refill it, if only there was a man, any man seated to her left instead of the computer bag. If only Arush were there!

She glanced away from the red of the bike idling to her right. She caught sight of a pair of faded jeans cut at the knees, its threads hanging loose. Two more red bikes moved in to her left and at least a couple more were visible in her rear view mirror. It was easier to pretend she hadn't seen the leering bikers and for a change she desperately wished for the eunuchs begging at traffic halts. One of the bikers had his hand on her door handle like it was his right...the same proprietorial way a husband sometimes lays his hands on his wife's shoulders.

Instinctively, Kavita opened her handbag and rummaged through it, pretending to look for something. She felt the stick-on-pad, a pen, some papers and a book ... Obama's *Audacity of Hope.* Then, all of a sudden, her fingers traced the rounded silver curve of steel shining against a black frame. Nokia! Hope! She grabbed the instrument and with a clean purposeful flick of her thumb she had slid the top cover up, and the screen was aflame.

She rolled her window down briskly in a sudden rush of adrenalin, rested her elbow on the frame, slid her dark glasses up and looked straight into the eyes of the biker. She was not alone anymore. She called her friend and talked and laughed. She leaned forward to take out a CD; she drove the stillness away, and the fears and the obstacles. The lights were turning green; the gear shaft fell to the first, the second, and the accelerator pumped in gas just at the audacity of hope.

Anuradha Nalapat

God, Why Me?

All my life, all I ever wanted was to be happily married with four children, preferably all girls, two dogs, a loving husband (who said 'I love you' at least twice a day), a house near the sea and probably one up in the mountains. I never did wish or want to be a high-powered businesswoman with a burning desire to grow beyond my imagination. But God works in mysterious ways. From my wish list I did get what I wanted most, one beautiful strong, courageous daughter who is the core of my being, my life. Being twice divorced did nothing to my ego, in fact I felt like a failure. My soul mate was nowhere in sight. Strange how life deals out the path one is forced to take much against your wishes or so it seems. People tell me my success story is inspirational. I take it in my stride and constantly ask God, why me?

There has to be a reason why life turned out just the opposite of what I so desperately wanted. I think I focused so hard on my destiny that He had no choice but to point it out to me. It all happened in a very mysterious way. It was a mother-daughter bonding night out. We hung around the lounge of a restaurant waiting for our table when an elegant French lady walked up to me and asked, 'You are Ambika, aren't you?' At my nod she went on to tell me how her life had changed after a hair cut by me a year ago. I think I must have questioned her with a slight snigger, wondering how one hair cut could possibly change anyone's life. She just looked at me, shook her head in wonder and said, 'Wow! You really don't know, do you?' For weeks I thought about what she could have meant. It intrigued me. Night after night I slept with the question reeling in my head. What was it that I didn't know? I probably would never have found out if she hadn't come back to me for a haircut two months later.

I didn't want to sound too eager but I had to find out. I waited patiently for her to settle in the chair. I got ready to start but driven by a stronger need, put down my scissor and comb and asked her what she had meant. It wasn't her place to tell me, she said, making me even more curious. She booked an appointment for me to have a telephonic session with a mystic lady in Los Angeles the following weekend. Aurilla, she said, would clear all my doubts. Aurilla was half Cherokee and half African American by origin and lived in Los Angeles. I couldn't wait. I had no idea what I was getting myself into. 'Session,' she'd said. I had no clue.

On Sunday morning I made my call. To get and keep a good reception in my phone and to have this 'session' in peace, I stepped out of my house to sit quietly on the front doorstep. Aurilla started by drawing a golden circle around both of us to keep us safe through the session. She asked me to make a list of all the questions I'd never gotten answers to in this lifetime. My list was long and tedious. I needed so many answers.

All my 'why' questions got answered one by one to my utter astonishment. The last few and most important of them all, 'God, why me? What have you put me on this earth for? What was my calling?' I got the most unexpected answer. It took my breath away. I shook my head in amazement and wonder and most of all, I questioned it yet again. Was it possible she had got it all wrong? I questioned her further. How could I tell if this was true? She must have seen this coming. She calmly said, 'Ambika I can see you. You are sitting in the front of your house. You have a mop of curly hair,' and while she spoke, out of nowhere a big monkey jumped onto my balcony wall to gaze at me. I swear I'd never seen a monkey in my colony before. I was in shock. She said calmly, 'Sit still. I see it. It won't harm you, it'll go away if you don't scare it.' Now I was totally blown away with no choice but to believe everything she was saying to me. Healer, she said, is what you are. You touch a part of a human body that is the most vulnerable, the crown, the soft spot of the head with your left hand to heal, to take away pain. People come in droves to you to heal. My head was spinning. I am a make-up artist and hairdresser by profession. Through the make-up session with a client my left hand stays lightly on the 'soft spot' to give me support while my right hand works on her face. Through haircuts my hands constantly touch a client's 'soft spot'. Suddenly my whole world was making more sense to me. My career was meant to be. All my previous episodes came to me in flashes. A week ago I had broken out in a cold sweat half way through a bridal make-up, seconds before my bride leaned against me in a dead faint. In a daze she had opened her eyes and called me 'mom'. Only later did I find out she had lost her mother six months ago.

I remembered a client telling me she had ulcers all over and inside her body. The next day I woke up with my mouth covered with ulcers. I told Aurilla story after story. Then she told me the real reason why my French client had wanted me to call her. She said, 'Ambika, you heal but you don't know how to safeguard yourself and that could someday kill you if you are not careful.' She gave me one remedy after another: 'Hold your hand under running water or knock on wood or shrug and wriggle your hands to free yourself of the pain you take from others.'

I am calmer now since my 'session'. I go about living my life exactly as I used to but am no longer plagued by questions. If I can help another soul, I am only too happy. Now I go through life with a purpose. I feel like a whole new world has opened up for me.

Ambika Pillai

Shaped by Nature

'Activate the will to do,' said Malati Teacher, giving one of her pep talks to her eighth standard girls, 'and sustain it. Only then can you achieve anything.'

The well-intentioned teacher wanted the kids to overcome their laziness and learning difficulties. One of her students, however, activated her will to experiment with something close to her heart — poetry. This little incident happened decades ago. And that eighth-standard kid was me. I discovered that I could summon words to evoke things I imagined and I wrote a poem. It turned out to be a magical experience, private and secret, giving pleasure and pain in equal measure.

It was a product of — among other things — the solitude that has been a part of my life ever since I can remember. Several factors contributed to this solitude. As a child, there was no peer group in the neighbourhood. Besides, I was a latecomer in my family, fourteen years younger than my sister who was four years younger than my brother. Furthermore, I did not go to a regular school till the age of nine. There was no school in my village or in the neighbouring areas, and in the fifties, there were no school buses picking up students from distant places.

I had no companions. My friends were stray cats and dogs and the cows in the cattle-shed. This solitude was enriched by an awareness of beauty that seeped in through my senses. The doors to the perception of beauty were thrown open for me by nature very early in my life.

I was a child of four, or even less, when my father planted the branch of a rose bush on one side of the yard outside the house. I watched excitedly as tender, reddish leaves appeared on it, then, how they turned green and how the branches sprouted. I was thrilled when the buds appeared and readied themselves, day by day, to bloom.

My mother woke me up early one morning and said: 'Get up, if you want to see how the rose buds have opened ...' I jumped up from the bed and ran out of the house and, in my haste, I fell down the steps of the portico into the yard. Instead of weeping and screaming, as was my wont on such occasions, I picked myself up and ran to the rose bed. And there I saw two of the loveliest natural pink roses I have ever seen in my life — two large roses, not fully opened and two or three buds awaiting their turn to blossom. I bent the prickly branch and inhaled their gentle fragrance. That plant became the medium through which I knew how a part of a plant, well tended or in congenial circumstances, developed into a new plant. It also taught me to love all plants.

One day, around this time, I was frolicking outside the house on a pleasant forenoon. All of a sudden, a radiant jewel-like blue struck me like lightning. I was petrified. It took some moments for me to grasp what it was. It was a view of the distant Western Ghats, resplendent in the sun. On looking back I see myself as a wild being, happy in a very natural environment.

There are no extremes in Kerala. A healthy person needs only cotton clothes throughout the year. Each season is lovely in its special way, but perhaps I loved the monsoon the most. I could watch the rain endlessly and it often rained endlessly.

Rain or shine, the kerosene in the lamps we lit those days would dry up in a couple of hours. So we would have our supper by seven. The village would be asleep in another hour or so. Silences punctuated the sounds of this existence. As a solitary child I grew very aware of these silences and often experienced a fullness, which, at times, was tinged with sadness.

A fairly wide sand road passed by my house, crossed a low bridge over a water canal and moved further between stretches of paddy fields on both sides. Then it turned and disappeared into a thick clump of trees. An occasional cart would pass, filling the calm air with the clatter of wooden wheels and the sound of bells around the bullocks' necks. There were other sounds too — the drone of beetles, the wind on Palmyra trees, bird calls, vendors selling ice-candy or vegetables or palm jaggery or brooms. From my doorstep I could watch the villagers walking on the road — all of them familiar. Once in a week there would be a purpose to this pastime ... I would be on the lookout for my grandfather, who would bring home a Malayalam weekly, which had a children's section I loved to read.

Although I had no schooling till the age of nine, I somehow picked up the Malayalam alphabet very early. I probably wanted to imitate my brother and sister who were college students and very involved in their books. As there were no children's literature available, I soon started reading novels and poems my brother and sister brought home. I could understand quite a lot and enjoyed reading. My mother tongue, Malayalam ('language of the hilly terrain'), has a rich tradition of poetry composed in a variety of metres, both Dravidian and Sanskrit. Lines of poetry stayed in my memory without any great effort on my part.

Thus it was Kerala's nature and its silences, which shaped my inner life. It was into this inner space that poetry made its quiet entry. As years went by, that magical experiment inspired by my teacher made me realise that I could pursue this craft myself. And as a single person, especially, poetry has been a great companion, for what I write brings fulfilment.

O.V. Usha

A Dream and a Mojo

The day begins at midnight as a one-year-old monster yelps in his sleep. It drowns out the din of the street dogs that have gang fights every night and the creepy sounds emanating from pests slinking around from somewhere. They're always around, you know. He howls and cries. I say, duh, tonight it's the pacifier's turn to calm him down. As I rest all my hopes on this invention-of-the-century and plug the little monster, he effortlessly pulls it out of his mouth, shouts, screams, howls, puts it back in his mouth, has fun chewing it, and pulls it out again for an action replay. The night goes on without a wink of sleep and I wake up feeling like a guitar that's completely out of tune.

From writing an innocent children's story, I can easily switch over to a mystery based on a serial killer who kills the milkman who rings the bell not once but twice before the crack of dawn, the cook who always turns up after lunch is packed and the mysterious maid who mops and cleans only in my dreams.

It was never so tough to write even when I was in college. As I stood on one leg in an overcrowded, sweat-flooded, fish-stinking local train compartment on the Harbour line or hung on a hope in a BEST bus in aamchi Mumbai, my mind was constantly at work. Creating characters, whisking, buttering, spicing them up and baking them to a beautiful golden brown till all of it made sense — it was a great pastime while travelling.

Now I not only need motivation, inspiration, and all the blessings possible, but also cooked meals, twice a day. A writer, in that sense, would seem to be the most idle creature on earth. He broods more than he ever writes. He lives like a single soul and when he dies his soul remains throbbing like a heartbeat in his work. It is that sense of immortality that drives a writer to abnormal extents; like insulating himself in the bathroom for hours on end, waiting on the railway platform, not for the train, but for his line of thought to end, or making notes on the reverse of bus and train ticket and treasuring them like gold.

But life always has something else in store for you. Whoever said we live on the edge? That way we have only one way to go. Down and out! We always live at crossroads. Those again have lanes and by lanes. And finally small little gullies where you need to tip toe. For there isn't any room for two happy feet to find ground.

I got married to a wonderful man who is still as wonderful, for his latest, most recent gift to me surpassed all others that he has given me over the last dozen years. A dimple-cheeked miracle, who laid siege on my life. And of course, life skidded around the corners and took a three hundred and sixty-degree turn, creating sand clouds that made goals distant or even invisible.

I wished solitude at times, if only for a little while, where I could wear the garb of my single status and type out my thoughts at the speed at which the auto rickshaw metre soars to dizzying numbers. At the rate at which Gulzar Saab gets younger with his poems. At the rate at which Ram Gopal Verma churns out flops.

Become Mr India. A gentle press on the tiny button of that gigantic golden watch and bang! I'm invisible! I could be just lying on my lazy chair, exploring new plots, new characters, perhaps in 'phoren' locales like Karan Johar. Gallivanting in my own world and my son gallivanting in his world around me. We are in our own worlds, yet we co-exist in one. Wow! It's like eating a Death by Chocolate at Corner House and finishing it too!

Or, then, maybe I could have super powers! Be one of the blessed weirdoes in the TV series heroes. Like Hiro Nakamura, who could teleport himself to any place, past or future! I could go back to the days when I was single. Just sit by my window with my notepad and Reynolds pen, gawk at the foliage and crows shedding good luck on car roofs. Daydream of Tom Cruise all day long. Travel places in my head. Enjoy a perfect date with Mr. Freedom. Brood and write more while I devour maa ke haath ka breakfast, lunch, snacks, dinner and more! Stay up all night, not changing diapers, but just staring at the creaking old Khaitan fan with its rusty blades, and dream! Run away into the clouds and drift to wherever the wind takes me. Burst into raindrops and become one with the earth, where again no one could outsmart my camouflage! Only difference being I'd fall with a thud and the dream sequence of my real life would come to an end.

But it was not me who fell! My little toddler fell from the bed, face down. As soon as he realised it, he quickly looked up, saving further injury to his jaw and unborn teeth. He cried. Not as bitterly as I did. But through his blood-masked face and a severely cut upper lip, he smiled when he saw me and the smile grew wider as I smiled back at him, my tears saying, 'Hell with you, Mommy, I'm gonna flow today!'

I don't know how he could smile in so much pain. How I still cry as I type this. Every time life decides to act funny with me, I think of his smiling face and all my troubles seem to fade away into oblivion. Now I've found my inspiration, motivation, the biggest blessing ever. I still wouldn't mind the cooked meals, though....

So like they say, I learnt the most important lesson in life from this tiny little single soul that hovers around me like a butterfly all day. From whom I tried to lose myself into the world of words. The one thing that distracted me the most is now my soul-inspiration to write. Yes, my days are numbered and gone. It's my baby who's at the fulcrum of everything. I had God in my womb. The most unsullied, shining chi!

Amid all the realities of a normal married life it was time to write new goals. Set new targets. So, between the sweet clamour, dirty diapers, soiled bibs, unwashed dishes, impending laundry and strewn toys, all I do is dream. About being the best mother and a writer, for if you have a dream, nothing can take it away from you. All you need is a Mojo, like my dimple-cheeked miracle who can't wait to see my face every morning and before going to bed, who smiles at me every time he gets a glimpse of the split-ends in my hair, recognises my breath as I tip toe into the room while he's asleep. Now I have mastered the art of making time to brood and to write. And guard my little angel, see him unfurl his wings, see them take flight!

Yes, I got a dream and a Mojo and now I let life live itself.

Vaishali Shroff

The Little Girl's Town

It was on a whim that I was driving to the airport, both amused and a little intrigued. I had picked the place off the top of my head and here I was setting out on my own adventure ... my first solo holiday.

Sure, people do that all the time but for me it was a first. A coming of age in many ways, I could do this I could do anything! Taking a break from work was tough enough and when I got time off, planning a break suddenly became stressful. I knew I needed time to be with myself and take stock of where I was headed. Part of me was tempted to stay home and do just that. Better sense prevailed when I had a sneak peek of the pending chores that I would have to look into.

Goa seemed like the most obvious choice. It was literally in the backyard and I knew the place like the back of my hand. I had forty-eight hours to decide where I would go and Goa seemed simple and uncomplicated. I did ask a few pals if they wanted to join in. Then, other options came to mind. Some places were on my 'to do' list; some came heavily recommended. Yet there was a voice telling me that I needed to do this by myself and go some place that just sounded exotic and felt like it was calling me.

A friend recommended I try a new company in Karnataka, called The Bucket List, which tailor-made holidays, and that had me hooked. Seemed like they already had what I was looking for. So when I was sent pictures of a gorgeous resort in a coffee plantation, with a great spa, I instantly said yes.

I didn't realise it was six hours away from Bangalore and when I began the drive I was wondering what I had got into. That's when I realised that sometimes going with the flow and trusting the universe is the only choice you have. Solo time is what I had yearned for and here it was. So I ventured ahead into this not-so-familiar territory.

Of course, calls and messages from family and friends didn't help. Some thought me mad and asked me to come back. Others said the peace and quiet would drive me insane. That egged me on. Surely I couldn't be such a slave to the bad life?

Mr Srinivas, my guide and driver, set the tone for the next four days. Tough but interesting, if I made the effort. He looked like a bank manager and spoke like a doctor. We honestly didn't know what to make of each other. He told me that Chikmagalur, my destination, actually meant 'the little girl's town' in Kannada. It was gifted by a rich merchant to his little daughter as part of her dowry. Seemed ironical that I had chosen a town thus named when I needed to feel that I was no longer a little girl who needed to be chaperoned, even on a break!

Google threw in more surprises. This was the place from

where coffee, my constant companion, first entered India. It was also Indira Gandhi's constituency before Amethi. A friend had a charming anecdote about how her brother called a lady Chikmagalur as a kid. With my camera, the landscape suddenly began coming to life. It was a festival of sorts and women, in all their finery, lined the streets at times blocking traffic. Mr Srinivas pretended to be angry, which was quite endearing. En route we stopped for south Indian filter coffee and steaming hot idlis. I was enjoying myself. I got into the groove listening to cheesy Tamil songs and discussing the phenomenal 'Rajni Sir' with Mr Srinivas. My phone and computer were allowed to take a break as well.

There was an aroma of coffee in the air as we drove uphill. Chikmagalur has the vibes of a hill station, even though it is not at a great height. It has a colonial air with old British structures and green roundabouts and if you saw an Englishman riding past you would be tempted to tip your hat.

Then there was 'The Serai'. Calling it just a resort would be unfair; it honestly is something else. Luxury takes on another meaning here. What is about this place is it's amazing yet understated elegance and the way they unobtrusively spoil you. It takes a couple of hours getting used to a private villa with a diving pool, a Jacuzzi and an outdoor shower!

Early morning walks in the coffee plantation is what I decided on. Well-trained staff showed me around and let me wander at will. The place is in the Cafe Coffee Day plantation. Felt like I was home; maybe I was a Colombian coffee planter in a previous birth? I saw coffee seeds in different stages — from green to red to brown. I also got to know how coffee and pepper grow together in these parts. Both need each other to flourish. Set me thinking. Peace and chaos in the right proportions?

Hot stone massages, meditating in the forest clearing and sampling the local cuisine in the finest china. I knew I had made the right choice. What for me was a first and a great beginning, was the fact that I did not miss my phone, TV or social networks. It was a revelation and an achievement.

I was asleep by eleven and up at seven. The best part is that the routine continues even now that I am back to real life. If I can keep to that timing and my no smoking stance, my life will be perfect. Of course the clincher for me has been the life-changing holiday. Did some amount of writing, a fair amount of reading and lots of thinking and rid my mind of toxic people and situations.

The sheer joy of not having to second-guess what your partner is thinking is inexplicable. The more I think about it the more I am convinced that I had to go to Chikmagalur because I was the little girl in the little girl's town! Solo holidays are hugely recommended!

Shifa Maitra

Amma

I first met Amma in Simla in 1975 in Burj House, an elegant residence allotted to the IAS officer who served as Secretary to the Governor of Himachal Pradesh. That officer was Amma's husband. Of course, in those days, I was only 'going around' with Vivek, and therefore, and most inappropriately, called his parents Uncle and Aunty. Vina Srivastava had magic in her fingers. She had to just touch something and it bloomed, or turned itself into elegant upholstery or a gourmet dish without fuss. Her home was bright with flowers, budgerigars and Silky, a black Labrador. There were stables attached to the house and Vivek and I rode enthusiastically every morning cantering noisily up the slope to the Vice-regal Lodge as we fell madly in love.

Of course Amma ensured that I slept in a bedroom across her own so there was no chance of nocturnal adventures. I was as terrified of her sharp tongue as I was in awe of her obvious talents. Among all the exciting things we did that summer, Vivek and I got caught in a raging thunderstorm, and I ended up with a really bad head cold. Till today I have not been able to erase the memory of the stinging pain in my nostrils when Amma flattened me on my back every night to administer hot mustard oil into my nose. 'There's no need to waste money on nose drops when we have the best remedies at home,' she said sternly with the cotton wool hovering over my face when I protested that we normally used Otrivin and I didn't like this horrible oil. Needless to say I was well in three days. Amma had a solution to everything and it was always homemade. I never forgot the lesson!

Four years later Vivek and I married and in the meantime the Srivastavas had moved to Kirsten Hall. The house was over hundred years old and Amma transformed the top floor of the large rambling cottage into one of Simla's most beautiful homes with a gorgeous view of the sunset. The main door opened straight onto the Mall road between hillsides covered with geraniums, lilies, poppies, hydrangea and orchids. Multiple shades of green ferns and ivy rambled over the railings and climbed up the roof. I had thought hard about what to call my in-laws because the names had to be distinct from my own Ma and Dad, and so Amma and Papa it came to be.

'Do you cook?' Amma asked, as I tumbled out of bed at eight in the morning, newly married and guilty to be sleeping while she finished cooking lunch before leaving for her B.Ed. class in St. Bedes College. 'Well, don't turn the vegetables so many times on the fire, or they'll get mashed up!'

I did not particularly care for housework and Amma and I had many arguments in those days. She was house proud, super efficient, and academically brilliant in political science, history and languages, particularly Hindi. I was studying for my doctorate in sociology while working as a fashion model and theatre artist in Delhi. We clashed over the concept of privacy, language and the late nights that Vivek and I spent out of the house. Amma said privacy was an upper class phenomenon when I wanted to keep my bedroom door locked. She said middle class Indians put their clothes on in the bathroom before coming out. I was obviously bred in a western culture and lived as an alien in my own country!

'Can you write Hindi?' Amma inquired when I said I would deal with the dhobi who came in every Tuesday. Ashamed at my lack of proficiency in Punjabi, (my mother tongue, so to speak!), I tried hard to fast track into speaking the elegant Hindustani that was used in the Srivastava household. I accompanied Amma on the Mall walking at a furious pace to collect provisions from stores located at different levels below the Ridge, and earned her appreciation at my willingness to befriend my new life. I loved the mountains and the warmth of the people we encountered every day on the Mall. Amma and I soon realised that we were enjoying each other's company and I found myself occupying a daughter's space in a home that had bred only sons. I also learned to cook.

This would remain a sweet story on mothers-in-law if destiny had not plotted another path for me.

Within the next seven years, Vivek and I had parted company never to live together again as husband and wife. As that fairy tale was stumbling to its hurtful end, another story was being written. With Vivek far away in the US I hurled my hurt at the breakdown of my marriage onto my in-laws. Amma bore the brunt of it. I was working in Delhi and looking after a three-year-old daughter. The Srivastavas had retired to Dehradun and I visited them every year during Ishita's school holidays.

I berated Amma constantly for not being able to fix things between Vivek and me. In my head I carried a notion that if she tried hard enough she could persuade her son to return to India and somehow save our marriage.

'What should I do to him?' she said, 'Stop talking to him if he does not listen to me?' Only once during all those years did she suggest that maybe I was equally to blame, and that if I agreed to join Vivek in the US with Ishita, we might have a chance to work it out.

'Why should I!' I exclaimed, 'Am I a beggar?' After that I stopped talking to Amma for a year, and sent Ishita alone to Dehradun.

Simultaneously I fell in love again. My new friend was in a troubled marriage and had asked for a divorce. I was separated from my husband and considered myself a single woman with a child. My boyfriend and I presented ourselves as a couple in Delhi and made no secret of our affair. I stated our intention to marry as soon as he was divorced and commenced my own divorce process as well. Through all this Amma continued to support me as an elder. She stated openly that Vivek and I were equally to blame for the breakdown in our marriage and that I must not be criticised for trying to start a new life. She offered advice only when asked and never forced her opinion on me. I now realise that I still don't know what she thought of this affair though I am aware of the disapproval from the wider family, Vivek's and mine.

Then suddenly my boyfriend died of a heart attack. We had not managed to obtain our divorces and so were not married. I was forty-two years old and devastated. Amma came down from Dehradun to manage my daughter and my home while

I grieved. She stayed with me for one month, cooking my favourite food and entertaining guests who came over to commiserate. I introduced Amma as 'my mother-in-law' and never thought it inappropriate. One night, distraught with my loss, I told Amma I felt like a widow without thinking that I was actually talking to my legal and living husband's mother! She comforted me into sleep, and it was only in the morning that I realised what I had said to her. When I apologised, she said it had not even occurred to her to connect the two realities. I had not offended her at all.

Another fourteen years have passed and I have remarried. In 2002, I introduced my prospective husband to Amma before accepting his offer of marriage. I told her that I would only take that step if she promised that our relationship would not change. I would not consider a life without her support. Three sets of parents had to bless my marriage to Omkar Goswami ... his parents, my parents and my soon to be ex in-laws. Vivek and I were finally divorced twenty-four years after getting married. We had lived separately for sixteen of those years. I had quite enjoyed my status as a single woman, readjusting old relationships rather than losing any. In this metamorphosis I became Amma's daughter, though sometimes it is simpler not to name the relationship. The story is complicated though most people in our lives know it anyway. Till today some people find it difficult to accept that Amma loves me independent of her role once as my mother-in-law. Sharing the same shelf in her drawing room in Dehradun — she has been a widow for some years — is a photograph of Omkar and me and of my life as a Srivastava daughter-in-law.

Neither Amma nor I find this story strange but many others have exhorted me to write it out and so I have. All I have to say is that maybe I never knew the disadvantages of being separated from my husband and living as a single woman because of the space I retained under Amma's eyes from the time I first met her in 1975.

Radhika Singh

How I Found My Inner Dog

When I was twenty-one, I left Kolkata for Paris (where I would spend the next twenty years), the idea of love and the ideal husband were as firmly intertwined in my head as I hoped I would be, someday, in that man's arms.

Eighteen years on, nothing had changed but the second part of the equation: for Husband, substitute Dog. In that interim, my life had undergone many, many sea changes before I had my epiphany.

The best time to make dramatic changes is when there's actually nothing dramatic going on. My little universe was ticking over nicely (apart from a heart that weighed more than I did at that point, over a prolonged bout of unrequited love). But, during one of my annual rejuvenating trips back to Goa to see my family, I suddenly realised there was something missing: I wasn't as happy to go back to Paris that January as I generally was.

Back in my flat, for about the first time in my life, I sat down on the floor of my hallway, stone sober, and emptied my mind slowly of all practicalities ... job, business partner, employees, friends, lovers, lame ducks — until I had created a great, big, empty space. I took a deep breath and asked myself what I wanted.

'A dog!' my gut shouted back instantly. 'I want that cocker spaniel, that little black and white boy — I can smell that milky breath, I'm kissing that silky head, I feel that ice-cold nose, I want him, I want him, I want him. Now!'

'What else?' I asked my gut.

'A garden,' it replied, not shouting any longer, but crooning seductively, 'a garden to write and to paint in.'

'That's it?'

'That's it.'

I then rapidly calculated how long it would take me to get things in order so I could change continents with a clear conscience; arrived at the figure of two years; wrote down that date; put on Leonard Cohen (*Songs of Love and Hate,* an all-time favourite, some things don't change) and, already romping in that mythical garden with my mythical pup, proceeded to get happily high.

I never regretted that decision. For a while, nobody took me very seriously. My business partner, of course, buried his head in the sand and would listen to no talk of finding or training a replacement for me. It was only when I packed up my desk and told him it was my last day on the job (having already written myself a severance cheque and paid my taxes in advance) that he got hysterical. It was only when I started packing up my flat that all the comrades started wailing, ' But why now?'

'When, then?' was all I could reply.

Always better to leave at a high point (except for the still-aching heart, but that is unavoidable being a woman — that is, until you find your dog) when nothing except something primeval deep inside you tells you it's time to go. Never wait until some negative event pushes you onto what you have persuaded yourself will be a wonderful new road but which turns out to be either a dead-end or a loop back to the beginning.

At 3 a.m. on a Tuesday morning at Mumbai airport, after a blissful flight spent reciting poetry with the Air India steward all night, I was groggily collecting a trolley for my luggage when an overweight, middle-aged man hit me in the ribs with his elbow and grabbed the trolley from me.

Did that dent my euphoria?

Nah.

I hadn't come back to India to find a man; I'd come back for a dog to find me.

As a smug Jane Eyre says at the end of the novel, 'Reader, I married him.'

His name is not Rochester but Joshua, a blue roan cocker spaniel who lives simply for pleasure. As we have the perfect union, I have adopted his way of life, and that without the slightest trace of guilt.

I won't start producing nude baby photos at this point, but will only say he was the most beautiful boy in the world and, now that he is middle-aged (and blind, like Rochester, but so much nicer), the years have only added to his perfection.

'If I can't have too many truffles,' said Colette (who also said that our perfect companions are all four-legged), 'I'll do without.'

That is Joshua and my joint philosophy too, but, metaphorically speaking, we generally see to it that we have too many truffles.

We find each other the funniest, best and most fascinating beings in the whole world. What better foundation for the good life can there be than unquestioning mutual adoration? We like the same things and the same people. We never argue. We howl when we're sad and laugh when we're happy. Our two hearts beat as one. He leads me when we walk together but, then, there is his masculine ego to cherish.

It is an indisputable fact that dog lovers tend to be nice people — open, generous, creative and unconventional (our unkinder critics would label these qualities respectively as 'foolishly trusting,' 'spendthrift,' 'lazy,' and 'not quite all there'). But then, they know nothing of the joy of being so ecstatically greeted, even after a five-minute absence, they see only the muddy paw marks on their white shirts. You would think that anyone with a grain of sense would realise their amazing luck at having Joshua (so handsome, so urbane, such a gifted conversationalist!) as a dinner partner: but no, they're looking at their plate that has been wiped clean before they've had a single bite.

But all these kill-joys are forgotten in the company of one's fellow enthusiasts. These are the 'real' people, with real values. With four-legged bodies cosily surrounding us and sometimes on top of us, and plenty of good food and drink to be communally shared (Josh is especially partial to a good calvados) we swap stories of our partners.

Their astonishing intelligence ('You see, he has such an eye for people: he bit the electrician and they just found out he's dealing drugs — well, he's safe in the hospital now'); their latest fads ('It's really lovely to have to get up to walk at 2 a.m...you discover a whole new world!'); their culinary preferences (the first cake I ever baked was for Josh). There are hot debates on medication (this, of course, involves riveting stories of midnight anguish, last-minute crises and miraculous recoveries).

I do actually have a two-legged male, a great artist called Antonio, in my life, but I have to admit that the reason he is still in it is that, from the first, he immediately and wisely, ceded first place to Joshua, thus letting the best man win and ensuring harmony in the home. Secondly, he's almost as mad about the boy as I am, which makes for positively good music!

My best (male) friend Siddharth Dube (who has a Portuguese Water Dog as his love), said, while I was writing this, 'Say I'd be the perfect dog! I'm gay, I'm gay all night and day! Pick me instead!'

I have to say, Rana, that if there had to be an alternative dog, it would have been you.

So: one piece of advice. Listen to your gut and let it lead you to your inner dog.

That out of the way, we can now get down to the nitty-gritty: those nudie baby photos. Here's the one commemorating his first bark...look at that face...have you ever seen anything as marvellous as that look in his eyes? Is that adorable, or is that adorable?

Kiss me quick, Josh, before I swoon all over again.

Tanya Mendonsa

Holding Out for an Elusive Hero

'Does she have someone?'
'There must be someone but they aren't telling us!'
'I think so too for why would they say no to such a good proposal?'

Being single, on the uncomfortable side of thirty and hesitant to mingle, means I have heard the above dialogue too many times. 'Well-wishers' and the odd matchmaker are staunchly convinced that the prime reason I say no to some truly spectacular (read: scary) proposals is that I have some wholly inappropriate boy tucked away in my back-pocket!

It doesn't matter that I have a brain and a discerning one at that, which throws up 'caution — tread softly' sign when an unsuitable proposal finds its way into my 'singledom'. Say a firm 'no' or even a lukewarm 'can we think about it?' and I get subjected to disbelieving glances and disapproving sniffs. I can see little word-bubbles form above their collective heads that say:

a) Who is she waiting for? Prince Charming? b) She is so choosy. She isn't exactly a Miss India herself, and c) Girls nowadays think no end of themselves (this last accompanied by a very verbal snort.)

When all the arguments have been exhausted, I get the ever-popular crowd-pleaser: 'But you have to make a compromise!' Sure I'll make a compromise. I'll ignore the glaring dissimilarities and give my assent too. I'll be the poster-child for compliance! But doesn't one need something basic to build upon? Some initial spark? Some essential element that makes one want to risk the rapids and take a hesitant yet definite plunge?

I demand that essential all-important spark. I would like to hear some bells clanging or at least some fireworks going off in the distance. And where on earth did these fanciful thoughts find their way into my practical head?

Unrealistic dreams ... shining heroes ... happily-ever-afters. Sounds familiar?

I'm instantly transported into the world of fairy tales and the lofty expectations that filled our impressionable heads and hearts. Since childhood, my friends and I have grown up on a steady albeit sugary diet of far, far away tales. It was a time when chivalrous princes walked the earth with the sole purpose of finding their 'one true love'. They would flick their deliciously rumpled hair, fix a narrow-eyed glance at the vile villains and battle evil forces with skill and guaranteed good results. Fair maidens (who came with the clichéd baggage of raw deals, conniving step-mothers and moustache-twirling villains) were swept off their feet before the book/reel ended. The miserable tides changed and the picture-perfect couple waved benevolently to a cheering, bucolic crowd as they rode off into the horizon.

And as we friends huddled over bowls of buttery popcorn, we ooh-ed and aah-ed and waited impatiently to be swept off our sneaker-clad feet. We hoped for miracles and the urban legend of 'the perfect man' to materialise.

Time passed and we all encountered more than our fair share of warty frogs, fire-breathing dragons and the occasional crafty sidekick. Princes were a long-buried species and the only time we got swept off our feet was when work ran us ragged, our blood sugar plunged and we needed an instant sugar-fix! The rose-coloured glasses were knocked off (or so we claimed). We decided to tuck our fancy ideals up into the high-tower, lock the doors and settle for something lukewarm.

But the problem with a fertile imagination and a 'never-say-die' optimism is that the high-tower rarely stays locked for long. A heart-warming book, an Audrey Hepburn/ Shrek movie, a quirky quote or even a song with just the right level of mushiness — anything and everything acts like a trigger. The bugle blares and the walls of Jericho are down again.

And some may call us fanciful ... hopeless even. But for me, it shows that despite the bad twists, bouts of rotten luck and the elusive search for Mr Knight-on-a-white-steed, we can't really let go of our hopes and dreams. We all want a happy-ending and are willing to wait. And if we have to meet our fair share of villains along the way, then so be it. After all, which self-respecting fairy tale would be complete without the evil cackle of a nasty witch!

Namratha A. Kumar

Strange and Lovely Things Happen

On my way back home from Amsterdam, after an exhausting work meeting, I was seated next to two people on the plane, economy class of course, so you can imagine the cramped quarters. They entered into some sort of negotiation with a woman sitting elsewhere and ultimately seats were exchanged much to my relief because now there was an empty seat between the woman and me (they were a couple and she was alone as far as I could tell).

She looked to be approaching her sixties ... Caucasian, very beautiful, in a balding Greta Garbo way. Absolutely striking smile, like she had a million watt light bulb inside her. But I was more concerned about getting some rest. I live alone and I knew I would be returning to a flat I would have to clean and dust. So for a long time I ignored her.

At some point, we started to talk. She asked about what I did. I told her in a guarded way, some gibberish about women's rights, only a part of the work that I actually do with a non-profit organisation, because who knows, she might be one of those right-wing abstinence-only folk that I am happy to battle on the ground, but not at 35, 000 feet above sea level. She was intrigued that I worked for women's issues and rights and told me that she was married to an Indian and was on her way to some remote village in Haryana to dedicate the rooftop of a village school that her husband had donated. So of course, we spoke of women's empowerment and female foeticide in Haryana and all the usual stuff, meanwhile also warming up to each other and disclosing increasing amounts of personal information.

She said I must come to Kansas (where she lives) and shock all the old biddies the next time I was in the US and pulled out her business card, which is where time stopped.

It was not an ordinary business card. The face of the card was a painting of a woman's nude body in the most striking colours and composition. It hit me so hard; I stopped breathing for a bit. Then I slowly turned it over and it was suddenly 'normal' — the ususal name, address, phone number, etc. I told her I loved it and asked if the painting was hers. She said yes, she paints, and discovered this gift only after she was diagnosed with cancer.

And then we really began talking like two real people. And the best was that we laughed so much that other passengers wanted to know what was bringing us such joy, and her husband, Om, sitting in another part of the plane noticed the hilarity and wanted to be part of it. At this point, after Om and I were introduced, she went on to share incidents from her past. One such was particularly funny; Om asks: 'You know, it's a bit embarrassing ... when will you stop drawing these female nudes? Says she: When you agree that I can draw you nude.'

I just cracked up — this amazingly self-contained woman,

this sweet, loving guy with his Indian legacy of 'decency,' and her completely insouciant but honest answer. How could I not love her spirit? And her bald head, her beautiful face, her generous spirit.

So, as we flew towards India and across the borders of all these countries fighting below us, we found something beautiful together and I asked her if we could use some of her art for a quarterly magazine we produce. I gave her a copy of the magazine; she looked at it, liked it, and said yes.

She also generously offered to send me the original painting of the image on her visiting card that had so entranced me in the first place, saying that she believes that her art belongs not to her, but has a place in the universe and finds its own person, and she is happy to know that this piece has found its home with me. She actually, later on, sent it to me, beautifully framed. I am so amazed and delighted that these connections happen.

On the plane she gave me a book on renal cancer that she had written (after having dealt with it in her own life). Along with the painting that she couriered, she also sent me a book called *What Lies Within* (her breast cancer journal; she had breast cancer after the renal cancer). She wrote, or rather drew that book because it has more art than words. Her name is Cynthia Chauhan, and the book has been published by Tall Grass Books.

The reason I am telling you about all this is because it lifted me out of myself, out of my 'single' existence. Each time I look at her painting, I come back to my life delighted that there are truly good people in the world, that we are all connected at some level, and that life is bigger than we think, generously giving gifts, making strange and lovely things happen ….

Radhika Chandiramani

Awaiting a Wedding

It is so wonderful to be in love. I wish my wedding date would be decided soon but my parents are so superstitious. Don't fix anything important during the shraddh season (time for remembering ancestors), they say. Before that it was the monsoon that kept them from going to her village to settle things. How long can a young man wait, I ask you. Each night after I clean up the kitchen and switch off the lights, I go out to lock the gates. There are usually some girls standing there. Prostitutes. They smile at me. I smile back. Sometimes there are eunuchs. One night, there was one dressed real smart with high heels and black tights. Dark lips. Two hundred rupees, a special rate for you. I'm married, I lied. Special rate for you and your wife she leered and, turning, stuck out her bum. She sounded like a man, but flirted like a woman.

My wife will have a gentle voice, and wear light-pink lipstick. I already love her voice, my new wife to be. She talks to me whenever she catches me alone ... especially when I bathe. No, she is not shy at all. She looks at each part of my body as I soap myself, as water clears the foam away.

'I am dark skinned,' I say to her each day.

'My Krishna,' she replies. I have begun to comb my hair with the centre parting she likes, and shave more often to look attractive though she never minds when I don't shave for days. I turn my back to her when I put on my vest, she must not see the tiny holes. I'll have new clothes when we are wed. I am putting aside money. The memsahibs will have to give me a loan as well. Twenty thousand, no, I will need at least thirty-five. Ten grand can be a wedding gift from them. They'll not think of it, of course. I'd better start hinting.

I would put my entire salary in the bank, but my parents keep asking for more and more. Daily living, they say, costs are rising. That is why I am here in Delhi, cooking food for memsahibs. Though I eat all the food that is left at the table, though I keep aside some with an extra dollop of ghee in the kitchen, I am not putting on any weight. I want to grow taller and broader before I get married. My wife mustn't think I am from a poor starving family. After all she will not see only my smart clothes. Looking at me bathing is not the same as seeing me remove my clothes on the night of the wedding. That will be special. Flowers in her hair, on the door, on the bed. Roses and marigold. Jasmine strong and sweet, not like this silly tea memsahibs drink. They call it jasmine tea, so I made myself a huge mug. Now I know better. Tasteless city food. They drink this only to show off their glittering rings by lifting the tea cups, with nails long and strangely coloured. Their breasts pushing the smooth weave of expensive blouses. Hips bulging in tight pants that end above their ankles, as if the cloth shrunk after a wash with an additional bulge around their middles from sitting around so much. No men these city women have in their lives. Men visit sometimes, sit quietly, eat and drink anything offered as fast as they can, and go away. Mostly it is women who come, women who chatter, women who eat and drink. Not just the hot water they call tea — they drink beer, wine, and whisky. The whole house reeks of the fumes. Yet they don't get drunk. At least not like the men in the village. Memsahibs possibly have another way of getting drunk. They must do it after I have gone up to my room.

My wife will never touch alcohol. I have never tasted it till now, but my uncle promised me a stiff drink after my wedding. You'll need it for your wedding night, he said. I must do all that is proper for her. My wife must lack nothing. I will have my first drink and go to her like a tall broad man. I hope the wedding photographs won't show her taller than me. With the computer they can do anything. I'll pay them extra to make me fair and big.

I won't cook for her, no my wife is not ever going to be a memsahib. She will wear salwars or saris like she does now, and smile gently, looking straight ahead without tilting her head to one side like city girls. How do they work in offices when they can't hold their heads straight? They go to work, carrying computers and files sometimes. They spend money, lots of money. So they must be earning big time. No men here. They earn for themselves. I went to one office once. That was when I went to an interview for this job. 'Madam, Madam,' everyone was saying as they led me to her room on the top floor. A big empty room with a huge table and enormous windows and tall plants like chapprasis (peons) waiting. One peon whispered, 'Tea?' Madam shook her head slightly. She wasn't wearing pants then, just a silk kurta with silk scarves like flags over her shoulders. I will get silk dupattas for my wife. When we go to see a film after we are married, or to the zoo with our children on a sunny afternoon after school, she will have scarves hanging from her arms. The children will skip along holding our hands. There will be two, first a girl, pretty like her mother but with pink bows in her hair, then a boy, with bright shiny eyes who will play first-class cricket.

My cell phone rang. My father. What is my wife's name? I asked.

We haven't decided which girl. We have three proposals. You will be informed at the proper time.

When your nephew Chandu came to the village last month, you showed him a photo that came with a proposal. He photographed it with his cell phone and got a printout done for me. It is blurred but she is pretty. She looks at me straight and we often talk to each other. I am already in love, Dad. You'd better hurry. Your son is deeply, madly, in love.

I spoke loud and clear in my mind but I heard my father say, 'No sound, signal tower fail,' and he disconnected.

As told to Bharati Mirchandani

Married, Yet Single!

Most people believe that once you are married you're far from being in the single zone ever again. I believed it too — until I got married. Now I can only wish it were true!

The antithesis? Once you get married you have a partner, but you're singled out as a married couple especially when you have only single friends.

It's been three special years since I've been married, but I have never been more 'single' in my life than in these very three years. My husband and I live together, without my in-laws, in Mumbai. I am a stay-at-home freelance-writer whereas my husband is a professional working with The Times of India. He leaves early in the morning and returns late at night, leaving me 'single' at home all day.

It's definitely out of choice that I work from home, because I like a neat and clean house and the flexibility my freelancing allows, but having said all that, how much time do I really spend with my husband? Maybe, two or three hours a day, barring the seven hours we sleep together.

So how much of a 'married couple' are we, really? Yet, all my single friends say, 'you are so married!' Fortunately or unfortunately, I really don't know. Most of my friends are single, men as well as girls. So, to all the girls I am a 'married woman' and they avoid disturbing me as they presume I may be busy with my husband. My single men friends avoid being their natural selves or refrain from flirting, which they did all these years, because now I am married and that isn't cool for them anymore. All the married couples — the few that I know with children — tell me I won't understand their situation as I don't have a child yet. So where does that actually leave me? Married or Single?

Honestly! Each to his or her own! Of course, it does not matter if you are married or not. In today's world, you're 'single' any which way. Life is getting more and more individualistic, and that's the way most of us prefer it, too, so why complain about one's single status. Because, believe me, when you are married you are even more single and have to fight your battles on your own.

Your closest single girlfriends don't understand your need to complain about your in-laws or your life as they think you are married and happy. Your single men friends look at you as though you're an aunty and on the brink of being pregnant every time you meet them, as though the shock of your marriage was not enough for them and they need something new to talk about. Your parents avoid joining you for dinner or the movies, as they want to give you 'space'. Your sibling does not confide in you as much, as he imagines there is no longer any confidentiality, that there are no secrets between husband and wife. Worst of all are your friends who have been married for too long, they think you are a novice; and the ones who have recently got married ... they think you're too much of a pro for them to handle.

So, basically I am living through the best phase of my life married, and yet I am single. I can't wait to see what lies ahead for me on this journey!

Roma Kapadia

Status? Umm ... Single

Old habits die hard. And none harder than becoming single after a long stint in 'coupledom'. Even after I had found my bearings and adjusted, mentally and materially, to my single status, I often landed myself in situations where I had, metaphorically speaking ticked 'married' in the marital status check box. That one, unpremeditated act would unleash a chain reaction that would require a string of lies and excuses just to keep the married cover intact. At other times, when I decided to clarify my single status upfront, it would lead to hilarious, if not mildly embarrassing situations. Apparently, talking about a changed marital status is not as easy as ticking the right box on a form.

And certainly not easy when lying prone in the dentist's chair! It was a scary chair with all its motorised arms, lights, scalpel trays and spittoon. Dr N advanced towards me with a surgical mask already across his face. 'You've been here before,' he said.

I was glad he remembered. I might still be able to exit the chair alive.

'Yes, yes, I have. For a routine dental clean up, about a year ago.'

'That's too long to ignore your teeth.' He frowned.

What could I say? Time flies when one is trying to avoid the dental chair. Anyway, Dr N got down to business. To be fair, he's a good dentist. He's gentle, takes all the precautions and is acutely mindful of every flinch and whimper.

'There's too much crowding in there,' he said, gesturing towards my mouth, after he had finished.

'I know.'

'Your teeth are overlapping.'

'I know.'

'You should show it to an orthodontist. Get it fixed.'

My heart sank. 'Really? Is it necessary? What kind of fixing?'

'You need a realignment. It'll require the extraction of a couple of teeth. You'll need to wear braces, for about a year and half. And, yes, you may need to come in for monthly sessions here.'

I just stared at him aghast for a while. Eventually, he broke the silence.

'Are you married?'

'What?' I mumbled unthinkingly. 'Yes.'

'Then, what's the problem?' I think it was on the tip of his tongue to say 'the groom-hunt is over' but he refrained.

'How does my being married make a difference?' I asked incredulously.

'Okay, let's do it like this,' Dr N placated me. 'You go home and talk to your husband about this. Then take an x-ray and come back with him. We can collectively take a decision after that. Okay?'

Great, now this absentee 'husband' has been dragged into the dilemma. I scrambled to find a deflector.

'You are aware, Doctor, that I am in my thirties. You want me to live through a teenager's nightmare, braces and all.'

'It won't make too much of a difference,' he reassured. 'Apart from a few precautions while eating, the braces shouldn't interfere in your daily functioning.'

'Not interfere?' I snapped. 'Braces on a middle-aged woman! People are going to laugh at me.'

'You don't look middle-aged. So, no one will know.'

'My friends and family will,' I countered.

'Ah, your husband? I am sure he'll understand. It's only for a year and half.'

Easy for you to say, Dr N, I thought. It's not your mouth that will be wired up for five hundred days. In any case, it would have been futile to argue any further. The husband-who-doesn't-appreciate-braces would have kept featuring in the conversation. I left the dentist's office sulkily. Now, I have two options left...either I go back and tell him I am not married or I change my dentist.

Next time, I rebuked myself, next time someone asks about your marital status, give the right response, the honest response. To hell with what the world thinks.

That opportune moment arrived soon after. I had recently bought a car. Being a new (and admittedly lousy) driver, I pray hard every day that the big city traffic spare me, but alas. The humiliation was complete one evening, when I swerved into a service road hoping to avoid the speeding marauders on the main road, and found myself swarmed by a herd of goats and buffaloes making their own, sweet progress home.

I decelerated to a crawl, honked wildly, lowered my window and urged the mammals along, but to no avail. My biggest fear was that one of the bovine beasts would decide to scrub off the day's mud bath against my new car's gleaming exterior or worse, check the sharpness of his horns with a bump or two against the bonnet. Trying my best to wade through the herd, I almost grazed against a taxi parked on the service road.

Though I was pretty sure there had been no damage to either vehicle, I stopped, grabbed my phone and gingerly stepped out of my car to inspect. Distracted as I was, I had not noticed the policemen in the Traffic Interceptor van parked on the main road. The cop was beside me in a trice.

'What's the use of calling your husband now, Madam?' he sniggered.

'You can tell him later that the buffaloes dented his car. Now, wait, let me see if you have damaged the taxi.' He walked around peering intently at non-existent scratches. It took me a moment to register what he had just implied. The indignation flared in me.

'What makes you think it's my husband's car, Sir?'

'Then your car, aa? Okay, okay, Madam, your car or husband's car, same thing, no?'

Ahaa, here was the 'next time.' I would speak the truth.

'No, not same thing. I don't have a husband,' I retorted.

'Oh sorry, sorry,' he said hastily. 'You are not married only. Then you are calling your father, aa?'

'No, I am not calling my father. My father lives in my home town.'

This was one inquisitive cop. But, why was I proffering unsolicited information? I should have left it there. The cop already looked dejected that neither car had been damaged, so he could not issue a ticket.

But I blundered on. 'And, I was married. But I am not anymore. So, why should I call my husband when I am stuck in the middle of a herd of buffaloes?'

He looked at me nonplussed, sure that I was missing a few screws in my head.

'Okay, don't call your husband, Ma'am,' he said sheepishly.

'I said I am not married.'

'Don't call your father also, Ma'am.' He was distinctly uncomfortable.

'Am I in trouble? Can I go? Or shall I call my....' Before I had said 'lawyer,' he was shooing the rest of the goats and buffaloes off the road. I am pretty sure he thought I was one cranky woman. But let me highlight the positive here; my car was fine, there was no ticket to my name and the road ahead was clear. I drove away as quickly as I could.

It'll take some practice, I tell myself, to be able to talk about becoming single again. More so, to talk effortlessly, without faux pas or unintended misunderstandings. But, practice makes perfect. So, I plod on. Eventually, I'll get the hang of it.

Mumukshu Mohanty

Till Death Do Us Apart

She was single now. Not technically so. At ninety-six, she had lived a full life and spent many years with her husband till he passed away. The reason I knew Maria was because she was visually impaired and I volunteered with her. I had learnt the sighted guide technique, how to walk with and guide a visually impaired person in all situations. It was a training I was honoured to receive because it allowed me to do something meaningful with some free time that I had over the weekend.

I was introduced to Maria by the social worker. She lived in an assisted living facility, what we call a nursing home, except that it was really posh and she was in the 'independent section' where she had just transported all her furniture to an apartment and received only limited help. She was in relatively good health and was extremely cheerful and optimistic.

The first time I met her I discovered so many interesting things about her...that her dashing husband was in the Navy during the Second World War ; that she herself was on radio and joined him for some time as a civilian; that she went back to work in different fields, even played the piano once because her salary nosedived as it did for several women in the pre-liberation era. She was one brave, spirited, vivacious lady.

She told us how she enjoyed her reading group at the nursing home but her best friend had passed away two weeks back. She was matter-of-fact about death and composed about most things. She joked with me that she could hazily see figures and when she walked down the plush hallway, she would greet them. Till one day, a figure didn't greet her back! And it turned out to be a housekeeping cart! She guffawed loudly at that and my heart warmed to her.

She mentioned a trip to Egypt with her husband, with her playing the role of a journalist. She talked about having received teacher's training. What a lovely life, what wonderful memories. Her eyes lit up every time she talked about her husband. She never mentioned his name but all around her I saw pictures of both of them.

For some reason they couldn't have children and obviously I did not probe. I had thought she was in her seventies and was pleasantly surprised to hear that she was ninety-six. She would get up with some difficulty but hobble around with a certain dignity. Her home was as impeccable as she was and absolutely beautiful with artefacts and curios collected from all over the globe, so tastefully done and yet so warm and colourful. She told me she had some rugs but she had tripped over one so the wall-to-wall carpeting was all that she was allowed by the facility.

The nursing home facility was really nice, almost like a five-star hotel. I was impressed and my vague, nebulous fears about an Indian with not much family aging in America were laid at rest to some extent.

As time went by she told me a bit more about her life and there was never sadness or loneliness in her voice when she talked about her husband, it was as if he was still there with her. I loved it.

In my daughter's school, filled with students from different parts of the world, I felt at home when I read something in her library: 'Your skin colour may be different from mine, your language, your food, your religion, but we both cry the same tears and we both laugh the same laugh and we both love in the same way.'

I helped Maria in many ways...arranging her paperwork, putting things away, reading to her, talking to her. But one time I realised how much she loved her husband was when she asked me to file a paper right in the middle of her closet in her cosy living room, which had a huge sunny window and a lovely sofa. It was a kind of a personal temple. As I opened her closet, she asked me to turn to the right and switch on the light.

The closet was bright and colourful as all her clothes and dresses were as vibrant as her life. Interspersed with each dress of hers was one of her husband's suits. In that little room there were pictures of her husband receiving awards in the Navy, distinguished citizen awards and their wedding picture.

Was she single? Was she alone? Could she not see? She had seen everything that was significant. So many of us walk around feeling lonely and living through loveless relationships; here was a lady who could not be called single by any stretch of imagination because she had lived a full life and loved and carried her husband in her heart forever.

Anuradha Gupta

Escapade

'Where do you want to go, Madam?' a bearded man asked me, as I approached the makeshift office of the travel agency, a table and a bench on the pavements of Connaught Place, New Delhi.

'Where do your buses go?' I had asked him, not having any idea where I wanted to go. All I knew was I had to leave the city immediately. I smiled as a little voice inside me said, how brave ....

'We have been running this luxury bus service for over seventeen years. Haridwar, Dehradun, Mussourie, Shimla, Dharamshala, Nainital — we go everywhere. We are world famous in Delhi, see our buses,' the man had replied, proudly pointing to the fleet of buses parked in front of him.

I couldn't choose. Somewhere down the line I had forgotten that skill. 'When do the buses leave?' I asked.

'All leave Delhi by ten o'clock,' he replied.

I looked at the watch; it was about eight. I wanted to be out as soon as possible. 'Any bus leaving now?' I enquired, hopefully.

'Well, the bus to Nainital leaves in half an hour,' he said, a bit perturbed by my urgency. 'Well, one ticket to Nainital then!' I replied, feeling triumphant about making a decision.

So many things had bound me that I was forgetting who I was or what I wanted. Earlier, in Kolkata, it had always been about what I should do or want. I had smelt freedom in Delhi as he came along, filling my life with the fruity colours of love. But it didn't stay that way. Soon, I couldn't even figure out what my favourite food was or who my real friends were, always going with what he dictated. Then came the supreme betrayal. I knew I would have succumbed to him, yet again, if I didn't escape. It was the last chance of saving me, before I totally lost myself.

'You'll go alone?' asked the travel agent.

I had fretted for the last two hours battling with the question of being single. Single women, alone in the city, are always vulnerable. But then again what could be worse than being with a dominating turncoat? I had begun facing the fact that from now on I would be alone. The man's question concretised my stand. 'Yes!' I replied, proud of being able to make a decision without any pressure and solely for myself. As he handed me my ticket, I began relishing the taste of absolute freedom. I did something people would think quite unbecoming of me. I bought a cigarette and smoked it all by myself, standing underneath an orange streetlight, watching the cars and buses whiz by. In that same spirit, I switched off my mobile phone. I wasn't afraid of being single anymore.

Several hours later, as I stepped down from the luxury bus that had, in the course of the night, left behind a congested city and an even more congested life, the cold, fresh air of the hills burst into my lungs. Bright sunlight hit my eyes and I saw a yellow signboard that read 'Nainital'. I couldn't conceal my smile. No one knew where I was. The childish feeling of adventure that had filled me as I had switched off the phone before boarding the bus, returned with a vengeance. I had finally managed to cut away all the strings that had kept me attached; I wasn't a puppet anymore. Very soon I found myself in front of a huge lake, well barricaded by mountains. I don't know what exactly about the lake drew me to it. Though it was fenced, I found myself peering into it, wanting to jump into it. The mobile phone, still dangling from my neck, hung precariously over the still lake till the knot binding it mysteriously gave away. In a moment it disappeared. I remained hypnotised by the distorted reflection of myself in the silvery green waters.

Lightning interrupted my reverie. 'The weather in the mountains is unpredictable, it's sunny one moment and raining the next,' one of my co-passengers had said. He was right. Brightness gave way to a dull grey sky as the small little drops of rain turned bigger. A feeling of loneliness set in. Good times flashed before my eyes. What would I do next? He would always know, I thought, my mind suddenly going weak. But I had to let go of him. Tears welled up as I sat on a bench nearby. I cried my heart out in the rain. It made me feel better, as if I were getting rid of my submissive and dependent self. I didn't realise I already had done so the moment I decided to leave him, leave Delhi and venture out on my own.

Nothing tastes sweeter than freedom. Maybe it was the freedom that made my escapade so memorable. Maybe it was the freedom that made the mountain berries or their vendor, the fourteen-year-old Kamal seem so sweet. 'Have some berries. They will make you feel happy,' said the little boy settling down beside me with a basket of strawberries. I looked at him, dazed. No stranger had ever spoken so kindly to me. 'Don't cry and have some,' he insisted, smiling. As I tasted his wares, he went on talking.

He told me his father was a driver who drove to Almora, Ranikhet and even Delhi. He himself had never been out of Nainital but he would go, once he grew up and became a driver, too. His mother wanted him to become a boatman, on the Naini Lake, so that she would be able to see him from their house up in the hills but he wanted to go to big cities like Dehradun and Delhi. He woke up at four every morning to pick the berries, so that when the tourist buses started coming in at seven, he would be there. He loved looking at the visitors and thinking about what kind of lives they have at home.

Intrigued, I asked, 'What did you think about me?'

His reply was prompt. 'You have come from Delhi to teach in the girl's boarding school but you miss home, so you were crying.' I laughed and replied, 'I wish…'

I stayed in Kamal's two-room house for a few days before returning. I picked wild berries every morning and ventured to places most tourists are unaware of — haunted houses, secret caves in mountains, sacred temples and hot water springs.

Since then, rarely have I not followed my heart, rarely have I cried.

Joie Bose Chatterjee

Find Yourself

Born as a girl in a typical Punjabi family, I was always treated like a princess. I was the eldest kid in my generation and my parents' first child. All the members of my family adored me. When I say princess, I mean I had every possible toy, clothes, books, music, etc. Anything that one could want was in my cupboard! Life was wonderful for me but that was exactly what pushed me to struggle. Since everything came so easily to me, I intentionally started searching for a less easy life. Weird as it may sound I have purposely given up on a lot of things to lead a little less comfortable life.

In an ideal world, my life should have been as follows: a graduate at twenty-one, a postgraduate at twenty-three, a working woman six months later, a married woman by twenty-four and a mother by twenty-five. But here I am, at twenty-four, I am done with my post-graduation, worked with two firms, have had a series of relationships and break-ups, and am now working with an NGO. I left my amazingly well paid job in a sleek office to teach seventy kids in a dilapidated municipal school building. I work with one of India's education movements and feel proud to say that I am the class teacher of Grade Two in a municipal school based in Mumbai.

I completed my graduation from one of India's best colleges and started working with a corporate firm in Delhi. When I couldn't handle the pressure of politics at work, I called it quits. I started working with another company soon after I left the first. As I loved challenges, I started studying for a distance-learning course, preparing for my MBA, volunteering with an NGO and interning with another over weekends, while working fulltime as a research analyst. I had packed my life with all the things that would make my resume look great!

Life was very convenient and comfortable but I chose to struggle. Not to get away from the life my parents had planned but to find myself. When I was working in a plush office and earning a hefty salary, I was happy since I could afford every luxury in the world. But what I am getting now is immeasurable. No feeling in the world can be compared to the satisfaction I get when I see my class progress. The kids in my class come from small communities and slums around the school. Each one of them has a story to tell, whether it is Devi, whose father is a drunkard and beats up her mother or Faiyan, whose father left his mother while she was pregnant. Seven-year-old Zeenat's mother is my age! Sameera's father stays away from the family in a different state to earn a livelihood and Dilshaad and Raza's fathers don't have jobs, pushing their kids to work at the age of six! Yes, these are the stories I struggle with every day. These kids are my life. They have helped me discover a new side to life.

When my lesson doesn't go well or my students are restless or in no mood to study, I feel I have failed. At such moments,

I wonder if I made the right choices. But then I look back on how much my kids have made me smile that day and I feel it's all worth it. Now, every time I think of my life, I remember the slogan for MasterCard — There are some things money can't buy. It is true that some people find happiness in corporate jobs or working in the government. Others find it in an MBA institute of their choice or their profession. I am still trying to find myself.

It was never easy for me to give up my family and friends and move cities to do what I am doing, but I feel if it were not for them I wouldn't have done this, either. Sometimes I wonder if I weren't here, I would either be doing another masters or would have been married or at least engaged. I am not sure if I would have been happy had I not chosen to do things differently in life.

On days like these when I think of how things could have been and how they are, I listen to the song by Brad Paisley — 'When you find yourself, in some far off place … and it causes you to rethink some things, you start to sense that slowly you're becoming someone else…and then you find yourself…'

Ritika Chawla

Single at Forty

I have never had any luck with lasting romance and this is being said without any under or overtones of tragedy! The fact is I have shot opportunity in the foot whenever it has surfaced. Like the time when a boy I kind of liked in school, came to our class to monitor us and asked me to sing, and I lost my voice because I started on a higher note than necessary to impress him! Portentous? Maybe. Then there was this senior boy in school with the eyes of an angel for whom I had nursed a serious crush for a few months. Once, when he fell sick, I remember sending him a hand-painted, get-well-soon card with a note that began with 'Dear Bhaiya'. So there! And there was also the fatal tendency to see more in people than there really was. So my first heart-break happened over a boy whose pictures I came across recently and found myself thinking, 'Really?'

Though I am forty, I feel like fourteen and at the cusp of a life that has not yet begun. I have never had a real, adult relationship. Dating in small Punjabi towns is unheard of and in my time, there were no cafes, no Internet, no social networking sites, no opportunities to meet boys if you lived in a mohalla and came home straight from a government college for women! The only men I saw were eve teasers who rode their bicycles behind rickshaws carrying demure girls or accosted you in bazaars with, 'Hi Yankee' (the aforementioned address was reserved for girls who wore jeans!).

At University, a guy half-a-leg shorter than me and with a virulent attack of pimples began to follow me home and once caught up with me outside the library to say, 'Will you make friendship with me?'

I stretched to many righteous centimetres and said grimly, 'Thank you for the compliment but I am going steady with someone.' The last sentence was said with a little wistfulness because I wished there *was* someone out there. All around me trees flowered, as did romances, but all I had was poetry and Hindi film songs. It never occurred to me to respond to the occasional attention I attracted. Romance, you see, was a serious business for me, and love had to be the real thing. I never had any interest in short-lived summer romances.

I was the heroine of my own love story with no hero in sight. At twenty-five, marriage happened. But I am single at forty and strangely, it feels normal to live on my own with my child in a home where nothing is random and everything reflects the current state of my mind. But I am essentially still the same person I was when I sat in the university garden under a bougainvillea bush, singing a song and waiting for someone to come and sweep me off my feet.

Truth be told, today I would rather be alone with myself than be alone with another person. My son said earnestly the other day, 'If you were the desperate kind and somewhere abroad, you would have hit a pub (he meant a singles' bar) by now, Mom.' I laughed but he echoed what I figured a long time ago. If you haven't been successful in matters of the heart by the time you are a certain age, most people think you are desperate. But women my age choose to be single because they want more from life and not because they want to test just any puddle or fall into any ditch. I am as fastidious and squeamish today in my attitude towards unwanted attention in my space as I was when I was a teenager. Yet everywhere around me, I see portrayals of stereotypical older women or cougars salivating at the sight of younger men. From the manipulative older women in James Hadley Chase novels to Tolstoy's unfulfilled Anna to the many television and cinematic avatars of Mrs Robinson (*The Graduate*), it is almost as if a woman in her forties is doomed to either self-debasing desperation or deathly boredom if she does not have a happy personal life.

I remember when my son was around five, I had taken him to the launch of a new restaurant. We had barely progressed to soup, when a twenty-something PR representative I vaguely knew came to my table, reeking of vodka and a love story gone wrong. And then he went on to say, 'Now no young girls for me. I only want to have affairs with older women!'

I was stunned that he actually presumed I would be game for what he was suggesting, no questions asked! That I would fall in neatly with his plans, and all because I was seen everywhere without my husband! Just because I was now labelled an 'older' woman presumed to be alone or lonely or both, I had no choice or volition in the matters of the heart anymore!

It did not stop there. An acquaintance, who knew my husband was away on work, began to call up to 'chat,' reminding me not to tell his wife because she would 'misunderstand'. And all this when I was not even officially single!

I don't care how the world perceives me or what women my age are supposed to expect from life because I deserve exactly the same things a girl in her twenties hopes for herself. A lasting love, a man who thinks of his woman as the core of his life and not as an afterthought at its fringes. Not someone who makes the mistake of smiling lasciviously at me and asking, 'are you a single mom?' like someone did recently. I will never settle for anything less than a playful, joyful adult relationship where partners put each other first, share hearts and minds, conversations and silences, distances and intimacy, homely meals and dreams and not just household expenses.

No more waiting for a man to show me that I matter. I matter, with or without him. If he wants me in his life, he better show it and speak it and live it. Like Ross said once in the popular TV serial, *Friends*, in response to a statement that Rachel's love for him was implicit, 'I want it to be Plicit!' My sentiments exactly!

Reema Moudgil

Window to the Soul

It was another rainy April morning in Kashmir. The wet asphalt created shimmering reflections. The tourists that throng the valley during the 'season' had dispersed with the coming of the rain. A brave few walked along the pavement skirting the Dal lake, as CRPF troops eyed them suspiciously.

As I sat on the balcony of my hotel, which faced the Boulevard, I saw a girl and her little brother play in the rain. I grew increasingly restless as I watched them, so I decided to step out for a while. Leaving instructions for my room to be cleaned, I walked towards the lake. By now, the rain had subsided leaving a lot of slush everywhere. As I strolled along the Boulevard with my camera, I remembered my previous trip to Kashmir. Bittersweet memories surfaced as I sought the right subject to photograph. A few shots of the lake and I made my way back to the hotel.

The hotel was tiny, more like a guesthouse with very little Kashmiri carving, which was quite a rarity. I saw the owner of the hotel at the reception. He was a man of maybe forty, not very tall, but with a pleasing personality. He was well-spoken and well-mannered, very unlike the people I had met on my previous trip.

Some days ago when I had checked in, he was taken aback by my name. The reservations had been made for Diya from Delhi and when I walked in, I was Saadiya and my head was covered.

A few minutes of questioning followed. 'Are you really not Kashmiri?' he asked.

'No!' I replied, emphatically.

'How come you have an Islamic name? Is your mother Muslim?' The questioning continued. 'Coincidence' and 'no' were my respective replies to the intrusive questions.

'Why is your head covered then?' he asked, suspiciously. I gave him another justification and at last, I was given a room.

On this damp spring day, the owner of the hotel looked quite disturbed. 'Would you join me for a cup of kahwa (traditional Kashmiri tea)?' he asked.

Such invitations generally made me uneasy. Being a single woman travelling alone, this kind of conversation usually went one way, in this part of the world. But every now and then, I am overwhelmed by the concern an individual expresses about my travelling alone. It happened again, this wet April morning. Something in his manner made me feel comfortable and I decided to enjoy some kahwa.

As we sat across each other sipping the hot tea, he kept looking at me. It was a look I will never forget. He looked right into my eyes; he was not staring or leering. He just sat there and looked at me for a few minutes and then the words came out. 'How come your smile never reaches your eyes?'

For a few seconds I was stunned. I still don't know what

the appropriate reply should have been. Instead of saying anything, I just smiled awkwardly.

'How come your smile never reaches your eyes?' he asked, again.

'Of course it does!' This time I tried hard to smile properly. I grinned like a jackass just so that he would stop asking me this question.

'I can see the pain in your eyes,' he went on. Then the grilling started: How old was I? Twenty-nine. How many siblings? One. Older or younger? Younger. Why wasn't I married? Didn't I want to get married? Did my parents not worry about me? Yes, they did.

I was quite touched by this stranger's concern, so I sat there and answered. The questioning went on and on, interrupted by various insights into my personality and ending with, 'The man you are in love with doesn't love you. Otherwise, he would have never allowed you to come here alone.'

The last part simply baffled me; honestly, the whole conversation did. But as one who is not very articulate, I was quite used to people speculating about me. But this last statement was unreal.

'There's nobody,' I replied.

'I know there is!' he answered.

A little more talk and then I excused myself. I walked into my room, confused by the conversation. After a few minutes of sitting on the bed, I realised there was something amiss. My things seemed to be slightly out of place. One bag had toppled over. My books were exactly in the same order as I had left them but they were upside down and on top of the pile was the letter. I walked towards this almost open letter and read it slowly...

April '08
Srinagar
Dear Love,

I call you love because you're the one I remember loving. I arrived in Kashmir and it reminded me of you. I write to you knowing that you will not reply but I can't talk to anyone else right now. The only place I feel better is here and the ironic thing is if you were around you would have never let me come to Kashmir. There's so much pain and yet it is so breathtakingly beautiful. In one moment it seems like heaven and in another, hell. It is like an external manifestation of how I feel inside, so I guess I'll just have to keep coming back.

Love
Diya

As I folded the letter carefully, I felt the tears well up and then, a few minutes later, suddenly came a smile that actually reached my eyes!

I had just put two and two together. The previous day I had seen the owner watching TV in a room that was occupied by another guest, while his staff cleaned it.

My letter was lying outside. This had been written to my brother whom I lost in a car accident a few years ago. Since the owner didn't know that, he'd assumed the letter was written to a lover! A sigh of relief escaped my lips. As I looked into the mirror, I stared at my eyes and thought, it's words that are still the only window to the soul!

Saadiya Kochar

It's Only Fair

He looked up from his writing and smiled, that lopsided, disarming smile. I shook my head, laughed and sat down cross-legged on the floor beside him. He was a close buddy and he had called saying he needed to talk. We both knew exactly what the conversation would be! To his credit it had been six months since the last SOS. This time around a married woman, who he swears he had only a platonic friendship with, was losing it on him. He needed me to talk to her. This was going to be tough.

Before getting judgemental about him, you need to know a few things about S. His name, loosely translated, means the first among equals. In many ways I think he truly lives up to his name. I haven't met anyone like him. He is in his early thirties and single, is incredibly gifted and one of the most genuine human beings ever born. He is generous to a fault and that's what gets him into trouble. Maybe it comes from the fact that he was born and brought up in the hills, in a family that is deeply spiritual. So he doesn't quite fit in with the hip media gang that he is part of. S is genuinely interested in people and will do all it takes to engage with them. Loves to help, 'happy to help' is actually his tagline! So when he first moved to this city and became part of our gang, everyone was intrigued by him. From my Mom, to the building chowkidar, to our CEO, everyone adored him. The girls wanted to know if there was a girlfriend tucked away at home. The guys said this was an act.

Seven years later we know that it's not an act and that there is no girlfriend or boyfriend back home! He does believe in love and believes it happens only to a lucky few when it's destined, in whichever lifetime. So with that warped logic he goes about inadvertently breaking hearts.

Each time he is being his usual concerned self, a woman feels he has fallen for her hook, line and sinker. Not knowing that after the dinner he is as involved and attentive with the auto driver whose life story he insists on knowing. He is gradually learning, with a lot of help from friends, what not to say when he meets women the first couple of times. His praise is always genuine and his manners impeccable. He is such a rarity in present times. So women move to more personal territory, which is when the problems arise....

One woman, after four dates, told her family she was marrying him. He was called home and had the family delighted, till post dinner, dad took him for 'that' chat. He froze and said he had no such intention or inclination. He ran for dear life and then the awkwardness in office had to be handled.

Older women, young teenagers, married women, divorced women and hopeful singles...he has a repertoire that would leave most guys green with envy. Being who he is he would never kiss and tell but clearly he does sleep with some of them, the ones who are the no-strings attached types. An enviable exsistence? Actually, far from it!

So now he tells them upfront that he is not looking at anything serious or long term. No one has turned him down on that count. It's all just what they had in mind as well. Yet after a couple of weeks of hanging together they start resenting his spending so much time with X who needs help in shifting or with Y who needs emotional support since she lost her cat. Things start going downhill when women start asking questions. Like why do you need to go off to learn martial arts in Kerala and not come with me on a cruise to the Bahamas?

That's when he panics and calls us. He truly does not want to hurt anyone yet he needs to be out now. It's almost a pattern and one day, totally exasperated at three in the morning I asked him why didn't he just fall in love like normal people did? He thought for a second and patiently said, 'Because I have so much love to give that it seems a little unfair to give it all to just one person!' You can't beat that logic, can you?

Which is where selective listening comes in, we all hear what we want to. So when he told M, the lady he met online, that she writes very well, she heard it as he likes me. When a month later he offered to accompany her to a classical music concert that she really wanted to go for, she thought it was a date. On that freezing night over mugs of coffee I made him recap all that had happened. Clearly he had given out friendly signals that had got badly bungled.

We singles have frequently sensed how people misinterpret friendliness or concern as a desire to spend the rest of one's life with that person. To me that is a sign of the other person's insecurity and deep-rooted need to flee from their own situation. S is happy being single and successful and that seems to be what people hold against him. How dare he say nice things to me and not want to marry me? 'Get real' is what I want to tell some people.

Nevertheless early in the morning I made the difficult call to M. I told her who I was and why I was calling her. I apologised on behalf of S, she said he had done that himself too. She was feeling sheepish and was defensive. Two hours later, she, S and I were bonding in his flat. She made the most amazing adrak (ginger) chai and came to terms with the fact that much as she would have wanted it otherwise, S was sold on 'singledom'.

She needed to make her decisions regarding her marriage and situation based on her reality. S was not available as an escape route. She left looking cheerful and S and she promised not to keep in touch for a couple of months.

He thanked me and then asked the question that most singles do, ever so often. Why are my actions judged on the basis of my marital status? Why does every relationship have to be labelled and slotted? Why can't I choose to be and stay just friends with someone? If she tied a rakhi on my wrist I could pull her leg without her getting ideas, right?

I ruffled his hair and laughed, 'Being single can be complicated too!'

Shifa Maitra

The Single Soul

'Did you always want to remain single? Were you determined to become a career woman from the very beginning? Would you have accomplished all that you have as a professional were you loaded with domestic responsibilities like other housewives? Would you recommend remaining single to your younger friends?' are some of the questions I'm often asked by friends and relatives.

I respond to their queries depending on my frame of mind and their intentions. In my opinion, for the majority it is idle curiosity and small talk. Some are looking for a juicy, intimate story and hoping I will entertain them; I don't. Only once in a while I come across a genuine case when someone in a similar situation is seeking earnest answers. Then I lower my defences and share my thoughts and life.

Interestingly, nobody asked me such invasive questions a few years ago. Then it would have been inappropriate, even insensitive. Today, because I'm perceived as having crossed the marriageable age, they don't think it offensive to invade my privacy. It makes me wonder if they ever raise similar questions to a widower or a divorcee. I have my doubts because the widow and the separated are victims of personal tragedies and taking liberties with them would be inconsiderate.

But the single soul, for varied reasons, is a subject of immense curiosity and speculation. Everybody has a theory about the unmarried woman — her life, reputation and career. Everybody has a question to pose about her past, present and future.

Over the years I have got accustomed to being judged by strangers. They have concluded without knowing anything about me that I'm single out of choice, not circumstances. I'm successful due to my status not talent and finally, I'm free of responsibilities because I'm not committed to a partner. 'It must be fun living life on your own terms and not being answerable to in-laws or spouse,' they joke with me. I prefer to just smile and evade the topic. Like the magician who juggles new tricks to engage his audience, I assemble some funny and some irreverent observations of people who often don't know how to deal with my single status.

Many years ago when my ageing mother and I moved into our new home and were still settling down, the newspaper boy woke me up one early morning to confirm if I needed to hire his services. 'Sure,' I said and began to rattle my choice of weekly papers, when he interrupted me rudely.

'Have you asked sahib?' I was confused by his question. 'First ask sahib and then give me the list,' he added. He was not the only one who didn't think me worthy enough to make up my mind. A few days later, I was in for a second shock. My newly appointed part-time helper watched me working on the computer and said, 'I don't see any child around.' I ignored her.

She continued with the dusting and, pointing to my mother, asked, 'Does she live with you? Is she your mother or mother-in-law?' I was getting irritated but tried to be patient.

'Mother,' I responded briefly and resumed working.

'And where is your husband?'

'Don't have one,' I replied curtly.

She stopped cleaning and stood up, victorious. 'Don't have one? Is he dead or did he leave you?'

By now I had had enough of her interrogation. I shut the computer and announced, 'He didn't leave me; I have left him.'

It's uncomfortable answering intimate questions posed by strangers and very often I deliberately offer outrageous answers only to get the nosey parkers off my back. Recently, I was on a long flight home and had the misfortune of having a very talkative co-passenger. All through the flight he bragged about himself, his work and his family, and when he had exhausted information about himself, he turned to me. 'So what does your husband do?'

I shuddered at the questions that would follow and to cut short the conversation replied, 'My husband is no more!' He stiffened, a trifle embarrassed at having trespassed but not yet tongue-tied.

When the flight landed and I was on my way out he could not resist the last word, 'Looking at your bright sari and jewellery nobody could suspect that …' I walked past him mid-sentence.

Sometimes, I deliberately hold back information. Perhaps it just makes me feel safer. This usually happens when I'm in unfamiliar surroundings for work. Once I was attending a party with other delegates after a long seminar. A colleague, trying to make polite conversation asked, 'So how many children do you have, Madam?' I decided that this was not the time or place to talk about myself to strangers so I shrugged and shook my head. The poor guy felt guilty, as if he had touched upon a raw nerve and after an awkward silence excused himself. It suited me perfectly. I hadn't spoken the truth but I hadn't lied to him either.

Today, when distant relatives and strangers corner me with intimate questions, I look at them and wonder: are they even worth answering or reacting to? I don't think so. Why must I tell them how I get my groceries and fruits? Why must I tell them who pays my telephone and electricity bills or who does my bank work? What makes them think that a single person's life is any different from the others who juggle time between office and home? Is it worth sharing how I manage my deadlines and social commitments? I don't think so; and not out of resentment or irritation, but because I truly believe that each of us is eventually a single soul waiting to be connected to the Supreme Being.

Bhawana Somayya

Parallel Best

Make no mistake about this.

Being married to the right person is the best state of life to be in. You are there for each other — you whisper, you agree, you laugh, you enjoy, you bore each other, you disagree, you fight, you fume, but you would never be able to live without one another. By the time you reach the double decades, that's when the marriage gets most meaningful. You are glad you met, merged and will now melt into eternity together.

However, if life simply did not play you the marriage card, or if you were deprived of happily ever after because death or divorce did you apart, then there is another state that can, and does, spell bliss.

It is the 'parallel best' state of life to be in.

The state of being single and content.

I have a friend who is well into the fearsome forties. She is single and content. She has all life can give her plus some more. She did not want it this way. She fell in love with a colleague and they were together for more than eight years. Then he decided he did not want to spend the rest of his life with her; so he moved on, and married a fledgling his mother chose.

Though eight important years had ended in a void, my friend is wise. Before he departed, she spent a couple of evenings with him, in comfortable conversation, assuring him she bore him no ill will. She wished him well, and went on with her life.

She refused to abandon the marriage dream. While her career went on zooming upwards, she met other young men — she dated and even checked out several marriage dot coms. She met men of her age available in the marriage market. Nothing worked out. She was too intelligent to get married 'just for the sake of getting married'; she also discovered that most of the men who come through the Internet path were 'weird'. The other ones that were not weird were not her type.

At some point she gave up Internet dating and meeting and says she would advise all young women to avoid that path for the greater chances are that they could land in 'big trouble'.

Today, my friend has a multi-national job which involves global travel with every perk you can think of, including bungalow, servants and a foreign car — and a jet-set lifestyle in the capital city. Wherever she goes, she stays in five- or seven-star hotels; because of the kind of post she holds; she is wined and dined by those in the halls of fame or the corridors of power.

She is single and content.

She has siblings who are married and have children, and those nieces and nephews are to her, like they were born from her. She is comfortable with them and with other couples too. She knows how to handle men who make passes and is completely capable of protecting herself. People love her maturity and often seek her for counsel in their marital problems.

She has certainly not given up the marriage dream. Her parents are conservative; and though they are proud of her achievements, they tell her that they would be able to 'die happy' if they could see her settled in marriage before their eyes close. She hopes for their sake that it would happen sooner rather than later. However, today, her viewpoint is: 'If it has to happen, it will happen. I am not going around searching frantically for it. But I do not have my eyes closed either.'

She and I are friends because I am also living life in the 'parallel best' lane. And I have some rules of my own which have contributed to making the life I live one of great contentment.

Firstly, I take care of myself. I have a flexi-hours job, which I can do from home. I firmly resist the urge to dwell in nightgowns. By nine each morning, I am 'dressed with make-up' and at my work desk in crisp, fresh clothes. It makes me respect myself and work better.

Secondly, I do all I can to avoid potentially sticky situations. For instance, a judge friend of mine invited me over to dinner at his place. He has a charming wife, so that was not the problem. The problem arose because before putting the phone down, he said in a slightly lower voice, 'Do not come in your car, I will drive you home.'

I did not want to cause offence so I did not go there in my vehicle. When it was time to leave and he went to the inner room to get his key and jacket, I took the opportunity to link hands with his wife and to say lightly, 'Please come along, I'd love the company.' I did not need to say anything more. She understood, she came along; her husband scowled.

Another time, after a prayer meeting at the pastor's house, his wife instructed the Reverend to drop me home. I told her 'No, I would manage', that I could easily hop into an auto-rickshaw. She insisted that I should go with her husband. I refused again, saying I did not want to trouble him. She insisted a third time, saying, 'Please go ahead, I don't mind.'

A nerve burst somewhere. I retorted, a bit abruptly, 'But I do.'

There was a shocked silence. No one expects a single woman (very much like a fifth wheel, a stepney!) to have a mind, leave along a voice! In a kinder voice, I explained: 'I am new in town; most people know I am single and divorced. It will not appear proper to be seen alone in a vehicle with the pastor. It may be misunderstood and lead to rumours which would not be good for the name of the Christ's church.'

That night, they unexpectedly dropped in to apologise. 'We had not realised the consequences,' they said with remorse.

People will not realise the consequences, because to this day, 'singlehood' is a grey, uncertified life zone. So it is for the single woman to guard her worth, otherwise there will be challenge after challenge.

But once one establishes the ground rules and sets up the requisite boundaries, life's 'parallel best' state has more to offer than many troubled marriages. Particularly those marriages where spouses live under the same roof as strangers; or, as partners who cannot stand one another.

Anonymous

2

SINGLE AND HAPPY

You do not need to be loved, not at the cost of yourself. The single relationship that is truly central and crucial in a life is the relationship to the self. Of all the people you will know in a lifetime, you are the only one you will never lose.

—Jo Courdert

Following the Tambourine Man

And so I go into the spangled morning
on my magic bicycle of air, and birdsong
blurring the wheels of elsewhere to speed.

Goodbye.
I cannot stay
in tea cups or beds wedded to the floor four square.

You say it is a good life,
but it is not mine.

A life is to be lived, not inhabited carefully;
daily dusting the chairs and cupboards of normality.

I want to eat the unexpected
and have
a star guide me to my next sleep.

If I tumble, it will be into the future and not graze
my knees on the perpetual present.

Let me go with gladness
because you own no part of me;
yet I have given you all that I am when our
heads were beneath the same roof tree.

Even the birds leave,
the ones that were meant to leave.

Sing the songs that I taught you when you think of me.
They will do you more good
than if I came home for dinner every night.

Tanya Mendonsa

The Singles' Club

'You know why you're still single?' a friend's mom asked him, angrily. 'It's because your closest pals are all single and no one wants to end this party.' We laughed out loud, yet amongst the gang I know all of us said a silent prayer and thanked God for having each other.

The gang began with about seven of us who were in our twenties and full of dreams and ambitions. Twelve years later there are about ten of us, with a few from the original days. What our gang has is the fact that we are all single and that we are our own support system. Sure, we love our married and hitched friends. Yet, some hesitation has crept into our relationship, which both sides try to deny. Is it that smug married vibe? I, for sure, can sense jealousy, too!

For me, it was tough when, about five years ago, I wanted in again. From being single and loving it, I suddenly crossed over. Got married, moved cities, changed worlds and thought this was life. My single pals kept teasing me about how I had done a volte-face yet I knew they loved me all the same. I, on the other hand, was completely caught up in creating the perfect marriage.

It went kaput. I was woken up with a jolt and all I felt like doing was curling up and going back to sleep. I moved back to my city. Family and friends held me together, protected me like I was made of glass. Actually put me back together.

The way parents saw the situation, the way siblings wanted me to be, the take married pals had, it all made sense. Yet what the gang said rang even truer. They were home. They had accepted me back as one of them. I didn't feel like I was at a halfway home. I didn't have to laugh at couple's ribbing each other or get ecstatic when a four-year-old learnt how to say balloon.

I could just vegetate on the couch all day at my artist pal's place and know that she would go out and have a good time if I insisted I just wanted to watch TV at her place alone.

My crabby banker buddy would ask no questions but just land up at the crack of dawn to make sure I went for a run with him. I didn't have a choice. He never asked me what went wrong and yet he knew the answers. My physical and fiscal health was what he took over.

The 'dadima' (grandmother) of the group, who had been through hell in her marriage, started quietly nourishing my soul. We just did the things we did before I moved out. At first it seemed a bit forced but she just wouldn't let me brood. It was so endearing, this act, that neither of us dared to stop the charade.

Then there was the intense brooding pal who never had been a favourite. Truth be told, I had a crush on him and he was the confirmed bachelor. Yet once I was back the unspoken equation we built was comforting. With uncanny precision, he bailed me out of situations and conversations that were uncomfortable. Without expectations and the complications of sex, here was yet another space that helped the healing. A late night drive on a monsoon night with this gang worked so much more than any therapist's session.

In about a year, my well-meaning siblings and smug married pals were trying to get me hitched again. I came back from those evenings feeling like I was being stubborn and unreasonable. So I went on a couple of dates. Most of us in the gang date. Yet when someone gets serious, it's stocktaking time. So it happened in my case, too. Like S the banker says, each of us is the other's mom, dad, sister, brother, shrink, banker and confession box. So we have to know what we are going to be dealing with. Am sure it can be daunting to a newcomer — all that scrutiny and checking out, yet it is fun. So when, after a couple of times, we all realised that the guy was just not comfortable in his skin, 'we' decided it was time to bid adieu.

It's been almost five years now. Together we have made it ... for all of us. I have my own home, a job I love and the guts to dream again. That's a lot. We all have to be there for each other and that's a commitment this amazing group of people has. It's never easy, yet this is one roller-coaster ride nobody wants to get off! Someday we will all grow old together. In a commune, by the beach. Single, successful and senile ....

Shifa Maitra

Love in Licatuc

Coming back to Licatuc for good, after more than forty years, was no easy decision. But then, I guess it had always been at the back of my mind, through all those years of intense struggle in the corridors of power.

Licatuc is where I was born, where I spent those dreamy days of childhood before Mother died and Father took us away with him. The old house was still there in good condition — and where else could I go, anyway?

I eased back into life in Licatuc like I had never gone away. The town itself had not changed much from what I remembered of it. The streets were still narrow, the buildings were still those hangovers from the colonial era and the people were still friendly. The Club was still there, nestled amidst the Weeping Ashokas on the hill at the edge of town.

It was at the Club that I met lawyer Nair. Of average height, slightly on the plump side, dressed well though rather dull, he is about ten years older than I am. After a few days of smiling at each other at the bar, we struck up a conversation.

And then it became a regular habit. I am sure we must have caused a few smiles — two old bachelors relaxing over drinks every evening.

We would talk about everything under the sun — the local news, events in far-off lands, whatever took our fancy, but never anything personal. We preferred to keep our histories to ourselves. The drinking was moderate, not enough to loosen our tongues beyond the realm of the impersonal. Until the day the topic turned to love and lawyer Nair told me his story.

In his youth, he said, he had been the type that the good citizens of Licatuc took for granted, as they still did now — nothing much to look at, not very good at conversation. The type of young man you could see every day on the streets of Licatuc, hanging out with a crowd of several other young men of the nondescript variety. Not the type that any sensible matron would remotely consider a potential match for her beloved offspring.

Amidst his male contemporaries, Nair was well regarded, though. A good guy to have around, even though not very ornamental. A chap you could always depend on for help and cheer, even though your mom kept forgetting his name. As for Nair himself, he was comfortable with the way he was. There was no particular thing he wanted to achieve. He was content to let life take him the way it wanted to, the thought of swimming against the tide never entered his pointed head.

Nair's world turned upside down the day he saw the Princess for the first time. He had gone to an evening meet of the Nice Folks Circle, an event where the self-proclaimed cream of Licatuc congregated for enlightenment, fun and games. After a while, he retreated to the periphery, where he had always felt the most comfortable. And then the Princess got on stage to dance.

She was the most captivating creature he had ever seen. Enchanted, he watched her every movement as she timed them to a catchy rhythm. Every sweep of her arms, every swivel of her torso .... Nair's mind mopped them up like a kitten mops up a platter of warm milk. His concept about feminine grace would never be the same again. When the Princess walked off stage, he felt as though time had stopped ticking.

Nair was well and truly obsessed with the Princess. Ferreting out the fact that she was an active member of the Circle, he became a regular too, just for the sheer joy of seeing her once in a while. He observed her with fascination distinctive to the young, listened to her laughter and eagerly perked up his ears for the sound of her voice.

But all along, Nair knew the Princess was out of his league. She was meant for a Prince, not just any ordinary guy. Particularly not for a guy who had no idea where he was going or what he wanted to be.

Nair took to loitering around the path the Princess used to get home with her friends on the way back from college, hoping for a glimpse, maybe a glance or (scaling the heights of fantasy) a smile. Zilch. She paid him as much attention as the corner waste bin.

There were times when Nair wanted to just break loose, just tell the Princess what he felt about her. But she didn't even know he existed. And then, on the day he decided once and for all to confess his love to the Princess, his acquaintance Shankar turned up, on vacation from Singapore. Shankar — suave, handsome and brilliant in repartee. And soon the Princess had eyes for no one else.

That day Nair knew the heights of emotion, the pain, the angst of loss. He watched them talk animatedly, each peal of laughter a shaft searing into his bleeding heart.

From then on, Nair decided that he would never let anyone or anything affect him so much anymore.

But first there was something he had to do.

He had to make the Princess notice him, at least once. His opportunity came at a gala event of the Circle. A full-fledged band was available for all socialites who fancied they were able to carry a tune. And if there was one hidden talent Nair had, it was that he could sing. He could hold his own when it came to a good warble.

The melody that Nair chose was a classic from the Maestro Ramodafi. It spoke of a search for love, how a heart once lost would never be regained, how love is not for the likes of you or me. He sang as never before in his life, his gaze often flitting to the centre of the hall where the Princess sat with Shankar. He did the Master proud, for his heart was in his song.

Was it his imagination? Was she staring raptly at him? Was she shushing Shankar when he sought her attention? Afterwards, the crowd of surprised friends thumping him on the back blocked his vision. By the time he struggled free, she was no longer there.

Nair never went to a Circle meeting again. Sometime later, he did hear that the Princess had married Shankar and gone off to the Far East.

But he didn't let that affect him. Sometimes, the thought

passed his mind that there could be another Princess some place ... or not ....

Nair went through the rest of his life as he began it — content and going with the flow. He did this intuitively, understanding the wisdom of it much later. He did not come upon another princess. He did moderately well in his profession though now he has almost retired. He still sings, though, to himself. He's comfortable in his own skin, and in Licatuc. Licatuc has a place for everyone and everyone has his place in Licatuc.

I stayed back at the bar long after Nair went home, musing over when to tell him my story.

Srinath Girish

Alone is Not Lonely

I had never lived alone. From a multitudinous family, to a girls' hostel, to marriage and children and friends and family, with neighbours and servants and doorbells ringing, my life had been noisy and crowded. I lived joyously, irritated and sometimes resentful; my days were filled with conversations and laughter and sometimes silences that were far from serene. Life was accompanied by the cacophony of television, of music and of the sounds that inhabit a block of flats.

Until the year I turned fifty-four and my daughter and I moved to Chennai, she into a hostel and I into a room of my own. I was overwhelmed by relief at the calm silence, after years of silent discord and the intrusion of unwelcome music.

I would awake to the silence of pre-dawn darkness, lie listening to the birds and then all too quickly, to the clatter of vessels from a maid at work early next door. From a flat crowded with possessions and people and a structured day with many needs and demands, my life shrank to a single room in an almost empty house. Each day welcomed me into the contemplation of a wide sky seen through a canopy of neem (margosa) leaves. I had the option of instant coffee or 'tea bag' tea to drink, and fruit, curds and crackers and cheese to eat. Each day stretched spaciously before me to make of it what I chose.

In a new city, I had few friends. I had a job and the kind of freedom I had never known.

'You will be lonely,' a friend in Delhi had warned me when I decided to move. 'It is not easy to live alone. There are times when the loneliness can be very hard.' Yet books and a new neighbourhood, the sea and sky and inexpensive restaurants, a daughter to worry about and to release from parental bonds, a son making his way in a distant city at the end of the telephone, loving friends also within reach of the telephone, and kind neighbours to discover ... loneliness did not seem to come into it at all.

The few friends I did have in Chennai became anchors and supports, each in his or her way. Gowri pointed out the best places to have juice and 'degree' coffee with idlis and vada, and took me on a visit to the sabhas (cultural gatherings) during the music season, which was a particularly busy time for her. Geeta and Girish, who lived at the other end of town, introduced us to Pondicherry, on a weekend trip, and brought us gifts of avocadoes and organic mangoes. Girish took us under his wing and showed us places to shop and local fruit that he thought we would enjoy. When my car took several months longer to arrive than expected, he lent me his second car, which saw me through an especially rainy season. In material terms and in the forms of affectionate advice and emotional support, he shouldered me through the months of transition, making an effort to visit me, to invite me out and to tell me of his belief in what I was doing. Later, when he was unwell and even walking was not easy for him, he travelled across town with his wife Geeta, to attend my daughter's examination dance performance, calling later to tell her that she had danced exceptionally well. His kindness cushioned the change I was making, as did the kindness of other friends, such as Leela, who held out her hand even as she was struggling to encompass enormous new responsibilities.

Chennai is one of India's largest cities but the neighbourhood in which I found myself still followed the patterns of a small town, of a sense of community, despite the many blocks of flats rising swiftly and the traffic that increased with each passing day.

There were still old and spreading trees here and small shops and vegetable stalls whose owners wished you as you passed by and a sense of kindliness in the air. When the vegetable seller or the small grocer went off to deliver their goods, they left their shops untended, confident that their goods were safe. I found I could leave my front door open for much of the day and it is only now, after friends have warned me about being careless that I have grown more cautious. Once when I had fever and found I did not have any Crocin in the house, a call to the man who supplies water had him going to the chemist next door and delivering the medicine at once.

It is difficult to be lonely when you are greeted with beautiful music and sometimes the glow of an oil lamp from next door when you open your front door. You cannot feel isolated when the morning begins with the cry of the coffee seller, then the call of the man selling 'kolam' (geometric patterns created at the threshold) powder and the banana vendor and the tender coconut cart and the fruit man …. I find the silence I crave only before dawn, an all-too-short period before the koels and crows begin their chorus.

When I go for a walk, sometime later, I meet familiar faces, including a little girl who waves to me as she passes by in her school bus. We met on a nature walk in the neighbouring campus of Kalakshetra, where she listened with bright-eyed interest to all that was said and then shared her knowledge to identify a tree that no one else could.

When I return home, the tailors outside my house are setting up shop and my neighbour's open doors tell me that all's well across the wall that separates our houses. On some mornings, Sushila, my neighbour will emerge from her door with a steel tumbler brimming with foamy coffee. 'The best coffee in the world,' I tell her and it does taste better than any other I have had. Her culinary gifts extend to all that she makes and I am the fortunate recipient of extraordinary idlis and rasam, delicately flavoured vegetables such as banana stem and spinach, fenugreek and bitter gourd and even alu paratha. We met only five years ago, but Sushila is part of my life now, a happy, caring presence, a companion on trips to the theatre and the temple, to talks and festivals and shops. Her knowledge enlarges me and her kindness spills across the garden and over the wall to encircle her lucky neighbours. When Sushila's door is open, mine stays open too. Her open door gives me a sense of security in addition to the warm and friendly vibrations that flow from her home.

My days are filled with reading and writing and work with words that never seem to end. There is always a sense of anticipation of more to look forward to, of not enough time in which to do all that I would like to. I feel blessed.

The past year has brought me bouts of ill health, which have also served as signposts on my journey. In September I made elaborate plans to participate in a workshop in Chiang Mai in Thailand and to visit Angkor Wat. A week before I was scheduled to leave, a particularly nasty viral fever made me cancel my plans and slowed me down for months afterwards. Then, I went on a trip to places closer to Chennai and an asthma attack caused me to hurry back. It seemed as if being in Chennai was what I needed to be doing just now, until an unexpected asthma attack in Chennai has made me rethink all my certainties ... but that is another story!

My solitary state has changed since my daughter Vasundhara came home to stay. Her presence adds fizz and joy to my days. I was not lonely before she came home and continue to experience a sense of wonder at being connected in so many ways to loving friends in distant places, each of whom remains a part of my being.

Anonymous

Single in India

I've been single for nearly two-thirds of my life but was hopeful all the same, as I set out for a new job in a country I'd always romanticised about and read up everything by its native authors, way before Indian writers caught on and became popular. So here I am in my sixth decade, having just turned down offers from Dubai, Mexico and Italy, feeling surprisingly hopeful about meeting that special someone in New Delhi.

I'm convinced it's sheer luck, unmitigated chance when a romantic boon lands into one's lap from the chaotic void beyond. Having been a type 'A' personality for nearly most of my life, this is not too satisfactory an explanation though, as where is the 'me' in all this? Surely, I have *to do something* to deserve such a gift?

It's this inescapable paradigm that got me going, moving, taking on and trying out in the belief that with due diligence targeting a clear objective, I too could get rewarded like Goldilocks who exclaimed in wonder and delight 'Why, it's perfect! It's just right!'

After two 'not so right' marriages with interludes and in-betweens of loneliness and single motherhood, I alternated between the meat market and the cave — taking turns putting myself out there, expectant and open and then, retreating to solitude to lick my disappointment at the paltry fare. Silly me still looked for Lions, stalwarts in intellect and character even though I'd already proved inept in the judgement department as far as this goes not just once, but twice!

And so it was for the first few Indian men who entered my life. Instead of lions, I met an insomniac with one foot in depression even as the other foot was already being doggedly stalked by something serious. The rosy side to all this is that we are in India so there is always that much touted alternative path. There is always hope for such a lost soul. My insomniac put himself on some path to healing: soul-searching, self-discovering and communing with the divine. In fact, had it not been for his daily start-up ritual of yoga and meditation, he may not have made it through each day, day in and day out through the ongoing chasm. I had met lost souls before but not one imbued in the yogic and meditative. But what could be more natural after all, here in India?

Still, this Indian cliché seems to dog me unrelentingly as the next romantic foray saw me meeting up with an erudite and charming, fully Indian where the same scenario surfaced. As we flirted, skirted and explored, we shared stories and once more, I found myself with another 'wannabe sadhu'. I found myself confronted by a previously successful corporate type who'd just upped and liquidated his earthly possessions, said bye to wife and son, and yes, took himself off to some ashram in Vrindavan in search of that illusive something. Why me, pray tell?

I think I must have been primed to meet him. The universe surely sent him my way, seeing I am this unbelievable food magician. He was clearly being lured back into the material world because after three years of good works, duties and simple food, he'd started to feel thoroughly deprived of those finer things in life I'm a natural at dishing out as everyone tells me. A match made in heaven, maybe even that perfect fit perhaps?

Alas, where would the fun be if it were that easy, huh? So no, we really didn't fit much, actually, not at all. Once more, here I wait again, seemingly perfect, fully integrated with two feet planted firmly in all dichotomous worlds; separately, of course, just to make sure I'm balanced — waiting, but ....

Because I'm no dumb, I know with absolute certainty that this just ain't it. I'm that incurable romantic and optimist who just doesn't know how to give up. I really haven't. It's just that India and the Indian cliché do clutch and hold you to setting foot on that alternative path. It's my turn now.

That left-brain, type 'A' person I know so well is beginning to recede: not systematically pursuing some targeted goal is sitting well, now; staying in the moment and enjoying whatever comes along is just fine, too.

Simply 'being' feels pretty good and familiar.

Yes, I like that I'm laughing and even guffawing! And I'm sure I'll recognise and welcome that accident still to come my way when it makes its appearance or not. How can I possibly doubt that this is why I was meant to come here rather than go to glitzy Dubai!

Iona Lou Leriou
(As told to Sandhya Mendonca)

One Last Sip of Sap

I have always wanted to live by a river.

As a child I did, by the Hoogly in Kolkata and now I do, by a shining ribbon in the beautiful fields of Moira in Goa, but, in-between I met more rivers: the Seine in Paris, where I spent much of my working life; the Aude in the Oriental Pyrennes, that looped a little island where my French cousins lived; and then, one summer when I was in my mid-thirties, I met the quintessential river, in a tiny hamlet in the Ardeche, the region in France stretching from Lyon to Valence. I say quintessential, because it existed of itself; it was 'every river' and 'dream river' all in one.

There, too, I met two people who seemed as transparent as its waters, who taught me a great deal in a very short time.

It was a baking summer, and my friend Lavinia and I had decided to borrow a friend's car and head for two weeks in the country. Having, the year before, driven through the Ardeche and fallen in love with the region, I managed to find a cottage for rent by putting a finger on an isolated region with a river running through it and then calling the local agency.

Lav drove; my job was to keep her cat from garrotting himself with the bars of his cage. A thumping big grey tom with cold, fish-like eyes, he answered to the inappropriate name of Bunny and was to have his own (and much more exciting) adventures where we were heading.

As we passed Lyon and started climbing, the landscape changed dramatically. It was a poor one, for France, with none of the lushness of Normandy or the rich crops of the Lot et Garonne. Instead, there were low grey stone houses, walls and bridges, high plateaux, patches of grain or fruit orchards and, everywhere, rivers intersecting hills. Something about the simplicity of the region caught at the heart — at least mine.

We arrived at our destination at twilight. The hamlet of a handful of houses was on the ancient Route de Napoleon. Our cottage was opposite the large house where our hosts lived. They handed us the keys with a smile, and we tumbled into bed.

The next morning, we explored our domain: two rooms, one to sleep in and one to cook in — with metre-thick stone walls that kept us cool — giving onto a triangle of gravelled patio shaded by a lilac tree in full plumage, under which sat a tiny round tin table and two rickety chairs.

We met our hosts by daylight. Lucien was tall and spindly, with a shock of pure white hair, a pair of eyes so blue that it looked as if a bit of the sky had fallen into them, and a slow, soft smile. He was a beautiful man. He spoke little, but that was made up for by Annette, who was at least fifteen years younger than him. Small and nut brown, she was lively as a mockingbird, with a wreath of tight black plaits and sharp bright eyes that missed nothing. It was soon clear that she adored, and looked up to Lucien as the font of all wisdom. He, for his part, relied on her for all the things he was detached from.

They were both struck dumb at the news that two lone girls, had driven down all alone, with only a cat for protection, from that terrible and fascinating capital city where we lived ('incroyable!') all alone.

Lavinia was Italian (that was enough to stretch their eyes) but, as for my being Indian, that put the cherry on the cake. Red Indian, they asked? No. The Taj Mahal evoked no response, but elephants and tigers did. Annette, who had never left the south of France, jumped behind Lucien as if she expected a Bengal beauty to leap out at her from behind the wisteria.

The days that followed unrolled like an idyll. We were nestled in hills of peach orchards, at least twelve kilometres from the nearest village. Five minutes away from the cottage, down a grassy path bordered by poplars, one came to the little river. At that peak of August heat, it barely covered the glossy stones that lay on the riverbed like pillows. You could lie in it, with your head propped up on a larger stone, and read, with a canopy of shifting leaves overhead. Best of all, and I've never seen that anywhere else — it was bordered by narrow strips of pure white sand.

Lying in that cool stream, with the Oxford Book of English Verse, one could almost imagine Matthew Arnold's scholar gypsy parting the ferns and stepping down to join us.

Carrying a struggling Bunny, we would set off, after a late breakfast under the lilac tree to spend the day in the water. We would put the fruit in a shallow hollow to keep cool, and the wine in a deeper one; Lucien kept us well supplied with the latter, at five francs the litre bottle, made from his own grapes from his vineyards further down south, in Provence: 'drink, *mes enfants*, drink; it's only grape juice.' Needing no encouragement, we did. Of course, we had good crusty bread too, and the goat cheeses of the region, wrapped in chestnut leaves; *pate* and cherry tomatoes or smoked ham with the honey sweet melons in season. Bunny had the feline equivalent of all this in a tin.

Having no intention of wasting his time lolling around like us, he spent his days (and nights) scorching his paws on the hot sand, getting stuck up a towering oak tree, waging war on all his local brethren, and generally managing to get enough action to stir us up at least once a day. Annette was his fervent admirer. 'What a *numero*!' she would exclaim proudly, as she rescued him yet again and brought him back to us, hissing curses in her arms.

She generally crossed the road to visit us at breakfast time, ostensibly with a gift of fruit or vegetables from her garden in a cardboard box, but really to gossip. The sleepy village, according to her, was a sink of iniquity .... English lesbians, a deviant priest, the merry widows, the bent trades people, and as for the lawyer's daughter ...! We listened, bug-eyed, and didn't believe a word of it, though we enjoyed the stories immensely, and would egg her on to fresh excesses.

Contrary to what we'd assumed, she was Lucien's sister, not his wife. She had never married ('Who'd have had me? Look at my face!') but Lucien had once been engaged. While he was a young soldier in the last war, his delicate fiancée had died in an epidemic of influenza. Showing us a photograph of her, he said that he 'remained faithful to her memory,' playing all her favourite pieces of music every Sunday at the village church, where he was the organist.

It was a storybook life they lived: harvesting their peaches and grapes in season, growing their vegetables and flowers, cherishing their home and each other. They were never in a hurry; their days had the slow rhythm of a country-dance. In every matter, each was convinced that the other's opinion was the best way forward.

Most evenings, after dinner, Lucien would formally invite us to drink a 'digestif' with them. The garden he had created (Annette was happier with the vegetables) was like something out of a musical comedy: on a little lip of ground overlooking the valley showers of rosebushes ten feet high, banks of old-fashioned hollyhocks, larkspur, love-in-a-mist, lupines and wallflowers were crisscrossed with high hedges of lavender whose scent made the air almost too heavy to breathe. We then happily addled our senses further with Lucien's potent brews made from rosemary and thyme.

In that perfumed darkness, the stars shining above us like so many crystal lamps lit up the faces of that innocent pair, as they lifted their glasses to us yet again, to toast our new friendship.

We never went back.

When we returned to Paris, we sent Lucien a tie and Annette a scarf from Hermes and, for a few years, they would call us at the beginning of each summer to say that if we wanted to rent the cottage again, they would offer it to no one else.

But I never forgot them, and, years later, I must have been thinking about them, deep in my heart, when I wrote the poem called 'One Last Sip of Sap'.

One Last Sip of Sap
I have never seen the star jasmine
burn
so bright
as in this early spring:

It buds fiercely against the tough boughs.

Even withered, it clings to them,
as if craving
one last sip of sap.

So certain old people are,
with their eyes still as bright as stars;
their gnarled fingers still milking
joy

from the smallest of pleasures.

Tanya Mendonsa

Single Belle, Single Belle, Single All the Way

He was sixteen and I was fourteen when we last met.

Douglas and I were sweethearts in the purest sense of the word; lots of handholding and a few countable quick goodnight kisses after Saturday night jam sessions in Ajmer, the small one-horse town in which we then lived.

To get me out of the small town, my parents dispatched me to Mumbai to make a career for myself. Before I left, Douglas proposed to me. I said a tearful no. He wanted to know the reason. I lied: 'Because I am Mangalorian and my parents would want me to marry only a Mangalorian.'

The truth was somewhat different. My parents' actual objections would have stemmed from the difference in life stations. I was highly educated, and going in for still further professional study. He was an Anglo-Indian, a school dropout (Standard V) and had a low-paying job in the Ajmer railways.

I forgot all about him even before the train had moved out of the Ajmer junction. I went to Mumbai, made a name and career, got married, had three children, got divorced, made a new life for myself and my children in Bangalore, was fairly happy. In fact, miles and kilometres happier than I was when in an unhappy marriage!

Out of the blue, a few years ago, the phone in my house rang and Douglas was on the line, calling from the USA. After nearly falling unconscious with surprise, I responded to his questions, and the conversation proceeded. We exchanged quick updates. On his part, he had gone from Ajmer to Delhi, progressed in the telecom industry, moved on to America, married his brother's wife's younger sister. They had two children, he turned alcoholic, she left him, they were divorced, and at the point of death, he gave up alcohol and was now living a comparatively happy life in Maryland near Washington.

Much as I enjoyed his call, I wanted to be honest. A lot of water had flown under the bridge since we were in Ajmer, and the major event in my life was that I had met Christ in a 'born again' experience, and now functioned by a strict code.

I said: 'Douglas, I am not in the market for marriage or for an affair.'

Unfazed, he said, 'Why don't we try friendship?'

So we tried friendship. He called up often and we had long friendly conversations; between the hustle and bustle of being a single mom to three teenage children, I loved sharing events with Douglas who had always been very caring and considerate. He was interested in everything I had to share, which, as any single mother would agree, was balm for a wounded spirit.

What followed was inevitable. I have a media job that involves global travel and I soon accepted Douglas' invitation to stop by at Maryland on a return journey from Maui, Hawaii.

We were meeting after forty years!

The skinny Ajmer girl had turned into a grossly overweight mother of three adult children.

The good-looking Anglo-Indian boy from Ajmer was now bald but otherwise the same; he too adored his kids who now lived with his ex-wife.

We proceeded to have two memorable days in America's most environmental friendly state. Of course I stayed in Douglas' house, and our relationship was — if that were possible — even cleaner than the one we had known in Ajmer. His ex-wife came across to meet me and we got on like a house on fire. I loved his children, especially his daughter. His brother, whose wife worked in World Bank, had also settled in Maryland in a palatial house; they threw a huge party for me and it was like being back in Ajmer, guitars and non-stop singing, music and dancing.

But the best part of it was sitting and talking through much of the night, over hot mugs of coffee. Douglas and I shared all that had happened since we last met — the achievements, the progress, the trips downhill, heartbreaks, survival, learning to smile again. We agreed about everything but encountered an insurmountable problem when I talked about my walk with Christ. Douglas is a nominal Christian who does not even go to church. I live and breathe for my Saviour and Lord.

By the time he saw me off to the airport, we were both hiding terror in our hearts. The past was gone. But did the future have anything to offer us? Moreover, even if it had anything to offer us, did we want to take it?

I came back to Bangalore and to an email where Douglas wrote that he had gone home from the airport and cried for several hours, which shocked him. 'I did not cry even on the day of my divorce,' he said, sadly. He was petrified at the intensity of his feelings and in a subsequent email wondered if he was ready for another relationship.

On my part, I was joyful, enjoying the affection of a decent and caring man. I did not ponder much about the future because I have handed over that responsibility to Christ. That is the beauty of being a 'born again' Christian. Christ is alive in you and with you, and handles everything, including decisions. And you obey Him because He inspires trust. So after depositing the dilemma into His capable hands through a submission prayer ('Lord, should I proceed with this friendship with Douglas or not? Please let me know with complete clarity so that there is no confusion in my heart'), I went about my life and work.

I would be lying if I said my heart did not ache with trauma when in the days that followed, with complete clarity that left no room for doubt Christ made it clear to me through Biblical verses and my daily morning meditations that this relationship was not for me. I wept and stormed and went into mild depression. For the first time since I was born again in 1990, I was 'katti' (not-talking-to-you) with Christ and refused to speak to Him or touch my Bible at least for a week.

But one can't do without spiritual oxygen for long; I soon returned to Him and after our 'patch up' I myself got a glimpse of what my Saviour had been able to see through the x-ray of divinity: firstly, one cannot turn back the clock which is what in effect Douglas and I were trying to do. Secondly, other differences can be levelled, adjusted to or ironed out, but not when two persons are on different spiritual planes. Finally, when one has been single for as long as Douglas and I have individually been, one gets used to one's personal space, and it becomes very, very difficult to accept the idea of sharing it with another person, however beloved.

So for the second time in our lives, Douglas and I parted and this time we knew it was forever.

The tingle of single is not something that one can take for granted or endanger. There is always that frying-pan-to-the-fire possibility. Who wants to take a chance 'khalli pilli' (unnecessarily)?

Not this single belle!

Ingrid Albuquerque-Solomon

Twice Married

When I interview people for my articles, I invariably get asked, 'Are you married?' to which I reply that I am happily single.

Most people express disbelief, which is usually followed by a complicated listing of all the advantages of having a partner, which is followed by the part that really makes me groan. 'I know so and so's son. Would you be interested in meeting him and seeing where it goes?' I, of course, politely decline. Initially I used to get quite irritated by this sequence.

Now I take it in my stride as I realise their intentions are good. I still wonder why is it so difficult for individuals to let a single person be single and why they doubt that singles are happy. I, for one, am single by choice and not by force, and being single rocks. Many of my married friends envy me, they openly tell me so. Freedom, no compromises and the emotional roller coaster on which most relationships ride are thankfully not part of my personal life.

And if you have something you love doing, then it makes the journey of life all the more exciting. I love meeting people, listening to their stories, gaining an insight into their lives and getting paid for it on top of that. There are cynics aplenty who warn me against loneliness and depression taking over the later years of my life. I tell them, matter-of-factly, that both loneliness and depression could, at any point in time, become a part of anyone's life — regardless of whether the person is married or single. What matters is how loneliness and depression are dealt with.

Though I love my single status, I have now adopted a new policy. If people ask, 'Are you married?' I reply, 'Of course. Twice over. First, to someone who I believe knows me best and second, to that which gives me the joy of making a positive difference in people's lives. The first is myself and the second is my work.' The expression on their faces is priceless, some even nod approvingly.

Khursheed Dinshaw

My Story

I was born twenty-four years ago in a village in Assam, which can't be traced even on Google earth. Like every other kid, I was born naked but God marked me with three features, which were to have a great impact on how the rest of my life followed: I was a Marwari; I didn't understand numbers; and I was single.

For those who do not know much about Marwaris, we are a clan in which the first word a child is taught to say is 'business'. I didn't. I was different. No one told me this, but I figured it out by the look on my Dad's face every time he signed my Math paper. I remember having long conversations with God, trying to strike a deal with him if he cancelled my exams or at least whispered how to distribute 276 marbles equally between 14 boys. But that never happened and the marbles were often left undistributed. The only reason I did study at times, however, was to please my father. The occasional pat on the back, or words of praise which, if I was lucky, could get as flattering as 'keep it up', made the sleepless nights worth it.

My inability to add even single digits without the use of a calculator is also the reason I am not married with two kids. You see, the fate of most of my friends from the clan was decided even before they were conceived. Finish school. Graduate. Join family business. Get married at twenty-two. Make a baby. Well, what the hell, make another one? Live happily ever after. End of the story.

At twenty-two, I was still wearing striped yellow pyjamas and eating left over pizzas for breakfast. At twenty-two, I was also a copywriter, making a living out of adding words. Living a zillion light years away from home in a city, which introduced me to the fascinating concept of microwave, I realised whoever it was who coined the phrase 'life in the fast lane' was really serious. The robotic life sucked people's ability to express themselves. At home, I could complain, laugh or talk about anything. Here I couldn't. I didn't have anyone. Besides, it would probably have upset the person who coined the phrase anyway. Even when I was in love I recall — oh! I completely missed that part out. Love!

College is like a contagious disease where you need to have a really strong immune system to not to become a victim of beer, rock music and love. So coming back to the point, when I was in love with the most beautiful girl on earth, I felt it was both imperative and beautiful to express my love. It almost came as an epiphany. Say it. Or she'll find someone else!

Cards. Messages scribbled on notebooks. DVDs. Recorded messages. Conversations over coffee. Over the telephone. Sometimes during no conversation at all. Words always found a way through. Until one day, priorities came in between like an indestructible demon devouring all there once was between us. That day, words couldn't get through. And just as God meant me to be when I was born, I was single again. It wasn't a pleasant thing to happen in a city where you had to pay a fee to speak your heart out to someone. And it wasn't just me; it was the same story for most people. Either people had no one to express their feelings to or they didn't care to express their feelings to someone who cared to listen. I was suddenly hit by the realisation that I was among people who were, ironically, too busy to enjoy the very reason for which they stay busy for — to be happy. That was the moment for yet another round of soul searching of the kind most twenty-something-year-olds go through. Time to choose how I wanted to spend the rest of my life. Choices lined up as crossroads like in one of Robert Frost's poems, and I could pick just one.

Two years later, on a hot afternoon, a man was dragged into a bookstore by his wife to help her select books for her training in accountancy. He was a writing enthusiast but his profession never allowed his imagination to consider it seriously. When they walked in, his wife drew his attention to a poster about a book launch. The poster had his photo and name on it. It was his book that was being launched! Someone must have made a mistake, he thought. It couldn't be! But suddenly his family and friends turned up! They had come for the launch of his very own coffee table book, which had stories and poems from his blog. The wife was overwhelmed, friends were excited, family was pleased, and the husband, surprised.

My name is Varun Todi and this is what I now do. I organise surprises.

The idea was triggered in a 138 sq. ft. room by my partner who also had a sudden epiphany that there was more to life than making excel sheets for the MNC he worked for. He thought — why not organise surprises for people who are too busy to do it themselves? The more we probed the idea, the weirder it seemed and the more sense it made. Finally, on 3 June 2009, it turned into a company. We named it 'Oye Happy'.

But with time I've realised that surprises are not just about fun and being wacky. I think, in our own little way, we became a medium for people to express what they generally do not, or can't.

There was a guy in his early thirties who called me to say that he wanted his wife back but didn't know how to. Years of routine life had gradually but visibly taken away all traces of the chirpy, jovial person she once was. Now she barely smiled. He held himself responsible for what she had become. He wanted to apologise to her. Tell her he wanted her back. But couldn't. It naturally took us longer than usual to plan out the perfect surprise on her birthday. On that evening, after that surprise, she cried.

As I write this, I realise that none of it would have happened had I not been born with those three magical characteristics. Being Marwari built that natural acumen for business. I am still bad with numbers, but not quite so with ideas. And I am still single. The relationship phase of life, taught me the value of expressing myself and I must confess that I probably wouldn't have been able to make a difference in others' lives had it not been for the difference she made in mine.

I'd like to end this with a small incident. My Dad was in the city lately for a few days and during his stay, he kept a casual track on all the surprises planned in the city. A day before his flight was due, he walked in to my room while I was busy working on an order, stood there for a while, and said, 'Keep it up.'

Varun Todi

Free as a Bird

'Hey, how about a trip to Bharatpur and Rajasthan? The weather is perfect, lots of migratory birds to see and I can arrange the accommodation. We'll be driving of course.'

That's Rupa, my old school roommate and lifelong friend. For one moment, one glorious moment, I close my eyes and dream ... the only sounds, the hum of the engine and the wind rushing through my hair as we meander through a golden landscape dotted with rugged forts and crescent sand dunes, ancient havelis (mansions) and sprawling palaces!

The insistent doorbell pulls me back to my suburban home. The children, dusty and noisy, charge in throwing bags and shoes around. I smile as the youngest hugs me with joyous abandon. Rajasthan flies out of the window!

Rupa is single and the object of admiration (tinged with envy!) of all her 'married' friends, who look yearningly at her uncluttered existence, defer to her forthright opinions and respect her confident stance. No unseemly squabble mars the harmony of her household; there is no one to fight with! No one pushes the food away saying 'yuck'; she cooks only when and how she feels like! No frantic searching for the elusive pen; she knows exactly where all her things are. No need to concoct excuses, she always has time, especially for her friends! Neither guilt nor compromises dictate her behaviour. When things do go wrong, as they often do in this imperfect world, she accepts her responsibilities with serenity. There is no shifting of blame on others' shoulders. To her circle of friends, she seems as free as the birds she loves.

For bird watching is her ruling passion, and driving into the wide-open spaces, her great delight. At the crack of dawn on most weekends, Rupa sets off with friends, soft music on the car stereo, a packed picnic lunch and a flexible itinerary. Could anyone ask for more? Sometimes, thanks to an understanding family, I join her for the day trips. We argue amicably about the route, stop to admire the scenery or eagerly scan the birds perched on bushes and wires looped erratically over the countryside. There is no hurry, no deadlines to meet. The journey is of the essence.

But it hasn't always been so. Born into the quintessential army family, Rupa willingly followed in the footsteps of her doctor parents, content with the familiar antiseptic smell of the wards, the crisp starched uniforms, and the welfare of her patients. Just why had she remained single? Not by any design on her part. She was no man-hater, no fiery rebel fighting for female emancipation. Her parents, with very dissimilar backgrounds and from opposite parts of the country, had defied society to marry. Unwilling to settle for the conventional arranged marriage, Rupa had waited for the perfect soul mate all of us are convinced exists somewhere.

As an army doctor she had relished the challenge of living independently, often in the officers' mess itself, sometimes the only woman there. The security and camaraderie of the army cantonment had sustained her. Wide-ranging postings followed, some in busy cantonments, some close to enemy lines, fraught with ever-present danger. A spell in a remote outpost in Assam slowed her pace of life to that of the lumbering wild elephants that stole flour from the mess kitchens and sometimes stood athwart on the road, daring the drivers. A stint in Nepal, touring the villages of the legendary Gurkha soldiers, kindled in her a love for the outdoors and the magnificent birds and animals that share the environment uneasily with humans.

She had loved the familiar army routine and thought it was forever, but life has a way of taking one by surprise. The worsening health of her retired parents, living alone in Pune, compelled her to seek premature retirement. Her only brother, working abroad, was unable to help out much beyond sending money home regularly.

It was a life-changing decision. To give up a promising career midway, resigned to staying at home, dependent on a pension while still relatively young, was a huge sacrifice but one she made willingly. I remember her telling me with sadness, 'It hurts so much to see my parents like this. I have looked up to them all my life, for advice and support. Now it is my turn to give.'

Those were difficult years. Her batch mates forged ahead to increasingly important posts, while she struggled with chronic problems at home. Her parents required nursing round the clock. While her medical background helped, it was also sometimes a handicap. Too clear a picture of all that can go wrong medically is not conducive to mental peace. On particularly stressful days, worn out dealing with unreliable maids and careless nurses, she would yearn to break free, to go away, even if just for a day!

Determined to retain a measure of independence, she had insisted on living in her own flat in the same colony. This became her 'den,' her retreat away from the anxiety clouding her parent's home. Bolstered by her support system — her friends, Rupa slowly came to terms with her situation. Long leisurely lunches with her friends, nattering on all subjects under the sun, were a welcome break. A job as a part-time professor at a medical college had proved to be a lifeline, letting her hone her professional skills. 'I will never waste my life. I will live each moment as if it is my last,' she had vowed.

With the passing of her parents within a few years of each other, Rupa was truly alone. We worried about her. Would she sink into depression or just drift aimlessly? But she had her priorities well chalked out. Her new life was like a rebirth, a resurrection. Conscious of the fleeting moment, she was determined to relish and enjoy every opportunity life had to offer. This led her to reject tempting offers of full-time employment in favour of her part-time work. 'Not for anything will I give up my precious leisure time! Never again will I be tied down.'

A liberated Rupa now lives by her mantra of taking big pleasure in small things. Mistress of her fortunes once again, she has trekked through the magical Valley of Flowers, and verdant coffee plantations of Coorg, delighted in the challenge of identifying different bird species and exulted upon the sighting of the rare Great Indian Bustard. In her stout walking shoes, festooned with binoculars and camera, armed with maps and a copy of the indispensable 'Birds of India' by Salim Ali, she lives the dream most of us yearn for — the freedom to do as we like!

Her feathered friends are bound by invisible territories and migratory patterns. So, too, is Rupa bound to her home in Pune, the nest she returns to like a homing pigeon after every foray into the wild, every flight into adventure, her own nest cocooned by her family and friends!

One day perhaps, when my own nestlings have flown the nest, I too will drive with her up the sandy Rann of Kutch, and watch flocks of flamingos take wing into the sunset.

Sarita Varma

Culinary Adventures

'If you don't mind my asking, are you single?' said the mother of a five-year-old after I had finished her child's photo shoot.

'No I don't mind at all, and yes, I am single,' I replied.

'How does it feel? How do you manage?' she continued.

'It feels good and I manage quite well, actually,' I replied. Being a single man, I often get asked these questions and am rather proud of the way I have learnt to manage. For me, one of the most crucial aspects of being single was learning how to cook — not just survive on Maggi noodles and chai and fried eggs, if you know what I mean.

Cooking was something I learnt more out of desperation than by choice. After all, when your stomach is growling in the middle of the night you do have to satiate those hunger pangs. You can't be eating at a restaurant every day. A home-cooked meal is what you begin to crave for. So I took my first lessons in cooking from a friend of mine who dropped in from Mumbai. He helped me buy vegetables and pulses. He taught me how to make khichdi. It was my first attempt at cooking a proper meal.

But when I tried to make it on my own, I put too much salt and overcooked it and it ended up a gooey mix of rice and dal. So the next time I hesitated to add more salt and took the pan off the flame before the khichdi was ready. The result? It was raw and tasteless. By trial and error, I got the proportions and timing right and my first well-cooked dish was a dry potato vegetable.

Now I really enjoy preparing my food and eating it, too. Changing the gas is not a big deal, I am an expert at grocery shopping (the only time I was not alert was when I got a call on my mobile and the vendor weighed overripe tomatoes and slyly put them in the bag) and yes, my dishes turn out tasty. I am the master chef of my own kitchen!

Initially my friends, specially my lady friends, would refuse to believe that I could cook well, as I have not had any formal training. They thought I got the dishes from a restaurant and passed them off as my own. Their doubts were put to rest when I invited them over and demonstrated my culinary skills.

'Wow! Hemant, we had no idea you cook so well! You must give us the recipe,' was what I was told. From an egg bhurji to vegetable biryani, I can cook it all.

The other day I caught my neighbour staring at me as I was entering my home. 'Is something the matter?' I asked her.

She seemed a bit embarrassed but nevertheless asked, 'Is a lady staying with you? There was a delicious aroma wafting from your kitchen in the morning.' I was flattered; my fish curry couldn't have got a better compliment. And I do enjoy putting my married male friends in a tight spot as their wives admiringly request me to teach their husbands, if not how to cook, then at least how to help out in the kitchen.

The other day a relative, who is a self-confessed 'culinary disaster,' dropped by to catch up with me. I was leaving to purchase my monthly supplies and she agreed to accompany me. She watched as I searched the aisles of the departmental store for rock salt, checked the MRP and date of manufacture on the cheese spread, compared prices and quantities of three brands of basmati rice and chose the best one. Then she remarked, 'You sure have made good use of your single status. I had no clue you are such a pro. I am getting inspired to learn from you.'

The proud grin on my face said it all!

Hemant Patil

My Nomadic Daughter

My daughter, Khush, is excited. She is trying on the handmade bamboo earrings she purchased from Silchar, in Assam. Khush is pleased to see how well they go with her Japanese wooden footwear, the one that goes clickety-click. Today it is Khush's 'deck up' day as I call it. The first time my strictly jeans-and-kurti dress code daughter had decked up in an embroidered shirt and wrap-around skirt, I had asked her elatedly with whom she was going out. She had replied, 'Mom yaar, I am going out by myself. I felt like dressing up and looking good, for myself. Aren't I the most important special person in my life?'

Khush is in her thirties, unmarried and happily single by choice. She got her first marriage proposal when she was sixteen. At that time, we told the boy's parents that she was too young and we wanted her to be independent before even thinking of settling down. My daughter did become very independent. She also became very clear about what she wanted from her life — to be happily single.

She has her share of admirers and if any of them tries to

cross his limit, she tells me, 'I delete him from my inbox and my life.' Khush loves to travel and is a self-confessed nomad. So she will pack her bag and go see India whenever she feels like it. To be able to travel, she even chose a freelance writing career that would allow her to pursue her passion. In Mathura, she was mistaken for a foreigner because of her fair skin. As the 'lassiwala' told his friend to pose while she clicked photos Khush kept quiet and once she was done answered to his comments in chaste Hindi. 'The look on the guy's face was priceless,' she told me over the phone. In Gwalior the guide called her up five months later just to wish her for Holi. In a remote town in Assam, she sat with the blind bhajan singer and recorded his voice to be able to listen to him back home while Kanya Kumari's sunrise was totally worth the early morning waking up that my normally late-rising daughter had to do. In Bangalore, she enjoyed the idli variations while in Kohima she was given a traditional tribal welcome.

Exploring a new place, meeting new people, seeing and being a part of their culture, traditions and customs is an exhilarating experience for her. 'I want the freedom to do this,' she said to me. 'It makes me happy. Do I not have the right to be happy? Being single allows me that,' she told me when I asked her if this was what she wanted to do with her life. As her mother I have been worried. When she was in her twenties, I hoped she would find someone who would take care of her and settle down. I had mentioned it to her. 'You worry unnecessarily,' she said, with some exasperation. 'Why don't you understand that I can take care of myself? Do you have more confidence in a stranger looking after me than in your own blood taking care of herself?' she had asked me, rather wisely. She was right.

But a mother's heart needs reassurance. So when I see my daughter smile, wink at me and say, 'Mom, just chill, I will always be fine, I know what I am doing, trust me,' before she picks up the next travel brochure I know that my daughter has grown up, taken charge of her life single-handedly and is living it on her own enjoyable terms.

Nina Irani

Sister Lavinia

Adie and I grew up in the same neighbourhood. We attended the same school and were good friends right up till matriculation. She was a jolly person bubbling with life, and had an irrepressible penchant for mischief. In those days, Adie's love had been music and dancing.

Then even before we could join college, Adie announced that she was going to become a nun. 'Right now I'm not very happy about being forcibly thrust into a religious cage with my wings clipped. But I can't refuse. My parents have taken a vow that their eldest daughter would take the veil.'

Though there were no tears in her eyes, I could sense the turmoil in her heart. No more fun and frolic; no more dancing for sure; perhaps no more music too. Adie was sent off to a convent in a different town for her training as a postulant. I did not see her again for many years, neither did I get any news of her.

In 1990 when I came home for a holiday, I heard there was going to be a musical concert staged at my alma mater. I decided to go. There were thirty young students on stage with their different instruments. The conductor was a nun called Sister Lavinia.

The orchestra gave a brilliant performance and the applause they received was thunderous. When Sister Lavinia took her bow it suddenly struck me that this was good old Adie. I was in one of the front rows, and when her eyes fell on me, she beamed her contagious smile as much as to say, 'I might still have curlers in my hair under my wimple. But I sure made it.'

I hurried backstage to see her and went straight into her outstretched arms.

'We must meet,' she said, 'Can you have coffee with me tomorrow?'

The next day, our coffee mugs in hand, we moved out into the compound and sat on a bench under a mango tree, so that no one could eavesdrop. I said a bit awkwardly, 'So, how do I address you? Sister Lavinia or Adie?'

'Hey, I'm the same old Adie,' she said, taking my hand, 'But remember, not in public.'

We laughed and talked about our school days and classmates. Then the conversation veered to her life in the convent.

'I was sent to this convent three years ago. It brought back so many memories of our carefree school years. I was hoping that we'd meet some day. I heard that you were working somewhere in the North, where your husband was posted.'

'Yes, I'm on my annual leave. But tell me about yourself. Any regrets, Aida? Don't you miss family life — a loving husband and a houseful of mischievous kids just like yours used to be?'

She looked me straight in the eye.

'I know people think we nuns lead frustrating lives, always envious of happily married women. I also am aware that there are many crotchety old nuns who spend their entire lives fighting with God for imprisoning them in convents. But I can only speak for myself.'

'And you've never been miserable or lonely? You've never thought of handsome men who could have wooed and won you? Never dreamt of white flowing gowns and bridal trains held by pretty flower girls? Never regretted the fact that you missed the thrill of shopping for negligees to add to your trousseau?'

The sound of Adie's laughter was something I can never forget.

'Dear,' she said, 'Being single is not second rate. Neither is it a disease that can be cured by marriage. I have long been convinced that God never intended me to marry. I lack for nothing. I have a good education and am fairly knowledgeable in worldly wisdom. I'm well qualified in music because I was encouraged by my superiors to do so. I have the gift of humour and am able to see the silver lining even in the worst situations. At the risk of sounding pompous, I consider myself God's gift to the sisterhood.'

Once again, her laughter tinkled like a chiming bell.

'You saw my students perform last night. Could I have trained them like that if I were not happy at heart? I use my gifts to serve others.'

'But you do remember how crazy you were about dancing. How you used to pester us — one-two-three, one-two-three, turn to the right, bend to the left, twirl across the stage? How did you conquer that craze?'

She took my hand in hers again.

'I've never stopped dancing, dear. But it's no more with the likes of Fred Astaire and Gene Kelly. These days I dance with God. His strong arms guide me through the most complicated manoeuvres of life. I can assure you they are exhilarating moments.'

'Bravo Sister Lavinia,' I said, giving her a parting hug, 'After what I've heard, I don't think I can call you Adie. You have acquired such an incomparable status!'

Eva Bell

Ann's Date-o-logy

'Want to come for another session of my own personal torture?' asked my friend Ann, over the phone.

'Why not?' I replied, amused. Ann's love life or rather, the lack of it was a hot topic of debate in her family. They had tried to set her up with different men, each funnier or nuttier than the other. Now Ann and we, her friends, were so accustomed to these live comedy routines that we learnt to enjoy ourselves. Ann's parents just didn't want her to be single. They wanted her to get married.

'But look at my choices,' she would giggle. And we would join in.

Her first suitor, within the first ten minutes of their first meeting, had poured his heart out. It seemed he had taken the metrosexual male image too far. Ann didn't want to be saddled with a weepy partner nor did she appreciate being the agony aunt of her second date who ended up seeking advice on how to woo back his ex-girlfriend. The next guy was well dressed, his shoes were polished, and he was well groomed and appeared quite distinguished. Three dates later, he confessed to being gay. Ann had suspected it all along; she just wanted to hear it from the horse's mouth.

Meanwhile, the parents kept trying to find a suitable match for Ann who is not only smart and well educated, but a lecturer in a prestigious MBA college. Being financially independent and having a good intellect didn't seem to be helping with her dates and as she dreaded which man she would next be forced to go out with, her birthday approached.

We all gave her presents, but her parents stood empty handed. Because on this, her thirty-fifth birthday, they gave her the best gift of all — the freedom to find her own life partner or remain single.

'Ann we have always pushed you into going out with men who didn't deserve you. We realise that it was our concern about who would look after you if something happened to us. But we forgot that the most capable person is standing right in front of us — you. The way you manage yourself single-handedly makes us proud,' they said in unison. Ann was teary-eyed; this time they were tears of happiness.

Khursheed Dinshaw

Rocking K

I first met Kazveen or K, as I call her, at a friend's dinner party. She struck me as witty and intellectual. She didn't speak much, but what little she spoke made a lot of sense to me. Soon we started meeting more often and K became a part of our group of 'rocking singles' as we call ourselves. At the time she was the director of the Pune Zoo and I would often pull her leg about her passion for her 'wild babies' and why she chose this out of the ordinary career. 'Because it's challenging and exciting. There is never a dull moment. I simply couldn't see myself treating cats and dogs for the rest of my life. So I decided to become a wildlife veterinarian,' she said.

K loves being single. It gives her the freedom to follow her own dreams. And that she has happily done. From Pune, Goa, Morocco to now Singapore, she has worked with wildlife and says that being on her own allows her to indulge her whims and fancies. With a Master's degree in Wild Animal Health from the Royal Veterinary College, London, thanks to the numerous scholarships she received from charitable trusts and organisations, she got her first job with the Pune

Municipal Corporation, in charge of a zoo named Peshwe Park. She worked there for almost three years. Following the urge to work with free-living wildlife she moved on to work with the Goa Forest department where she was responsible for all wildlife health matters of the state. It was a wonderful experience to live in a forest and on completion of her contract she decided to look for another adventure.

It came soon enough and she left for Morocco. K worked in a captive breeding centre of Houbara Bustard, an endangered bird there. Her work there was an enlightening experience, for she learnt about recent advancements in the field of breeding birds in captivity. She also had the exhilarating experience of living in a totally different culture.

She returned to India as director of the Pune Zoo, The Rajiv Gandhi Zoological Park, which she took up in order to attempt to make a difference in people's attitudes at the way they look at zoos. Once when I had gone to meet her, she was not in office. I found her walking around the zoo picking up empty plastic bags and empty plastic water bottles thrown on the pathways. She told me that one of her babies had almost choked because of gross negligence of the visitors. 'These empty plastic wrappers can fly into the enclosures of my wild babies. Animals get attracted to plastic and can choke on them,' she had said in an irritated tone as she bent to pick up another empty wrapper.

An environment crusader, she henceforth made the Pune Zoo plastic bag free by banning plastic bags on its premises. Recently, K left for Singapore to pursue yet another dream — that of becoming the curator of the Jurong Bird Park. When I had asked her whether she was nervous or reconsidering her option to move, she replied that she loved the challenge of moving out of her comfort zone. 'Plus, I have no responsibilities to bog me down. My decision of leaving and starting all over again will only affect me. I like that. That is why I consciously choose to be single. I love my work so I never feel the desperate need to be with someone. Sure, on an odd day I feel that it would be nice to be pampered but then that feeling passes soon enough. Being single is totally worth it,' she replied as she gave me her dimpled smile.

I am happy for K. She is living the life she wants — combining her love for travel and wildlife and enjoying every moment of it. And for me she is a shining example of her core belief, 'If you love what you are doing, life becomes meaningfully complete.'

Hemant Patil

3
SINGLE PARENTING

There are two lasting bequests we can give our children. One is roots. The other is wings.
—Hodding Carter, Jr.

Family in Court

Welcome to the Solomon Family Court.

Meet the family. There are three children — Johann, Jacqueline and Janet; then there's me, single mom and author of this piece. My husband had abandoned the family when the children were very young. After we had exhausted our tear ducts we decided among ourselves that the world had not ended and we were going to do all we could to make family life fun. The Family Court was one of the creative traditions we designed to resolve conflicts and clashes.

A formal description of the court: The 'chief arbitrator' had to be a family member who was not part of the difference on hand. There had to be a 'Note Taker' who was not directly involved with the problem being dealt with. The two persons connected with the problem had to shake hands and agree right at the start of the court session, that they wanted to resolve the problem, and would abide by the rules and regulations set by the arbitrator.

Here is just one of the problems that got resolved in our family court —

Problem: Johann, aged sixteen, wanted the right to lock the door of his room from within. His mother, that is I, was not in favour of that. He said he was old enough to have privacy. I felt but did not say so, that this was the age when children got into bad habits like smoking or whatever, and it usually started behind locked doors of their rooms. Anyway, we had begun to have prolonged arguments on the subject and before it got any worse, we decided to have a 'family court' on the matter.

We chose a Sunday afternoon because that was one day, which would allow the court as much time as was needed to reach a resolution. The neatly covered 400-page notebook that served as the Family Court Logbook was brought out.

Jacqueline, aged fourteen-and-a-half, was appointed Court Arbitrator and Janet, aged eleven and a half, the Note Taker, since neither was part of the problem.

Johann and I shook hands and agreed that we both wanted the problem to be resolved; after that Jacqueline read out the rules:

- No raised voices
- No talking out of turn; everyone who wanted to have a say had to take her permission
- No one was allowed to walk away until the matter was resolved

Thus the court moved into session.

Step One: Proper identification of the problem

Johann and I, turn by turn, identified the problem, as we perceived it.

Johann: I would like the right to bolt my door from within. I am in college now and think I am old enough to be allowed to bolt my door because I need privacy.

Mother: I am not in favour of Johann's bolting his door from within. Most responsible parents do not allow their teenage children to bolt the door from within. I was interviewing Jaya Bachchan once, for Savvy magazine, when her daughter Shweta came in and asked her mother permission to bolt her door from within for an hour during which she wanted to have a head bath; she said she did not want to take her clothes into the bathroom in case they got wet. She wanted privacy in case her brother Abhishek walked into the room suddenly. If in spite of their studying in Switzerland at that time, the Bachchan children were not allowed to bolt their rooms from within, then I don't think that I am being unreasonable when I tell Johann not to do the same.

Step Two: Brainstorming session

The Arbitrator then announced the start of the brainstorming session in which all present were called upon to give their views about how to solve the problem. The Note Taker took down every view, however outlandish it sounded. No one was allowed to laugh, pooh-pooh or comment on another person's idea. The ideas that got listed:

- Johann could bolt the door when Mother was not at home.
- The bolt should be removed then Johann would not be able to bolt it.
- Johann should tell Mother the reason for which he wanted to bolt the door; and Mother would, at her discretion, allow or forbid it.
- Johann could bolt the door, and one of his sisters could peep from the window to see what he was doing, and then report to Mother.

- Johann should be allowed to shut the door if not bolt it, and no one should enter without knocking first and receiving permission from him to enter.
- If Johann was not allowed to bolt the door, then even Mother should not be allowed to bolt the door of her room which she often did.

And so on.

Step Three: Idea discussion one by one, each idea was picked up and considered until it was discussed threadbare, and finally, after a good half hour, we hit upon a solution. As had been decided right at the outset, it had to be a solution agreeable to both of us.

Step Four: The Solution and The Agreement

The solution was that Johann would not bolt his door but he would shut it and no one — including, and especially, Mother — could enter without first knocking and receiving his permission. Johann and I both had to compromise and meet each other half way to accept this solution, but it was a win-win situation since both of us were happy with it. We shook hands on it, and signed the agreement as written down by the Note Taker.

Dealing with problems thus became 'fun time' within our family, without losing out on the seriousness of situations. There was also an element of 'fairness' (so important to teenage children!) about the proceedings and about decisions made in our home; which eliminated the scope for bitterness and long-term ill will.

Why do people refer to single parent families as broken families? In our home, one parent did walk out. But the rest of us did not break.

In fact, I dare to say that thanks to the many traditions we created, there was more laughter and joy in our home than could be found in many two-parent homes where 'mom and dad hate each other' and each one in the home does his or her own thing.

And this is not 'khatte angoor' (sour grapes) speaking but succulent, mouth-watering seedless black grapes.

Ingrid Albuquerque-Solomon

Jacob's Joy

Jacob sits hunched on the floor, busy trying to fit the pieces of a jigsaw puzzle, pretending not to get them right. He fumbles and looks puzzled.

Six-year-old Ryan looks exasperated. 'Dad, this piece goes there. This one fits here. I think I am cleverer than you. What would you do without me?'

Jacob smiles. He has succeeded in making Ryan feel the smarter of the two. Jacob is not Ryan's real dad. Ryan's parents died when a tanker collided with their car on the Mumbai-Pune expressway, killing all the occupants on the spot. They had gone to receive a relative from abroad, who was to stay with them.

Jacob is Ryan's uncle, his mother's only brother. When the tragedy occurred, three-year-old Ryan was playing with his toys at his uncle's house, blissfully unaware of what had happened.

In the days following the funeral, Jacob was faced with a number of tough decisions. Could he adopt his nephew and bring him up as his own son? Was he mentally prepared to take on the responsibility of another human being, that too, of one who was just three years old? Was he ready to give up his free, casual lifestyle, which revolved around his own needs? Babysitting for a few hours and living with a three-year-old were two different things. It was not easy for Jacob, for as he kept weighing the consequences of looking after Ryan, the doubts mounted.

It took him a few days to realise the strength of the conviction that lay within him — that he had to do his very best to make sure that Ryan did not feel neglected, did not grow up an orphan. This feeling emerged so strongly, it overshadowed the doubts. Ryan became a part of Jacob's life.

It wasn't a smooth ride. Jacob struggled with Ryan's tantrums when the kid didn't get his way, balancing the demands of his own work with time spent with Ryan, putting Ryan's interests above his own, giving up his old habits and carefree lifestyle.

'Single parenting is not easy. There is a new challenge to be faced almost every day. But it is also the most fulfilling experience you can have. One smile from Ryan and I feel blessed. When I watch him sleeping, so innocent and angelic, I feel peaceful,' says Jacob.

One day, as we watched Ryan play a football match, Jacob said, proudly, 'He is my very own Maradona, my Ronaldinho!' Ryan managed to score a goal. Immediately, his expressive eyes sought Jacob's approval, as if he were asking, 'Dad, did you see it, it was a good goal, right? Did you see the goalkeeper's expression when the ball flew right above his head?' Later the team's victory was celebrated with burgers from McDonald's and ice cream from Baskin Robbins. (Jacob is particular about Ryan's eating habits and fast food is reserved only for celebrations.)

Ryan once got into a fight with his classmate who taunted him about not having a mother. Ryan replied, 'I have a Dad and he is the *bestest* Dad in the whole world. My mom is that star I see at night and she watches over me.'

When Ryan told Jacob about it, he felt both proud and rewarded by his son's reply from the heart.

Nina Irani

Sisters-in-Arms

I am blessed to work with children and their families. Day after day I witness miracles of courage wrought by ordinary human beings who display extraordinary resilience and strength in the face of serious challenges to their health and happiness.

I count Sonia among my heroes. She came into my office on a bright summer's day dressed in clothes of mourning, sadness etched into every line on her face. She reminded me of a black and grey cut-out pasted on a background of vibrant hues. Sonia sat in the chair opposite me and poured out her story. She had been blissfully married for six years, content to put all her energies into looking after her home, husband and two young children. Then one day without warning her idyllic world fell apart. Sonia's husband died suddenly of a massive heart attack. She was devastated and still reeling from the shock of abandonment when I first met her, a year after the sad event. With her husband's death her secure existence crumbled. Overnight her status changed from 'simple housewife' to 'desperate job seeker'. Fortunately she was able to find some part-time employment that provided a meagre income to the family. However, this meant long hours of work accompanied by mental, emotional and physical exhaustion.

Despite the burdens of job, home and family that Sonia had to shoulder, she made the time and effort to meet me. She wanted guidance on how to deal with her children. They were not listening to her, squabbled over silly things and constantly demanded her attention when she was at home. They lacked confidence, she said. When Sonia fell ill for a couple of days with viral fever, her five-year-old daughter asked 'Will you die too?' She was particularly worried about her son Tony, who offered monosyllabic answers to her barrage of anxious questions about his studies, friends, health, sleep, appetite and life in general. One day she was shocked to hear from the mother of a classmate that Tony had been punished in school for incomplete work. Sonia flipped and slapped him, shouting, 'Why could you not tell me yourself and spare me the embarrassment of hearing it from someone I hardly know?'

Her face quivered with remorse as she asked, 'Am I going crazy? I've never hit the kids before. But my friends tell me that if I do not correct them now, they will sit on my head when they are older. If my husband had been here, he would have handled it so much better. How can I manage without him? I cannot stay home and concentrate on the children because I have to work and earn the money. I feel so confused. Am I being a good parent? Why can't my kids behave themselves after all I do for them?'

As she spoke, fighting back tears and immersed in her anxiety, Sonia's problems seemed insurmountable. What could I say to her? Help her to think positive and see that despite her difficulties she was doing a good job? Explain about attention seeking behaviour and how she should catch her children being good? Suggest that she see a bereavement counsellor to help her deal with her grief? Caught up in the maelstrom of emotions, I myself felt confused. I had no ready answers to Sonia's questions. Her distress washed over me leaving me at a loss for words. What could I say to her that gave validity to her anguish? What advice could I give that she could effectively use? Whatever came to mind seemed so painfully inadequate and trite. I thought of my own family and what I would go through if my husband were to die suddenly. Would I find myself sitting in front of a professional seeking help for my child? What could that person say to me to assuage my heartache?

As I tried to empathise with Sonia's experience, I realised that it was only in the act of listening to her, that I could connect with the depth of her desolation. So I stopped thinking of 'the right answers' and stayed present to the narrative of her life as she gathered the shards and put them back together again. And as I listened beyond the words I could hear, I witnessed the miracle of a mother's endurance, reaching through her despair to care deeply about her children. By the end of the session, I was filled with deep respect, admiration and gratitude for the person who faced me.

As Sonia stood up to leave, on a natural and spontaneous impulse, I put my arms around her and hugged her tightly. I held her close just like one would a child. Her body relaxed against mine, and her tears, fiercely held back until this moment, started to flow. I felt profoundly moved and my own tears joined hers. We stood there for several minutes, our shared weeping forming a buttress against the loneliness of loss, two women enclosed in a circle of sisterhood created by arms, heartbeats and souls.

Nandita D'Souza

Remembering My Father

Today I remember my father. He would have been eighty years old. But he died thirty-five years ago when I was a freshman in college. The manner of his going was not an accident — it was by his own hand. And that left my brother Adit and me to struggle with his legacy — of what it all meant — but without him being around to explain it.

Now that I am fifty-two years old and a father of two teenage daughters myself, I am better able to understand. I know how hard he tried to properly bring up the two of us boys, to instill in us the right values, to have us aspire to lofty ideals, to be the best we could be. So many children from broken homes and difficult childhoods go off the track. My brother and I have stayed the course, more or less. And the lion's share of the credit goes to my father.

My father and mother met as students against the background of post-war Britain where my father was studying for his Tripos at Cambridge and my mother was at Badminton, the eldest daughter of a senior Indian diplomat. Beautiful and vivacious young woman meets intense and intelligent young man — both from 'bhadralok' (refined, upper-class) Bengali families. What more could anyone want to write an ideal love story?

Except that their union contained the seeds of its own destruction. My mother was a spoilt child of privilege, accustomed to being looked after while my father worked his butt off all the time, weighed down by the incredible pressure of unreal parental expectations. When goaded beyond endurance, he would fly into an uncontrollable black rage, which was a most frightening thing for a child to have to face.

Their quarrels and fights got progressively worse. As a child, I remember cowering in bed, listening to the sounds of shouts, screams and slammed doors. Soon the marriage was well and truly on the rocks and we got bundled off to Mayo College while our parents tried to sort out their separate futures.

Towards the end, my father found solace in the arms of his secretary to whom he had grown increasingly close. On the face of it, this was seen as a sordid little office affair and it effectively ended my father's sparkling career at Burma-Shell. But it was much more than a fling and today I do believe that Glenda gave my father the happiness and comfort that my mother never could.

My father moved away to Goa to a new job as marketing head with Zuari Agro Chemicals. Our school holidays were split between Delhi where my mother had moved in with her parents and Goa where my father lived alone in a beautiful bungalow in Dona Paula. There was never any question which was more fun for us boys — and I remember many halcyon hours frolicking with my brother in the sun, surf and sand of Colva beach.

But for my father, it was a lonely and unhappy existence. I remember clearly drenching him with seawater one day. Such a provocation would normally have engendered a massive water fight. But he stood there all alone, lost in his thoughts looking out to the distant horizon as if carved from stone.

So, three years later, compounded by the travails of working for the Birlas — Marwari businessmen with whom he had nothing in common — he left to take up another job with Empire Dyeing back in Bombay. This also brought him back to Glenda whom he still yearned to be with. But she was married with children and Roman Catholic to boot, so divorce and re-marriage was an even more difficult proposition to contemplate in her case.

I remember Jimmy Malhotra, one of my father's close friends telling me decades later that my father was an honourable man. I never really understood that until Uncle Jimmy put it all in context. After his involvement with Glenda, he wanted to do the right thing and marry her. And so he was prepared to take that final leap of faith — of converting to Christianity.

In my family, none of us were devout Hindus by any stretch of imagination, but at the time this inexplicable step both dismayed and perplexed us. I remember sitting at the back of St. Stephen's church in Bombay during Mass on Christmas Eve 1975 while my father, so long the rational non-believer, so much the man of science, took communion. I listened to the priest's sermon, uncomprehending, unsettled and unhappy.

By the following spring, my father was gone. He had sunk into deep depression, torn between being in an illicit relationship with the woman he loved and doing the right thing by his boys whom he adored. And so to paraphrase the hauntingly beautiful words of the song written about Vincent van Gogh — when no hope was in sight on that starry, starry night, he took his life as lovers often do.

What I do remember now is how much my father loved Adit and me. Through all his trauma and travails, he never lost sight of the fact that we were the most important things in his life. And he always tried to do the right thing by us — sometimes a little forcefully — but always with the best of intentions. To him, I owe my early exposure to such great writers as Galbraith and Hemingway. My decision to study Economics in college. My ability to type with both hands. My early understanding of male sexuality. My lifelong struggle to do the right and honourable thing.

And now when I read the last lines in his last letter to me, written four days before his death, in which he says: 'It is the power of Almighty God that you must draw upon in the important moments of your life,' I think I know what he tried to say to me. How he suffered for his sanity. How he tried to set me free.

Ranjan Pal

A Debt for Life

My mother is a sixty-two-year-old lady with the vigour and spirit of an eighteen-year-old. She is tall and chubby and loves all the good things that life has to offer. She is strong-willed, religious and feisty. Just looking at her, you know she is someone to reckon with. She can appear to be intimidating, strict and at times, even dominating. But beneath this 'tough-macho' exterior of hers, lies 'my mumma' as I know her, a softy to the very core!

I often wonder how she handled everything as well as she did. Not just for a year or two but for fourteen long years. I know that even now, every morning, she battles with herself as she gets up and puts on her brave face, just so that my brother and I know we are not alone.

Being a 'papa's baby' till the age of twelve, I never saw beyond my father. I was unfortunately unaware of my mother's pain, her struggle and above all, her integrity. I learnt of all this only when my father left us. No, he did not leave us for another woman. The sad truth is that he left us because he had no choice. He was in debt and we as children were being harassed by phone calls from creditors day in and day out. Even worse than the creditors were the cops, who turned up at odd hours of the day and night.

My mother never wanted my father to leave, she wanted to bail him out, but we (my brother and I) knew that was not possible, so as a family we took the decision that he had to leave. Handling two teenagers was not easy for my mother. I especially gave her a lot of trouble while studying. I partied a lot and was also aloof. I just could not let go of the pain of not having my father around. My brother on the other hand, shoved everything under the carpet, never discussed my father and became the self-appointed clown in our house. He took it upon himself to keep us all in high spirits. But beneath these dual exteriors we were pained and hurting individuals who my mother, single-handedly and with extraordinary grit, healed, revived and brought back to normal.

She never complained, she never hesitated in praising my father for the good he did to her and us when we were younger and above all she showered us with unconditional love.

She knew she would have to be a single parent. Being strict with us was not an option. Being lenient could encourage us towards the wrong company. So she struck a balance: she never became our friend, something I respect about her the most even now. We needed a mother and she went beyond that, she became a father, too: the breadwinner, the caretaker as well as the best homemaker.

Even though she worked, she never neglected us. There was always fresh, nutritious food on the table. We never ate fast food and even though she worked nine to nine, she would cook for us in the morning and come back at night, tired, and cook again. She inculcated in us a love for sports, encouraged us to follow our heart and speak our minds. The best part was her involvement in all the important events in our lives. She made sure she never missed them. She also kept in touch with my father's family and saw to it that we attended all family gatherings.

My mother imparted a sense of values, not by spelling them out to us, but by example. She taught us to be righteous, loving, expressive and disciplined and above all to stand on our own feet. She encouraged us, sometimes, even pushed us to go beyond what we wished. More importantly, she took major decisions for us, making me — a borderline dyslexic student — a writer, and my brother, who always had an aptitude for finance, a whiz kid in his field.

I believe all children are indebted to their mothers for giving birth and so, giving them a chance to embark on this journey of life. But for myself I can say that my entire life is an homage to the woman who made me the person I am today so proud of being!

Roma Kapadia

An Army 'Couple'

If there were statistics compiled on what takes its toll on married lives, staying separate because of work would definitely be one of them. My parents would be there amongst the statistics and viewing things in that impersonal light is somehow cathartic for me.

My Dad retired from the Army and he has no regrets about it. He really wanted to be an author, a scriptwriter for plays and movies, a lyricist. But his father told him our ancestors were freedom fighters and so had never had a chance to serve the government. Now that India was independent he wanted one son to serve the nation, honourably. That son was my Dad. In those days, people unquestioningly followed their parents' dreams. Later, my Dad did write as a hobby and after he retired it helped as a primary source of income.

While he was in the Army, he had several field postings. I'm sure there were many marriages that did not flounder as a result. But some did, and ours fell in the latter category. Sometimes, my mother stayed with my Grandma; at others, in the separated family quarters. Right after their wedding

Dad was away a lot, often gone for some course or to some border area. My mother gave birth to and raised her kids for some years while my father was still posted away and they would only meet now and then on scheduled or surprise visits from him. There were many women in the unit under similar circumstances. There was a time when they had help from orderlies and another when help was withdrawn.

Of course in the unit they had facilities, such as a mess, or an M.I. (Military Inspection) room where they could take sick kids. All three of us sisters would fall sick at the same time and God forbid if Mom got a contagious illness from us, it was so rough. One time she remembers putting all of us on a rickshaw and crying half the way to the M.I. room where a senior officer's wife met her, hugged her and took her in the staff car.

The flipside of being lonely was that Mom became increasingly brave and independent. She played squash, she read a lot, the women spent time together and soon Mom would drive our Ambassador everywhere, doing all the chores herself. Even today, as she gets older, those years are a blessing in disguise because she is so fiercely and inspiringly independent. But at end of the day she had nobody to talk to about little worries and big troubles. The telecom system wasn't the kind that would permit communication on a regular basis.

So when did my folks drift apart? I don't know. They seemed so much in love. They had a love marriage back in the days it was unheard of.

Dad had met Mom during a posting; she was his senior's sister-in-law and he was absolutely taken by her intelligence, kindness and breathtaking beauty. On top of that she has a singing voice that can charm a bird out of a tree and make the bird want to take lessons. Mom is a classical singer now. My parents supported each other in their creative explorations. My father became an author and my mother a singer.

Soon after he met her, Dad went to his village to talk to his father, Dadaji, about Mom. My grandfather was a deeply philosophical, simple and saintly man. He acquiesced. Mom's family agreed, too. D-day was set.

The wedding took place. They were both north Indians, Punjabis, but from different communities. It is interesting how in India our personalities and our ways of life are so often guided by the community to which we belong. Perhaps this may well be true for a lot of places.

The past is like a dream, they say. I look through my parents' wedding albums and family photographs — my parents on a mountaineering trip, we kids peering into the camera, holidays on the beach, in hill stations and places where we're not there. They seem idyllic. And then I see letters from us to Dad while he was posted away, photographs taken on holidays when we were apart and barely able to spend time with him.

I know now, as a mother living in a suburban home while my husband works in a city, that though he dotes on his kids, his schedule is such that he leaves when they are barely awake and gets back when its almost their bedtime. The weekends are dedicated to the family and yet we find it difficult.

Like this morning when I rebelled and said today is my day. I need to be by myself, I need to write. I need downtime.

For ten years or so Mom had no downtime.

It was their marriage that suffered. And now that they're old it has been ten years since they have actually conversed.

As I was growing up, we sisters started noticing how the disagreements got more frequent. Our hearts would ache sometimes; would long to reach out to them, long for them to reach out to each other. But they were remote because of issues they had with each other. They were amazing parents but a distance grew between them. The bitterness surfaced in little insignificant things, because who could talk about the larger issues, the lost years and the loneliness?

There was no recourse. Everybody has to earn a living. Do things they are committed to, like run a household, feed the children, educate them and provide for everybody's needs. Dad couldn't leave the Army.

But there were great times, too — camaraderie, Army parties, cultural shows, and Mom organised so many of them. There were songs and skits and one in particular, 'Faujiyon se dil na lagana' (don't fall in love with Army men) was hilarious. I recall the women laughing as they wrote about what Army men are famous for — promising to come home for an occasion and not showing up. There were jokes about the tears and fears that the wife has to deal with and of the little betrayals that the couple can do nothing about because in the line of duty a husband has to sometimes forego family life and put the nation first. It makes complete sense.

Over time it gets too late to repair relationships, to go to every crack and examine it. We can't turn the clock back. But when I see my contemporaries, my friends whose parents did get along and who are totally secure, I wish that mine did.

But this sense of regret is very soon replaced by a positive thought. If my folks couldn't do it, I can do it for my kids. My husband and I can be the kind of couple that will not let the cracks creep in. Both my folks have been wonderful parents — separately. My mother was practically a single parent. I want us to be great parents but I want our kids to remember us as a couple and without any pangs of sadness or insecurity. And may God grant us that wish because we are certainly trying our best.

Anuradha Gupta

My Dad, Superman

Rahul was the only male among the group of ladies seated in the school corridor for the parent teacher meeting. He didn't mind it, and neither did they, as they discussed their kids' progress or the extra-curricular activities they had enjoyed lately and exchanged tips on how to improve concentration.

'I cooked my son's favourite meal today as he has done well,' said one mother. Each one mentioned what she had done — be it rewarding or reprimanding her kid before she came for the meeting.

When it was Rahul's turn, he simply said, 'I took the day off and once I am done with the meeting I will spend it with Anand however he likes to. It is his day after all, and he should decide what to do with it! His marks have improved but even if he had scored less, I am happy that my son is taking responsibility and becoming a little adult.' Rahul had been both father and mother to Anand for the past two years.

His wife, Medha had passed away suddenly; cardiac arrest, the doctors told him. A healthy twenty-eight-year-old just collapsing and all they said was cardiac arrest. Rahul was a wreck. He had to cope with the loss of his beloved wife and look after their five-year-old son. Anand, unaware of what had happened, kept asking for Medha and Rahul had to control his tears. He missed Medha and would weep once Anand was asleep.

Rahul realised he had to be strong for both of them. Medha would have wanted it that way. As he coped with the shock of losing his partner, being a single parent and managing a high-pressured job, Rahul had once broken down. 'I just want this pain to go away. Anand needs his mother. What can I do single-handedly? The other day he asked me to help him with his homework. I had to submit a report the next day and told him to do it himself. You should have seen his face. It broke my heart to hurt him but I just couldn't help it,' sobbed Rahul.

After a few weeks, I saw him playing with Anand in the park and the two seemed to be enjoying each other's company. Rahul was learning to balance his work and be there for his son, the apple of his eye and a remembrance of Medha. Anand was happy that his dad was spending more time with him. He was told that his mother was with God and that Rahul was responsible for him. 'Mamma loves you and wants me to take care of you. She knows I can do it. She is helping God to look after those children who don't have parents,' was the explanation given to Anand. The father-son duo found homework challenging. Rahul would often be surprised at the high level of Anand's syllabus because earlier, Medha had handled his homework. On weekends, the pair would go for a long drive.

Anand also learnt to do things on his own, like prepare his own evening snack, count and pay for the ironed clothes when they were delivered or call for essential groceries from the dial-a-vegetable service. Rahul learnt all about theme birthday parties, summer camps and how to deal with exam jitters.

The other day, looking very pleased, he told me, 'My son thinks I am Superman. Could I ask for a better compliment?' The father-son duo was going to make it after all. Medha would be happy.

Sanaea Patel

Oh, Alisha!

Somi Tiwari's life epitomises Oscar Wilde's statement, 'Behind every exquisite thing that existed, there was something tragic.'

Somi had no complaints in life. A loving husband and a great relationship between them was revealed in the joy they together radiated. But as sometimes happens with beautiful things, their happiness didn't last forever. Somi lost her husband in 2002.

Somi knew she was going through the worst patch in her life. But an unfulfilled dream gave her a reason to stay on and begin life afresh. The decision that she and her husband had taken to adopt a child soon turned into a mission for Somi. However, it was not easy for a single woman to adopt a child. Friends advised her to marry again rather than adopt a child. But during the two years it took to get through the red tape, she knew what her life's calling was.

In 2006, four years after losing her husband, Alisha, a cuddly eight-month baby entered her life. The end of one bond led to the beginning of another, based on a strong foundation of love and unconditional commitment. Friends, neighbours and Somi's family welcomed little Alisha into the household. 'I was extremely lucky to have a supporting family. My dad, brother and sister were with me throughout,' says Somi, who is an educator by profession.

Tending to the needs of an infant wasn't easy, but Somi said, 'I was mentally prepared for Alisha; I took the decision with an open mind. Like any mother, I had to go through the rigmarole of sleepless nights, changing diapers and singing lullabies. But I have no complaints.'

Now, five-and-a-half-year-old Alisha is a livewire. Cherubic, naughty and talkative, she keeps everyone in the household on their toes. 'Alisha has totally changed my world. She is my life and the sole purpose of my existence,' says Somi.

The challenges she faced as a single mother were less daunting as Somi's family stood solidly behind her. 'I work from home, so I have never had to leave Alisha alone, I have never been faced with a situation where I didn't know whom to turn to,' says Somi. When I asked her if, being a single woman, society was critical of her decision to adopt a child, she said, 'I have always had great support from my neighbours and peers. They know that my life changed after Alisha came into it. She is the apple of everyone's eye.'

Somi also feels that children are more adaptable and have a better understanding of certain situations than adults. But they are also inquisitive and ever ready with an unending volley of questions, Somi, too, was eventually faced by questions she had been long preparing to answer — Alisha's questions about her father. 'I showed her my husband's picture. I tell her that her father has gone to meet God. I know she feels the vacuum sometimes. But my students double up as her extended family,' says Somi.

Celebrating the mother-daughter bond, the duo makes it a point to go for picnics and annual vacations. "I don't want Alisha to feel the lack of a father. I have ruled out a second marriage. My life revolves around Alisha and hers around mine. I have never lied to her about how she came into my life; I told her that she was given to me by God. Later, when she grows up, I will tell her the truth in parts so that she will slowly understand.'

Call it maternal instinct, or plain love — Somi as a single mother has braved the odds and come up trumps. And she isn't over-indulgent; she is not bringing up Alisha any different from other kids. Somi is as strict as any other mother when it comes to play and work. But she feels that Alisha should understand the challenges Somi faces as a single mother. 'I see to it that she understands my financial limitations. I don't feel handicapped as a single mother. I have seen women in bad marriages, without any financial support from husbands. Compared to them I am happy as a single mother.'

The beautiful bond of love and an equally magical relationship of caring underline the relationship between Somi and Alisha. Their ties are an example of how love conquers all. From the pain of losing her husband and the joy of being a mother, many lessons remains to be learnt from the love they share.

Preetha Nair

Pop Tate, Take a Bow

My earliest memories of Dad are of his bringing home hot, boneless chicken kebabs and chapattis from his restaurant. It tasted much like Mum's cooking. Though he would only return around midnight, I was happy to stay hungry in anticipation of the treat. Mum would quickly lay out the food and watch me gobble it down, with Dad indulgently patting my abundant cheeks.

Circa 1980, the world seemed like a secure and joyous place — with ubiquitous parents, a caring elder sister (is that an oxymoron?), a mischievous Dachshund called Bingo, friendly neighbours, loquacious aunts and jolly grandparents at one's disposal.

1986. Mum had passed away, young and suddenly. The elder sister was married and, seemingly, the world was not as smug as it had been a few years earlier. Dad had the unenviable task of rearing an eleven-year-old Cancerian lad, who was all this while the quintessential Mama's boy. A single, grieving parent could do with some space and possibly some new relationships. Dad was, however, a different kettle of fish.

He found in the situation, a sense of calling. It was doubly difficult that the son was a chubby unwilling cricketer, whose sole interests were being fed fatty home-food and getting 'good marks' in school.

A Quetta-born, Partition migrant who grew up in Shimla, Dad had moved to Bangalore to venture into the hospitality business in the 1960s and ran the rather popular 3 Aces on MG Road (or South Parade as it was then known). Food, cricket and a little bit of Flush were enough to keep him content. (Perhaps a bottle of Black Label, too, from what one heard, but one couldn't say for sure since he now only drank club soda). In the classic mould of 'just letting your kids be,' Dad let his ward figure himself out without much pontificating. He saw his job as the Provider — of drivers, cricket-gear, pocket-money, affection, head-massages, visits to restaurants, tracksuits, and the like.

Delicate (and painful) things such as PTA meetings were left to the elder sister, while Dad was happy to conduct fielding-practice sessions with a brand new cricket ball, plucked from his own sports' shop. (Now, that is cool.) Needless to add, his son was now a less unwilling cricketer. And it helped, that the lad was getting runs as a left-handed opening batsman and even taking some neat catches in the slips. Of course, superstition prevented Dad from showing up at any of the games.

Soon, it was time for the first shave under a father's watchful eye, and it helped that the Dad had a spare razor on hand. One couldn't easily break the ice when it came to confessing the female interests in school (or college) but when one's father asks you how your 'projects' are getting along with tongue firmly in cheek, there aren't many secrets left anyway.

It was even more endearing when one's friends grew close to Dad after college. The fashion designer loved Dad's fancy for tweed, corduroy and dark-tan, while the restaurateur adored him for his sagacious advice on how the 'look' of the rogan josh (lamb curry) should be consistent or the ice cream shouldn't be too creamy. Girlfriends found Dad suave and charming and seemed happier chatting with him about life in general, rather than chatting with the son about nothing in particular.

Once the son was a lawyer, Dad was at pains to understand the intricacies of litigation and the Constitution, and of professional ethics and arbitration. Many hours were spent grumbling and boasting, and extrapolating on matters that ill concerned a non-lawyer, but Dad listened patiently. Guidance was proffered strictly on a need basis, and was never superfluous or patronising. What was even more profound (for the son) was that Dad never pushed him into 'the family business' - an awful metaphor for the relinquishment of one's ambition and spirit.

Dad often mentioned that the birth of his son brought him copious tears of joy, and every time the little fellow laughed, Dad was thrilled to bits. Now, this is not something a dad should ever confess to a young, selfish son, who will undoubtedly abuse the situation. (Not that I did.) And the depth of the affection and concern was writ large whenever the son underwent turbulence in his personal or professional life. Dad was at hand — constant, unobtrusive and strong. Like an ideal friend.

Dad shared with me his love for public speaking and letter writing, cricket and tandoori chicken. Sunday dinners at Koshy's have watched us span a formidable generation of male bonding. Through all of this, Pop Tate (as I have him saved on my phone) rarely ever mentioned his loneliness or the bitter loss of his life-companion. He exemplified an altruistic, unrequited love that spanned a lifetime. At seventy-two, he still oozes the things that seem to make up his grain. Things such as honour, humour and grace.

Parents, they say, are meant to teach their kids sublime life lessons. My father certainly did — that the best things in life are free.

Aditya Sondhi

Thunder of a Blunder

I can understand their doing it, for I almost did it myself.

The urge for a woman to remarry immediately after the divorce comes through is overwhelming.

The 'single again' journey, among other things, is a grief process. During this time of sorrow and loss the single parent must go through several emotional stages. It is nothing short of a shock to be suddenly without a husband. You have children to raise, but that is not the biggest load you have to carry. Fear and panic dominate your feelings. You want to cry out, 'Help!' but the world is not really interested. You want to die, but you don't really want to commit suicide. All you want is for someone to 'fix it' so that the anger and pain recede and you can feel 'normal' again.

Unfortunately, the biggest mistake some single mothers make — after being separated, divorced or widowed — is to look for someone else to be dependent upon. Still trying to save your fairy tale, you dream of another Mr Right who will come riding over the horizon on a beautiful stallion to scoop you up (with an arm big enough to scoop your child or children, too).

I'm not saying this is a dream to doom; what I am suggesting is that it is a little premature to dream that dream now. Because it can turn out to be a horrible mistake and transfer you from the frying pan straight into the crackling fire.

'Don't do it,' said Bob Barnes, as he responded to questions put by American family expert counsellor, Dr James Dobson. 'Under no circumstances should a woman remarry for at least two years after the divorce. It takes around that much of time for feelings to stabilise, for her to heal, and for clarity to come into her thinking. If she rushes into another relationship, in nine times out of ten, she ends up with a man or a situation that is ten times worse than the one that led to the divorce.'

Dr Dobson asked Barnes (who incidentally grew up in a single parent home and today runs a home and counsels children of single parent families), 'How then should a woman deal with loneliness and depression during those two years?'

Barnes replied, 'I don't mean to trivialise her hurt or sound spiritually flippant — but for this time, she should in a very real sense make God/Christ her spouse, and turn to Him for everything — counsel, provision and comfort.'

I was listening to the tape of this interview on a return journey from Coimbatore to Bangalore and I remember gritting my teeth as I heard the exchange. Bob sat in the audio studio doing this interview while his cool wife sat in the lounge outside the studio waiting for him — it was fine for him to talk about a divine spouse when he had everything going good for him. What did he know about times of trauma and terror that a single mom has to cope with by herself?

The train chugged into Bangalore East station around five in the morning. My home was a short walk from the station but I needed an auto-rickshaw because I had a laptop and teaching aids that I'd taken along to the seminar at Coimbatore. Realising I was alone, and that I needed help; the rickshaw drivers were not going to miss the opportunity to make a quick buck. They made exorbitant demands and no amount of bargaining or pleading would get them to change their mind.

I grunted in an undertone: 'Make God your spouse indeed! So okay, divine spouse, where are you now and how am I supposed to handle this situation?

I'd barely muttered the words when a voice near me spoke out of the darkness. "Hi, do you want a lift home? My children have come to fetch me and we pass your house, so I can drop you if you want.'

I got goose bumps. The voice belonged to someone I knew only faintly and while I was recovering from the surprise, she and her children picked up my luggage and led me to their comfortable van.

'Okay, okay,' I said to the Lord, sensing His smile, 'I get the message. You don't have to rub it in.'

From then on I stopped keeping an eye open for superman to come and whisk me, and my three children, away to a faraway haven. Since I had launched a single moms' association, to encourage and support single mothers and their children, I shared the Barnes principle with them.

Not all of them received the advice well. One of my closest friends — lets call her Joan — got involved in a relationship through the Internet. She had a troublesome teenage child and was desperate to marry so that someone could help her put that son in line. The man posed as a level headed missionary who said he longed for the day when they could become a family. He also called up her son and had encouraging talks with him, all the time building up a picture of a wonderful future. I could not make out what his intentions were because when he eventually came to see her, he convinced her it was not the right time to meet her friends and family; he said he would do that on the next visit.

Their romance grew in leaps and bounds; but all she had was an email ID, no postal address. The wedding was fixed; she cut down her assignments, gave up her job, and at his behest, she began looking around for rental accommodation. He invited her to accompany him to Mumbai for an assignment. We, her friends, refused to let her go.

A week before the wedding, she received an email from him: 'I married Dr — yesterday. I was corresponding with her simultaneously and she is more a soul mate for me. Forgive me if you can.' There was no further word from him. Poor Joan is still trying to pick up the pieces, even though seven years have passed since the episode. She has turned bitter and warped, and it is difficult to have a normal conversation with her.

It is not God's will for man to be alone. He knows the end from the beginning and also what and who will be best for you. But before that, there is some work to be done within you and your children. Before one can walk or even crawl around in the forced wilderness it is unwise to get up and start running. The single parenting wilderness cannot be conquered overnight. It is a matter of putting one foot in front of another and walking in the right direction — toward God who is the only one who can heal that gnawing pain within you, and create in you a new heart. We will need to trust, love and forgive and share our struggles while experiencing the changing climes of this zone we are passing through.

The knight on the stallion will certainly come your way at the right time. Haste in this case, would not only make waste, but also leave a bitter taste!

Anonymous

No Child's Play

In a dog-bite-dog world, rarely does one come across a story of selfless and unconditional love. Geet Oberoi's life is one where pre-planned notions and social norms take a back seat. Mother of two adopted kids, Geet is a thinking businessperson, caregiver and mom and pop rolled into one. Remaining single and daring to adopt wasn't due to any jilted affair or failed marriage, it was a conscious move by the forty-year-old.

Geet feels adopting a child should be a choice that people make even if they have their own child. She isn't screaming from rooftops, as she knows certain things are easier said than done. She had to wait for three years to realise her dream of adopting a child. Red tape in courts only extended the painful wait. 'I was thirty-one when I applied to adopt Indya. Agencies never took me seriously. I had to keep pressurising them to let them know how serious I was. In courts, the house is divided; some judges weren't in favour of the idea of a single mother. Some judges favour adoption, some don't,' said Geet.

But the transition from courtrooms to the drawing room wasn't easy either. Her real challenge began when she had to strike a bond between twelve-month-old Indya and herself. With her family extending full support, Geet soon plunged into the task with love and tenderness. 'It's a false notion that a woman has to go through labour pains to give unconditional love to a child. Having a child of one's own blood is an overrated notion,' says Geet.

The first time Indya called her Mama is a moment still etched in her memory. 'I didn't know what she loved or hated when I got her home. But I wasn't the one to feel let down or panic. It took almost six months for her to call me Mama. But it was something so real and loving,' recollects Geet.

Geeth was so overwhelmed by the experience of having a child that she decided to give Indya a sibling. Soon, she began the paperwork for her second adoption. However, she reasons like any mother would: 'Bringing up a single child is more difficult than rearing two. Besides, being a single mother to a single child is a situation that's more oppressive for the child. A single child needs more attention; having a sibling, on the other hand, helps in a child's emotional development.'

So with Indya firmly holding her mother's hand, the two trotted into an adoption agency to find their new housemate. That was a learning curve in their bond, too. 'Indya knows she didn't come from my tummy and not all babies have papas,' says Geet. A year later, they welcomed baby Maya into their home with a grand party. Geet's mother and two sisters extended their unflinching support, which helped ease out things at home. As Geet began to divide time between her two children, Indya also realised that she, too, came home the same way ... from an adoption agency. With Maya, Geet was luckier, as she settled in very fast. Things had changed since her first adoption; it had taken only a year to get Maya compared to the long wait for Indya.

Just as all changes bringing in a new set of challenges, Geet had to ensure she divided quality time at home with pressing job requirements. Running one of the most successful school chains in Delhi for children with special needs, Geet couldn't let her official commitments slip. It was the experience of a boy whom she met in 2000 that changed her life. As a special educator, Geet met a child who was ridiculed by his classmates, scolded by his teachers and beaten by his parents who had no idea of his inherent disability. The incident turned into a calling to do something bigger. Soon, she quit her job to establish Orkids. Now with a dozen branches in Delhi and one in Bangalore, the school provides multi-disciplinary education for kids.

One would imagine that being pretty, smart, successful and single would make Geet the target of eligible suitors. Geet has been quizzed, advised and sweet-talked about the subject of marriage. But her take on life is different. She believes that the knight in shining amour can wait, as she is not ready to trade her freedom and happiness for anything else. Geet admits she, too, waited for that elusive 'dream guy' till her thirties. 'I did my bit meeting prospective husbands-to-be and at one point, in my twenties, I even thought that marrying was the most natural thing to do as all my friends had settled down. By the time I was thirty, I knew I was happier single. In retrospect, I thank God things turned out the way they did.' She adds that even if Mr Right walks in, 'he is miserably late.' With Indya and Maya making her life happy and complete, she says she has different priorities now.

But it isn't curtains yet. The Oberoi household is all excited about the likely next entrant. Geet has applied for her third adoption, this time she wants a boy. Indya butts in with a suggestion: 'We have decided his name will be Ram...'

Preetha Nair

4
INSPIRATIONAL SINGLES

Sometimes you have to stand alone to prove that you can still stand.
—Anonymous

Dreams are Forever

A time comes when we dream of a new life away from the care of our parents, we dream of a life of our own, of a companion, children, money and even more importantly, being an independent woman.

It's humbling how dreams can be shattered in an instant. In the time it takes for a doctor to say, 'Oh, no!' dreams can turn to nightmares and hopes can turn to fears. My first question was, what? That was quickly replaced by, not me! All those long held dreams of happiness and independence melted into devout prayers and frantic thoughts — what am I going to do? How did this happen? Why me? If only I can be well again ....

In a matter of moments I had traded marital bliss for CAT scans, my first salary for blood tests, rock solid normality for lunacy. I hung about in a state of shock, watching helplessly as my body was poked and prodded by strangers who neither had the time nor the sensitivity to answer my questions or allay my fears.

Hours became days and days turned into weeks and months and all the while I coped with a roller-coaster ride of good news, then bad, of hopeful signs, then puzzling questions. I was unable to think of anything beyond the next doctor's visit or test, hoping that this time someone would be able to determine the problem and my future. But I became frustrated with each visit and test, as still more were needed. Finally, everyone said that only time would tell what the future would hold.

In the meanwhile, I lost hold of my dreams. I was never to walk again.

Slowly, very slowly, I realised that I would never know exactly what was going to happen until it actually did. At first I was angry, I wanted answers, but it dawned on me one day that I was really no different than any other patient. I was one of the hundreds on a wheel chair, paralysed, with a broken body.

In Vellore, the darkness on my horizon gradually started lighting up in the company of the staff and doctors. I began to believe. From belief emerged hope and I started to dream again. To be sure, these were not the same dreams as before. I tried to be realistic. I tried to understand how to live happily in my wheel chair. I had to do things differently — it took longer to do everything — and I had to redesign my house so that I remained independent.

I journeyed through denial, anger, bargaining, depression and finally, acceptance. It was not an easy journey, but it had a purpose and it has its gifts. I grieved for the loss of my 'normal' life but finally returned home with the hope of a different but still meaningful life. I was neither afraid nor anguished about the future.

Bhubaneswar came as a shock. I was different. It was spelt out to me in many colours. The fact that I do not belong was underlined in red! The more my family encouraged me to feel good about myself, the more society's attitude depressed me. I heard a variety of comments: I was condemned for life for the sins committed in a past life; it is destiny, and many more to that effect. My dreams died another death. My job was terminated, my fiancé moved away. Life became a long wait for death.

My father's arrival from Madras, after a kidney transplant, gave me a new lease of life, for he made me dream again. A PhD and MPhil done, I dreamt of becoming an asset, not a burden. Then started my odyssey. My wheel chair became my stigma. A research institute in Bhubaneswar rejected me because of my curled fingers and the wheel chair. A private college in Bhubaneswar found me unfit to join as a lecturer because their building was inaccessible. I did not give up. There was one dream I clung on to. I decided to be self-employed, run a study circle and teach.

That dream has come true. Today I am financially independent, I have my own house and car and my mother's immense support. And of course, as ever before, I remain the idol of my siblings.

The people who helped me most on this road to recovery were Dad and Mom. Every little achievement became a milestone, a matter for celebration, be it sitting straight, holding the fork or buttoning up my shirt. My brothers and sisters have helped me immensely, both physically and emotionally. I am the eldest of four sisters and one brother — Swati is in Boston, Gayatri in Canada, Raju in Bangalore and the youngest, Munnu, works in Bhubaneswar. My mother is a doctor, owner of one of the leading nursing homes in

Orissa. She and I live together. My siblings have never made me feel like a patient or a disabled person. Swati and Gayatri are married. They took turns to look after me when I was in Vellore. My subdued voice is enough for them to make frantic calls home. One tear and they turn the world upside down. I participate in everything, from deciding the Sunday menu to organising parties, just as I did before my accident. I can only say, 'Love cannot be defined in words.' The sense of belonging and the feeling of being needed helped immensely. With my students also, I enjoyed a wonderful rapport. In the classroom I was strict, after class hours we are friends. Here, too, the key was love. They love and respect me deeply.

Well-meaning relatives and friends constantly ask about my health or insist upon informing me about every newspaper article they feel is related to my situation. Even strangers on the street have advised me about some treatment or clinic they think might help me. Others have suggested I would be made whole if I pray in a particular way or held on to certain beliefs. This irritates me no end.

But my best friend, Manoj, has helped me cope. He tells me repeatedly, 'Your anger or rudeness will never stifle these well-meaning persons. You cannot change them, but you can change yourself. Don't waste your time being hurt or angry. Just accept their good intentions, smile and thank them — friends, and strangers alike.'

I was afraid of being lonely and I am, even now. But here again, Manoj helped. In his words I discovered the huge difference between being alone and being lonely. I am slowly learning that I can turn aloneness — the state of being away from people and by oneself — into solitude, that lovely, silent seclusion. In solitude, we can re-learn how to understand ourselves in relation to people and nature. This subtle difference can make a huge change towards living happily.

My disability has made me able in many other ways. It has slowed me down to a point where I can appreciate nature much more. I have time and the yearning to take pleasure in all of nature. I have discovered new dimensions within myself — creative writing, poetry, and painting.

Today, sitting in my wheelchair, I symbolise the cause I am campaigning for. Fighting for the rights and dignity of differently-abled people, I have emerged as a perfect role model for the physically and mentally challenged in Orissa. I have initiated a process that clearly focuses on the rights and capabilities of the physically and mentally challenged, a major shift from the hitherto fatalistic and charitable attitude that the state authority, officials and people in general harboured towards us. Having been personally challenged for over twenty-three years, I can say I know what depression is. I know what it feels like to lose hope for the future. My answers may not be your answers, or my ways your ways. But I can promise you there is hope.

Am I a disabled person? No, I am a person, first; second, a person with a disability. There is a difference! Because I have started believing in dreams again....

Sruti Mohapatra

A Turn of Events

I am a Malayali raised in Tamil Nadu, where my parents were employed. My mother was educated and smart, but she was not one to pamper me. One day she didn't return from work and we made the bitter discovery that her certificates and clothes were missing. I was a child of eight and my brother, a baby of three. My father began to spend more time with us and I was eager to help him and attended to household chores as well as I could. I cooked our meals and, under the guidance of neighbours, experimented with snacks for my brother. May be it was the playful instincts of a child that enabled me to take on these tasks.

My father had in the meanwhile, started attending to some diabetic patients in the locality by cleaning and dressing their festering boils. Eager to assist, I used to accompany him on these visits. My father's act of service impacted me and I developed sympathy for those in distress.

Our village, Cinthamanipudoor, near Coimbatore, was extremely backward in those days. But it was a friendly place. Houses were not locked, even at night. We all knew one another. Births, deaths and marriages were occasions for being together.

I was a part of this relaxed and friendly lifestyle till the fateful day of my mother's disappearance. Then the attitude of the villagers changed. They became anxious and helpful and somehow, this hurt me and created a complex. I wanted an escape, which I found in reading and I was soon drawn to the world of ideas.

Bharatiyar captured my imagination. The great writer's strikingly feminist leanings impressed me. Women have taken birth to exert their authority, to make laws and to receive awards, Bharati said. In acquiring knowledge woman is equal to man, he declared. That Bharati's influence had a far-reaching impact on me would be clear from the incident I am going to narrate.

It occurred in 1981. One morning at four, I went out and was walking in the dark towards the open ground — our village toilet. I caught sight of a figure at the nearby village well. Startled, I ran back, mistaking it to be an apparition. Out of curiosity, I watched from a distance. It dawned on me that it was a woman bathing. She turned to the east and appeared to be offering her prayers. I approached her and it was her turn to get frightened. A girl of fifteen, she was the younger sister of the new postmaster in our village post office. He had moved in with his family recently. She had lost her husband in an accident a week after her wedding. She was only twelve then. To my horror, I came to know that she was condemned by society to remain a widow — an inauspicious person. So she stayed indoors, babysitting her brother's tiny tots. At night, she slept in a dark corner of their small rented house.

My heart went out to her and I kept meeting her in the early morning when she slipped out to bathe. I gave her the books I got from the library. What upset me most was the fact that she had no freedom like us to use our 'village toilet' during the day. Also, our secret meetings were making me tense. So I decided to meet her brother. He was shocked to know that I had spotted his sister and horrified when I argued that she should be allowed to mingle with her peer group. He dismissed me, saying that I was a mere child, ignorant of tradition. Burning with moral indignation, I threatened to reveal the secret.

I narrated the incident to my father when he returned from work that evening. Seeing me in distress my father decided at once to meet the girl's brother who refused to discuss the matter. My father did not give up; he needed a solution to console his daughter.

Eventually, the girl's brother relented. My father convinced him that his sister was a stranger in the village; nobody knew that she was a widow. She could be presented as a fresh arrival from their parental home. She could wear ordinary clothes and her tonsured head could be attributed to the fulfilment of a vow at the Palani temple. Two weeks passed by in preparation. We had to get clothes stitched secretly. Also, her hair had to grow a little. The change brought relief not only to her but also to the whole family.

This young widow resurfaced in my memory when I became a widow in May 1997, at the age of twenty-six. I recalled how lost she was! How cast away by society! Although other communities are not as strict as the Brahmin, to which she belonged, most people considered a widow inauspicious. No, I said to myself; that is not to be. I shall create another positive image.

My father had died in 1994. I was single, with no one to advise or help me. But I decided to gather my resources and work hard. And thus, Santhi Medical Information Centre was created on 24 August 1997. My training ground had been the Sri Chitra Medical Institute where my husband had been on the ventilator. I had waited outside the ICU for ninenty-six days. Patients or their relatives were looking for information of all sorts. As I had time, I started helping them obtain information and guiding them about procedures and services. I also got blood donors and financial support for some. Rendering information and help became my life's work.

I did face several challenges in the beginning. But thanks to the idealism of my father and to the thoughts that have inspired me, I overcame them. To be a woman, and a single one at that, is not easy. But when you have a mission that demands single-minded attention, being a single woman is an advantage. A woman's actions are touched by her heart, and dedication is no small achievement in life.

Uma Preman
(As told to O.V. Usha)

Arunchandra, My Teacher

How would you react if you lost your spouse to a heart ailment that she bravely fought for eleven long years? Would you be shattered, angry at the unfairness of it all and haunted by memories? Would you be cranky? I think you would. I believed that all of us would be so, till I met Arunchandra at the hospital. The sixty-one-year-old was rushing in to provide moral support to the family of a teenage girl who had been in an accident. The girl had lost a lot of blood and was being rushed into surgery. Arunchandra sat with the family till the operation was completed and the girl transferred into a private room for observation.

I had gone to visit a friend who had delivered her first baby. I went again the next day, and again I saw Arunchandra. This time he was helping an obviously illiterate patient fill out the requisite forms. He slowly read out the details, then wrote down the answers for the patient, a shepherd, who was dressed in a dhoti. The man had a blanket draped over his shoulder and his Kolhapuri slippers were worn out.

Curiosity got the better of me so I approached Arunchandra. 'What exactly do you do here?' I asked him once he had finished helping the elderly shepherd. Instead of rebuking me, Arunchandra smiled and told me that the hospital was his second home, 'I do whatever is required of me. I assist, counsel or chat with patients, purchase medicines during emergencies, get that much needed bottle of blood, explain post-operative exercises to the patient and family or simply be the shoulder for someone to unburden themselves on. I believe that after my wife's death, I am meant to bring some sort of relief to others and this inspires me to keep going. I have learnt a lot from patients. I have interacted with terminally ill patients or those suffering from life-threatening diseases, who still continue to smile. And I ask myself, if they can smile, why can't I do the same?'

His wife, Sunanda, passed away in 1998. When she was hospitalised, Arunchandra got an opportunity to interact with many patients on a personal level. It was here that reality hit him; there were some patients who had no one to care for them and others who needed emotional support. So despite his grief, a fortnight after his wife's demise he decided to dedicate himself to taking care of hospital patients. 'Have you ever seen how sad and lost patients look, especially when no one comes to visit them. I had the opportunity to interact with a young dynamic accident victim who was from out of town. His family was unable to come for the first three days and I could see the emptiness in his eyes, the sadness writ large on his face as he saw families and friends visit other patients. I chatted with him and we became good friends,' recounts Arunchandra.

Yes, at times he feels the loss of not having Sunanda around but believes that she would be happy with what he is doing with his life. 'She was a fighter and I want to honour her memory by helping others. For me, these patients are my family. They keep me constructively occupied and that helps ward off depression, boredom and loneliness,' he said before rushing off to get a rickshaw for a patient who had been discharged.

To me, Arunchandra has become a fine example of how to face personal tragedies and emerge triumphant.

Khursheed Dinshaw

The Caregiver

It's barely daybreak and she's there with her raucous voice to wake me. Even after death she won't leave me. Forty-six years she lived with us, from the day I got married. Kajoli, my husband's sister. Body distorted with childhood polio. She was a schoolteacher and then, later was headmistress for many years. At the crack of dawn she'd be making a racket, preparing for school. By the time I was through with breakfast, organising the house, the midday meal, she was back. Shuffling and pottering through the afternoon when even the servant was off for a nap. After serving her a tray of food and mug of lemongrass tea, I would try to squeeze in a five-minute shut-eye before evening activities began.

There must have been some love somewhere to make her don the body of a crow just to be near me. There must have been something wonderful in her that she was so cared for in her last days. Not once had I felt any hint of love or of her being special in any way. Stern and distant, she was just a presence, never pleasant, never overtly rude. Not friendly, always prim and distant, but never distant enough to be forgotten for a moment.

When she retired from her job she hung around me even more. I got used to keeping my feelings hidden, suppressed. Then she got sick. Cancer was discovered after much of her body had already been ravaged from inside. Doctors, investigations, treatment became the new routines. When the hospital discharged her I had to nurse her. She would press her thin lips tight and turn her face away at my touch. She hated her situation. Her hatred extended to include me; scorched away all sentiment. Caring for her body was like a cold surgical procedure. Unpleasant but necessary. Over forty years of living in the same house, we never got close or comfortable with each other. Cancer brought me physically close but the closeness was torture for us both.

Then one day a tiny old lady in a crisp white sari was at the door. She had heard there was someone who needed nursing. She was available to stay and take care of Kajoli day and night. I was so tired I let her in. I thought. 'She looks much weaker than me, she will not be able to cope. But let her work as long as she can. Even a few days will give me some rest.'

Her name was Rima. She stayed till the end. She took over all the work required to give Kajoli care and comfort. She gave medicines on time. Gave her a bath, kept her clean. She even sang songs to her, cradled her face, and kissed her forehead. I saw this a few times, Kajoli half comatose with eyes shut, yet she would smile. A little movement of her softly moustachioed upper lip, distinctly a smile, when Rima touched her, like a mother, like a lover. I watched from the doorway, amazed.

I learnt to relax. My home began to feel mine. No rasping commands, no whoosh-thup, whoosh-thup of her walk, no dragging of chairs. Sometimes I almost forgot she was there.

One day Rima chided me. 'There's no papaya. You know that's the only fruit she eats. You yourself said yesterday that was the last slice. Such a small thing! Even that you cannot remember.'

'How dare she address me so rudely,' I thought. 'All foods and medicines have been provided regularly. One morning, there's no papaya and I have to hear such words.'

Years of training to keep silent saved the day. I knew better than to chase away this amazing nurse for Kajoli. I dragged myself out in the midday sun and brought two huge papayas.

The end came, as we knew it would. I thanked Rima for all her help. 'Let me get you a placement with some friends,' I said. Many people were asking for Rima's services. 'No. Thank you. I am tired. I need to rest.'

I had forgotten how thin and frail she was. Yes, caring for Kajoli had taken its toll. She looked so much older than when she had arrived. Suddenly Rima bent to touch my feet. 'I can't thank you enough for all you have done for me.'

'Oops. She's gone crazy,' I thought. 'She's the one who slaved, and she is thanking me. Lucky that Kajoli's days passed peacefully. We didn't know we had a loony in the house!'

But stone-faced, she spoke on, looking blankly past my shoulder. 'I, too, am sick, with the same disease. But I am poor: can't afford treatment or nursing. When I looked after your sister-in-law I felt God was looking after me. The more I did for her, the more Krishna did for me. And you paid me well. So I saved money, it is a fortune for me. I know my son and daughter-in-law will never spend a paisa on an ill-fated widow like me. I know I have only a few days left in this body. I have no expenses; I can't digest anything now anyway. I have more than enough to pay for my funeral rites. In a separate packet I have put money with the list of people to be fed on the thirteenth-day ceremony.

'A million thanks to you. You provided me the means to arrange my last rites the way I want. I take your leave now. Krishna is waiting. Namaste.'

I was shocked; my mind raced through the previous months for telltale signs of illness in her but could find none. She was sick, dying, had none to care for her. I grabbed a bunch of unused medicines and rushed to give them to her. She could have Kajoli's bed, other equipment. I could hire nurses for her. If she wasn't crazy maybe she's a saint. Perhaps both. But she was gone. Outside the gate the street was empty, on both sides, all the way to the end.

When the crow caws at dawn I linger in bed and wonder. What bond tied Rima and Kajoli in bygone eons? Who were Kajoli and I in prior lifetimes? What are we carrying into the future?

As told to Bharati Mirchandani

Against All Odds

It takes immense courage for a single woman to resist the combined pressure of her parents, society and her orthodox community. But Irfana Ismail Mujwar did just that! She is a young, intrepid, thinking and spirited woman.

Irfana lives in Mumbai. She is a teacher by profession, and she found it disturbing that the school she worked in provided scholarships only to Muslim Shia students. So she decided to do an unusual, remarkable thing.

Irfana, along with her colleague Gazala, used the money set apart for her wedding and started a school, which provides education at a minimal cost to those who cannot afford it. This school is path breaking as it does not have any gender or community bias. All students are welcome and are given equal opportunities.

The decision was not an easy one, nor was its implementation. And it is all the more remarkable when seen against the backdrop of her sheltered existence. For ten years after her twelfth standard, she had never left home or been exposed to the world outside. Describing her journey, she says she faced immense resistance from her conservative family, as no one understood her intention or venture. Her father and brothers saw marriage and the life of a dutiful wife as the only path for a woman. Naturally, they felt it was what she should opt for. So it took a lot of talking, explaining and rebellion for her to first start working as a teacher at Anjum Islam School. There, she saw social discrimination and poverty, things she was completely unaware of.

After interacting with like-minded people like Gazala she decided to open a school with her, which would benefit the poor.

Starting this new venture without finance or support was not easy at all, but she says she took the plunge anyway. Neither Irfana nor Gazala had any support from their respective families. What they did have was direction. And Irfana did have the support of her mother throughout. She has been her champion and without her mother, Irfana says she would never have achieved any of the success she has. It was with her mother's help that she was able to convince her brothers and father that this was the direction she had chosen. This is what she wanted to do with her life.

After a lot of convincing, after people started telling her family what a noble cause she was working for, they finally accepted her mission and gave her the money they had saved for her wedding. She says, 'Today, my father and my brothers are proud of me and it makes me happy that I chose to follow my heart. I see the value of doing that.'

But the money saved up for her marriage was not enough for the venture, so Gazala took a loan and they got some help from Mr Keki Unwalla and Kirti Unwalla who still provide money, sponsorship and scholarships to the children.

Today, the first batch of SSC students has passed and Irfana and Gazala have reason to be proud, but feel there is a lot more to be done. Irfana is sad that her students have no playground. She wants to expand the school, and would like her students to participate in inter-school programmes.

A staff of twenty teachers runs Irfana's school. She would like to have more staff and students. As of now, the students are predominantly Muslim, but she sees a change taking place and says she makes sure of creating awareness about this matter. She tells people that her school charges a meagre Rs180 per year per student and for those who can't afford it, education is free. She also has a scholarship programme for extraordinary students, who are exempt from paying fees; in fact she supplies them with books and uniforms.

She believes teaching is her mission, helping is her aim and expanding the school is her target. To be able to dedicate your life, your youth, your money, your time and above all your future to others is not easy. But Irfana has proved that she is a woman of courage and a woman to look up to in this world dominated by men.

As told to Roma Kapadia

A Count of Blessings

My friend Anita had married David when she was nineteen. Her mother, a Christian widow, had struggled to bring up four children and had made a solemn promise to herself that she would find better lives for her offspring. Her eldest son had immigrated to England and never returned. Her daughter Karen had married Peter, whom the mother had found by avidly scouring the newspaper, and was settled in Australia. Anita's mother had worked as diligently to find thirty-one-year-old David for Anita, relieved at the thought that she now had to worry about only one more child, a boy of seventeen.

At first, things had seemed to go well. David's family loved Anita, who set up a warm and inviting home in Connecticut. She wrote about the wonderful things in America that helped make life easier — the dishwasher, the washing machine, the dryer, the microwave, the vacuum cleaner, the absence of dust, the organised roads and the even more organised traffic, things that Anita's mother liked to read over and over again, believing that she had made the right choice for her daughter. Over a period of time though, the news didn't seem to be as good. Anita wrote about not being able to conceive and about David blaming her for it.

Her mother encouraged her. She wrote, 'Pray, my child, don't forget to pray to God. He will give you everything you want.' However, God didn't seem to be listening because five years later, Anita was back in India, childless and dejected.

I was excited when I went to see her. Being unaware of any turbulence in her life, I was shocked to see the change in her. She was listless and had lost her spark. She told me about her life. We were both twenty-four at that time and I had been married for two years. I wouldn't say that I had a lot of wisdom or experience under my belt, but I had enough to realise that what she described was disturbing.

'He doesn't even look at me. He turns his head away if I try to kiss him. I've done everything that I can but I can't win him over. I just can't seem to get pregnant,' she confided, as we sat in her old room just as we had when we were teenagers.

'You should not have to win him over. That's ridiculous! Have you guys gone for tests? I'm not a doctor but I know that both parties have to go for tests to find out where the problem lies. Have you done that?' As I rambled on, Anita started to cry. I could see that she was greatly troubled.

Finally, in a whisper she said, 'I think he might be homosexual.' She had looked up at me as she said this, with fear in her eyes and a deep shame. I wondered why she felt ashamed.

'What?' I stood up in shock. I didn't know how to react. Homosexuality was not spoken about in those days. Of course, we knew there were gay people but as long as their sexual orientation didn't affect us directly, we had no problem with it. But here we were, and it was affecting us.

'How do you know that he is gay?' I asked her, hoping that she was wrong.

'There are all these magazines that arrive in the mail. When we got married, I didn't know what they were. They would arrive covered in plastic and he would never show them to me. After a few months, I got curious so I opened one of them. The cover had two naked men on it. I went through it very quickly because I was so afraid and then I hid it. He got really angry. He looked for it and found it. He threatened to send me back home if I ever touched his stuff again. I asked him why he didn't like me. He said he had only married me to get his parents off his back, that they were the reason we had to have a child.'

I advised her to get out of the marriage. I threatened to tell her mother but she swore me to secrecy. Two years later, she was back in India, this time to adopt a child. It took her six months to complete the process after which she was given a child from an orphanage, a beautiful baby boy whom she named Christopher. When I went to see her this time, there was a substantial change in her.

'This baby will fix everything. Don't worry about me. I'll be fine,' she assured me. I couldn't see how bringing a child into a loveless marriage would help but I chose to respect her choices.

Six years later, after she had given thirteen years of her life to a relationship that hadn't stood a chance from the very beginning, she wrote to her mother: 'I am leaving him. Christopher and I are not loved or wanted here. I have to find a better life for both of us.'

Her mother was heartbroken. She called me up and asked me to speak to Anita, to convince her that this was a terrible mistake. I told her that I was proud of my friend, and that she should be proud of her daughter, too.

A year ago, Anita visited India along with Christopher who was now eleven. She had gone back to school after leaving David and become a nurse.

'Being a single mother is tough but I love it,' she said to me. 'I have this neighbour who has watched Christopher through the years when I've had to work. I have truly been blessed. I've found work that enables me to help others. If I hadn't married David, I would never have found my true calling in life. I work hard but I'm able to give my son everything he needs. David is still in our lives — the laws in the US are tough so he has to pay child support but I don't touch that money. I'm saving it for Chris; he can use it for college. I'm happy. Do you know how free I felt after I walked out? I should have listened to you earlier. But then, I would not have had Chris.'

Tears arose in my eyes as she spoke. The words 'I have truly been blessed' still linger with me. Despite what she had gone through and how heavily the odds had been stacked against her, and still were, my friend had chosen to count her blessings instead of choosing to be bitter. This, more than anything else she said, made me realise how each one of us could do more of the same — count our blessings.

Shaphali Jain

Amazing Grace

I noticed Sulekha a few days after I moved into the sparsely inhabited neighbourhood. It was the month of January. In those days the suburb was still unpolluted and the crisp winter mornings had the air of a hill station. Sometimes, nilgais strayed from the adjacent forest into the far end of the colony.

She was walking around the square and something about her, maybe her natural elegance, set her apart from the others. When we eventually met, I saw that her face was at once beautiful and tragic. She and her husband spent their winters in the suburb, nearby to their daughter. In summer, they returned to the hills. I never saw her with her husband. Sometimes, I would see him walking alone. He was a tall man, aloof and unconnected to the people or space around him.

I would exchange pleasantries with Sulekha. She usually had some complaint about her servant, the weather, the changing times. She conveyed a sense of being burdened, trapped in a situation. Yet, when she smiled her face lit up, momentarily.

I got to know her daughter and over the years she hinted at the sad truth about her parents' marriage.

Sulekha rarely spoke about her personal life. When her husband died, I visited her home for the first time. On a side table there stood a framed photograph of the couple, possibly soon after they were married. When I commented on her ethereal beauty, she merely said, 'He was a good man.'

For some years Sulekha remained much the same as she had been when her husband was alive — worn and burdened. Then, about two years ago, I noticed a remarkable change. She was older, naturally, and she stooped. But there was a spring to her step, she sang as she walked, a smile played on her lips and her face was so radiant she simply did not look like a woman well into her seventies.

One day I asked her how, after all she had suffered and endured, she came through with a smile. This is what she told me.

'From the start, I was rejected. I was born to my parents after eighteen years of marriage and my birth brought upon the worst post-natal depression in my mother. She became mentally destabilised. She would reach out for me, then withdraw her arms. She rejected me completely, lavishing all her love on her son, whom she had adopted two years before my birth. My father didn't have much time for me, either. When I felt the need to be comforted I would run to the old family driver. It was he, not my parents, who sat by my sick bed and tended to my needs. I don't know how I grew up. Memory plays strange tricks; large parts of my childhood are blank. I could forget what I had learnt the day before, yet I passed my Trinity College music exam without being able to read a note. If I received any affection, it was from the nuns.

'I had absolutely no confidence. When my parents sent me to a college in Delhi, I couldn't understand how I was chosen the most beautiful fresher. I went through college because a few friends took care of me. By the time I was eighteen, my father started sifting through marriage proposals. I had no specific demands except that I was particular about who could touch me. I agreed to marry a man whose family lived in the same town as my parents. He had a job; he was good-looking and well spoken. I knew nothing else about him.

'I think I enjoyed our honeymoon and initially, the social life that is part of being in the army. But it wasn't long before my husband began to betray signs of alcoholism. Money became scarce; there was never any available. Then, emotional and verbal abuse began. Rejected by my parents, I was now faced with the reality of being rejected by my husband. One day, when my first-born was three months old, I packed my bags and went to my father's house. He let me rest a while, but at the end of the day he said there was no place for me in his house. I had to return to my husband.

'So, for forty years I lived with a man who had nothing but contempt for me. I bore him two more children and though there was no physical violence, there was enough emotional abuse, enough of nasty scenes to numb me completely. As the alcoholism became worse we became increasingly less welcome in other's homes. So I had no friends. My husband's family had turned against me, too. Years of stress brought on illnesses, which evoked further indignity, contempt and harsh abuse.

'Did I feel anger or despair? The truth is, I was so numb I could not even pray, I was so numb, it no longer mattered if he came home, hurt and bleeding, having fallen in a drunken stupor. When he died, all he left me were empty bottles — under the bed, in cupboards, in storerooms....

'When he died, I was so lacking in self-worth that I was filled with remorse and guilt. I was plagued with bizarre thoughts. I thought, had I understood him better he might have been different. Did I not do enough for him? When I was young, men often complimented me. Maybe I flirted with them. Maybe, in my mind, I was unfaithful. Just in my mind. Nothing ever happened. I was filled with guilt about this. For months, I wept. Nothing seemed to help.

'Realising I couldn't carry on in this fashion, I told my children I was returning to the hills. I wanted to sort myself out and I wanted to do it alone. What made me take this decision? I don't know. I had no spiritual life then, no mentor or friends. I still couldn't pray. All I knew was that there was an overwhelming desire to break free of the past. To break free of all bondage. I wanted to be free. I didn't even want my children around me. I was almost seventy. I wanted the rest of my life to be peaceful.

'I returned to the hills and stripped my cottage bare of every remnant of the past. I gave away everything I could, and of those things for which there were no takers, I made a bonfire. It was the first step I took towards acquiring a sense of self-worth. I shed the baggage of the past. It didn't happen overnight, it happened over the course of years. The important thing is, it happened. I no longer dwelt on the past. This brought immense calm. I decided then to make peace with my husband's family. I went out of my way to do this, even inviting my sister-in-law whose very presence used to make me tremble, to stay with me so that I could care for her through her illness. Eventually, it was more than her illness that was healed.

'I am at peace now, happiest by myself and surrounded by nature. My children are still a bondage, but at least I can see them from a slight distance. I have my music, my prayers, my books. I have birds around me and I watch the seasons change. I want this peace to pervade my last days…'

Sulekha spoke dispassionately, without a trace of resentment or bitterness. I looked at her with silent admiration. An unhappy childhood, a forty-year-long wretched marriage, a desire to change things for the better at the age of sixty-seven. She truly is an evolved person, filled with an amazing grace. She is strong, positive, full of the joy of life. She is truly beautiful. May her remaining years indeed be peaceful.

Shalini Saran

Nobody's Single in a Community

Captain Ramesh Singh was the kind of man who looked comfortable being single. More than a choice, it almost seemed a necessity. He was an introvert who loved his books, his newspaper, and his daily walks with his Alsatian, Buster.

We lived in Shillong and we would often see him take Buster for a walk along the meandering, serpentine lanes of the lush, undulating landscape. We lived in Happy Valley, a Cantonment area, beautifully endowed by nature and maintained by the Army. There were little valleys and hills, pretty houses, breathtaking flora and fauna and I realised why Shillong is called the Scotland of the East. Not that I've ever been to Scotland, but when I see pictures of it, I can relate to them immediately.

Our house was a dreamy government house since Daddy was a senior officer. It was beautifully maintained with a little pond and a profusion of flowers and behind it was an awe-inspiring view of terraced fields of sugarcane. There were stairs cut into the hill past our fence that led to a gentle waterfall. We would take a picnic lunch when it wasn't raining and sit there, play games, throw stones or read a book. Those were idyllic days.

Captain Singh would come for some of the Army parties and nurse his drink or play bridge. He was a solitary reaper, in every sense of the word. He didn't mind if somebody came and sat next to him. He was courteous with the ladies. He may have been an eligible bachelor at some stage but now, despite being rather handsome and not so old, his reputation of being a gruff loner preceded him wherever he went. So nobody really bothered about matchmaking. There were whispers of a heart that was broken, and while there was no concrete story, conjectures were aplenty.

And then there were the young couples, all of them were happy and busy partying. The husbands worked hard but not beyond five so everybody was out for walks in the evening, there was a mess where one could meet up, all kinds of welfare activities, a school where some wives volunteered or taught and it was a good, strong community. That's where I heard the word 'community' so often since my Dad would lecture everybody about building one, like building a family through shared values and support.

Captain Lal was the absolute opposite of Captain Singh in every sense of the word. He was a loud and dashing extrovert and his charming personality and good looks made heads turn. His wife was shy and retiring, but he would drag her to parties, try to get her on the dance floor or force her to socialise with the other women. She would feel awkward but indulgently oblige. Captain Lal was fond of chess and he found a good partner in Captain Singh. They enjoyed each other's company tremendously and though Captain Singh was shy around Mrs Lal, they all ended up spending time together quite often.

Being in the infantry involved staying fit for war; for us kids it meant our fathers woke up early to exercise. They were kept updated through training courses, went to office, on reconnaissance visits or town duty if there were disturbances and for community building exercises. There were also war exercises, which meant they were gone for a few days.

One day, we heard Mrs Lal was pregnant; she was thrilled and glowing. Then, everybody, including Captain Lal, Daddy and Captain Singh, was called away for an Army exercise. Several days later Daddy returned jubilant. They had done exceedingly well in the war exercise; he had gotten a Param Veer Chakra on paper, implying that if this were real war, it would be a real award! We were all so excited! Another unit of men was supposed to return a little later.

But that's when the phone call came, late at night. Captain Lal's jeep had overturned near a ravine, and he had died in the accident. Daddy had to break the news to Mrs Lal. Her family was flown into Gauhati and then drove down to Shillong.

The funeral was held with Mrs Lal heavily pregnant. I remember going with my family to meet her. There were so many people there, it was so confusing. She was putting on a brave front. Captain Singh, the recluse, was notably chivalrous. Some people were huddled in conversation and I remember eavesdropping.

Mrs Lal had no educational qualifications, no fall back job and no option other than staying with her in-laws, since her own parents were no longer alive. The in-laws declared that if they could, they would get her married so that she would not have to live alone.

'It's not that bad to live alone,' piped in Captain Singh.

'It's easy for you to say,' said Mrs Lal, tearfully. 'I can't imagine living like this.'

Captain Singh drew my father aside. He told Daddy, 'I value living by myself but I cannot bear to see this lady's plight. I will talk to Captain Lal's parents. After she is done grieving, I will marry her if she will have me. I will lend my name and my support to Captain Lal's child.'

Did he always love her? Was he duty bound? What made him rise to the occasion and offer to marry his friend's wife? Daddy's puzzled look must have made him explain: 'It's easy for a man to live alone in India. Tough for a lady, though it will get easier with time. If I had a daughter, I'd make sure she was independent so that if she chooses to live alone like I did, she could do so comfortably. It is terrible to see a lady fall apart when she is widowed. And by the way, I was never in love with Leena (for that was Mrs Lal's name). She is my friend and I respect her like I respected Captain Lal. Isn't marriage about friends living together?'

Daddy and Captain Singh didn't realise that Leena had heard every word of their exchange. She burst into tears and hugged Captain Singh. 'The very fact that I know I have a friend whom I can count on, that my late husband had a friend who was so loyal, will keep me going. You'll see how well we do, my kid and me. I will study, I will work, I'll get the Army pension and I'll be brave. I still love my husband so I can stay single like you, Ramesh. Anyway, nobody's single in a community.' They hugged each other and Daddy moved away to give them some privacy.

Mrs Lal did not marry again and Captain Singh stayed single, too. They stayed friends for as long as we were in touch with them. He always made sure her every need was provided for. They were single but they were part of a community.

They say it takes a village to raise a child. Mrs Lal continued to stay in Shillong, Captain Singh retired there too and Siddharth Lal, Mrs Lal's son is part of a wonderful community of friends and family. His grandparents came to Shillong after some time and they moved in with his mother.

I learnt something from this experience — that some people are single by choice, that they can lead fulfilling lives and that we need to respect and celebrate their decision.

Anuradha Gupta

Cooking and Singing

Every time I visit my friend Sudhakar, I learn something new about cooking. His time-saving and practical tips have helped me to save many an inedible dish, like the time when I added excess salt and was in a hurry to leave for my errands. I didn't have the heart to throw away the dish but I also knew that my finicky family would not eat a morsel, nor would they even pretend to eat a bit just to make me happy.

So I called Sudhakar and he advised me to add a potato and promised my dish would be salvaged. It was, and my family actually liked the curry that had 'just the right amount of salt'.

I smiled as I thought about Sudhakar, who is not a chef at some fancy fine-dining restaurant. He is someone who decided to pursue his love for cooking seriously after the demise of his wife, five years ago. His gajar ka halwa (a carrot sweetmeat) has got me travelling halfway across town while his besan laddoo (chickpea sweetmeat) has melted in my mouth even as I have shamelessly asked for more.

When I visit Sudhakar, my kids tell me, 'Do not return without the laddoos. And we know the difference between uncle's laddoos and the ones available in shops,' they add, without mincing words. Sudhakar always obliges happily, because, try as I may, my laddoos don't taste quite the same. And my family is not the only one that is fond of Sudhakar's cooking.

Sudhakar is blind and hence I marvel even more at his delicious culinary creations. His sense of smell helps him with spices and condiments, he does his own grocery shopping and his microwave, gas stove, mixer and grinder are placed so that he can reach them by counting his steps. Sudhakar listens to cookery programs on TV and then experiments on his own with the recipes. He has not learnt Braille. At a cookery competition organised by a senior citizens club, he was the only male participant and it came as no surprise when he won the first prize for his 'shahi methi muttar masala' (a rich pea and fenugreek curry) from among the other twenty-four lady contestants.

Sudhakar was not blind from birth. He was struck by an ailment known as Retinaitis Pigmentozarfa with nystagmus due to which he knew he would gradually become blind. Once, when I asked how he coped with this tough reality, he said, 'It didn't make much sense to fight my impending blindness so I decided to accept it and mentally prepare for it. I began to cherish everything I saw, the bright flowers, the sky, my wife's face and expressions, things and people around me. Because of the nature of the disease, the loss of vision was gradual. So I slowly began to change things — for instance, instead of riding a scooter, I started cycling and when my vision became blurred I stopped cycling and began to walk. At home I used to practice walking and doing my daily chores with my eyes closed.'

When Sudhakar was thirty-two he had a bout of malaria that accelerated the pace of this degenerative disease and became the subsidiary cause of his blindness. He was then working with the Nahata Arts, Science and Commerce College at Bhusaval, as Head of the Commerce department. He continued to work there and got new topics read by four specially appointed readers and taped them. He would deliver his lectures by first recording them at home and then memorising them.

Sudhakar is now sixty-eight-years-old and retired. Determined to stay fit and alert, he does his yoga and pranayam (breathing exercises) daily and also works out on his stationary cycle. 'I try not to dwell on why this happened to me,' he says. 'Instead, I look at the bright side — the rest of my senses are active. Besides, I enjoyed the gift of sight for the first thirty-two years of my life.'

Apart from cooking, there is something else Sudhakar enjoys — singing! It is another hobby he decided to pursue in the last five years to keep him constructively occupied. It started off quite accidentally. While he cooks, he habitually sings along with the songs being aired on the radio.

When a neighbour heard him, she remarked upon the quality of his voice and suggested that he pursue his singing more seriously and reach out to a wider audience. She told him of an aunt who also had a good voice and suggested they both sing together. Soon, others followed and now Sudhakar takes his singing rather seriously!

Twice a week, the ten members of his orchestra come to his home to practice. The group sings bhajans (devotional songs), and songs by singers like Mohammed Rafi, Suresh Wadkar and

Arun Date. Later, they enjoy the snacks Sudhakar has prepared and they all have such a good time.

In fact, they have often joked about how they can't decide whether Sudhakar's singing or his cooking is better, and which of the two gets them diligently to his house twice every week. Perhaps the answer lies somewhere else. Perhaps it lies in Sudhakar's innate and infectious ability to enjoy life!

Nina Irani

In Quiet Confidence

I met her one evening on my walk around the colony. She had recently moved in.

'I'm Maya, and I'm new to this colony,' she introduced herself, 'Just finding my way around.'

'Hullo!' I said, 'You'll like it here. People are friendly and helpful. Come walk with me. I usually take three rounds every evening.'

This was the beginning of our friendship. Maya was over sixty, but very sprightly. I had to double my pace to keep in step with her. The more I got to know her, the more I admired her grit and resilience. She had weathered many a storm in life and came out victorious.

'You live alone?' I asked.

'Yes, but I'm not single by choice. I've been a widow for most of my life. My husband, a pilot, died in an air crash many years ago. I was just thirty-one, and my children were as young as eight and three.'

'I'm sorry. It must have been very tough on you.'

'Yes, life was no bed of roses. I had difficult phases. Either there was too much interference from well-meaning relatives or heaps of unsolicited advice, which didn't help but merely confused me. Then I made up my mind to find a job far away from home, so that I could be independent and organise my life as I thought best. It helped that I had a profession.'

Maya was a doctor. She took up a job in a busy rural Mission Hospital. The work was exacting and the salary was not much. But it provided her with security. She had quarters on the campus, and domestic help was available. There was a good school close by for the children.

'But after two years, I felt the need to pursue post-graduate studies. Medicine was being revolutionised in every field. I didn't want to stagnate, so I went off to the UK. Of course it was heart rending to leave the children behind. My relatives raised such a clamour, calling me a heartless, irresponsible mother. I didn't accept their offers to look after my children while I was away. I was sure they would brainwash them and turn them against me. Instead, there was a convent close by and the nuns were my friends. They assured me that my children would be well cared for.'

Maya spent five years abroad, but visited her children annually, and even took them for a holiday to England. When she returned with her degree, she was offered the Directorship of the hospital. She worked there till her retirement.

'Did you never think of marrying again?' I asked.

'Not really. I was too busy providing for my children. Between work and home there was no time for another relationship.'

'What about the lonely hours?'

'I never felt emotionally abandoned or consumed by insecurities. I guess I had faith that God would see me through any difficult situation. When in trouble, I used to cry to God, "Take my hand, precious Lord … Lead me on." It always worked.'

Soon after Maya's bereavement, she met a lady who saved her from self-pity. The lady told Maya that she pictured life as a colourful canvas. The depth and beauty of the painting emerged when the artist added contrasting tones among the colours. Similarly sorrows and setbacks in life brought out strength of character and hence, the discovery of one's potential.

'I have always reflected on the wisdom of her words. One feels lonely and filled with self-pity only when there is a vacuum in one's life. During my years of service, in spite of the heavy workload, I took up correspondence courses in counselling and journalism. My mind was always pleasantly occupied. And if you think I was some sort of recluse, you'll be surprised to hear that I had many good friends and a decent social life.'

'And now that you have retired, how will you spend your time? Will you practice privately?'

'Oh no,' she laughed, 'I've done my bit for humanity. Now I intend humouring myself. I've already started out as a freelance writer. Look out for my short stories and articles in magazines and on the Net! And I've just booked my holiday to South Africa. I mean to travel around and see the world whenever I can.'

'No regrets being single?' I asked.

'None at all! Can't you see? I'm in love with life!' Maya said.

Eva Bell

A Giver to the End

My grandmother had been widowed very early in life and had single-handedly brought up her two young daughters, toiling as a schoolmistress in the small town of Raiganj in West Bengal. That was in the 1940s; and what we take for granted now, was not so well accepted then. But, refusing to take any help from her relatives or in-laws, she had lived alone with two young daughters, doing all she could to make them happy, forgetting her own sorrows in their little joys.

My mother has told me stories about her that has made us revere our grandmother as a lady who had gone through adversities like a knight in shining armour. She had educated her two daughters and married them off without a penny borrowed from anyone.

When I was young, I used to look forward each winter to our yearly visit to my grandmother's place in Kolkata. It was a tenement, and she had one room in it. There was a common corridor, which led to different rooms on that floor, each occupied by different families. I did wonder at times why she did not have an independent house or flat like ours, but to a five-year-old, the excitement of living in a different setting overshadowed all other inconveniences.

In the drawstring bag that she carried, there was always a picture of Maa Kaali and a hundred-rupee note. As a child, I thought that was for something she wanted to buy, maybe for me. When I grew older, I realised that the note must have a special relevance. Maybe she was keeping it for an emergency or for a time when she might be in need of a little extra cash. It was much later that I discovered that she had kept it for the purchase of the bier on which she would be carried to the cremation ground. She had given strict instructions regarding this detail of her funeral to her daughters and sons-in-law.

She had also made some unusual requests to her daughters. She told them, 'I have not taken a single penny from anyone throughout my life. I do not want that someone should pay for any ceremony or ritual that will be part of my funeral. I have enough money to pay my way to wherever I may go after I die. I will never be at peace otherwise. It may or may not happen, but I do not want to harbour the thought that some day in the future, my children would sit and calculate how much money they had spent on making funeral arrangements for their mother.'

She also said to her daughters, 'I don't want you to keep my portrait in your house. It may be that you put a fresh garland on it every day for some months, and then invariably, the garland will not be changed for a couple of days, and some years later, it will be changed only on special occasions, perhaps only on my death anniversary. And even if you take care to wipe it every day of your lives, your children will one day, stack it away in the store-room with old newspapers and other junk, perhaps even muttering that an old portrait is not in keeping with the décor of their house. If you wish to remember me, do so in the sanctity of your hearts, in private.'

True to her wishes, every single penny spent for her last rites came from the money she had kept expressly for the purpose. Under her mattress, there were little bundles of fifty or hundred rupee notes, even some loose change. Her savings account was not touched. According to her wishes, her hard-earned money was divided between her two daughters. She was a true giver and she remained one till the very end.

Monika Pant

Vikram, My Inspiration

I was waiting for the lift, when I heard a man say, 'Excuse me, Ma'am, could you please keep the door open for me?'

I turned and saw a man in his forties. Each step he took was an effort, despite the use of a walker. We were both attending the Multiple Sclerosis (MS) annual social evening — me as an invitee and he as an MS person (patients are referred to as MS persons, not patients). MS is a chronic disease that attacks the central nervous system. It occurs without any known cause and is incurable, despite intensive research worldwide. Some years ago, I had read an article in the local newspaper about MS often being misdiagnosed. It was also stated that even by creating awareness about the disease, a person could help. That is how my involvement with MS began.

The man introduced himself as Vikram. Later, he told me more about himself. He was thirty-eight years old and unmarried when he was diagnosed with MS. At the time, he was living with his elder brother and family, and he earned his living by cycling long distances to deliver books to readers who had ordered them. But after the onset of the disease, he had to give up his job and sadly, his elder brother began to look upon him as a burden. So Vikram shifted out of his house and slept on a bed placed in the portico. Vikram paid his brother every month for food and for the use of the bathroom.

MSSI (Multiple Sclerosis Society of India) is the only support group for MS persons. The volunteers and the physiotherapist provided by them became his support system.

'When I was struck with MS in the prime of my life, it opened up a world of bewildering questions to which there were very few answers. My priorities changed from planning things weeks in advance to focusing on the present day and the blessing that it was for me. I began to look upon each day as another chance to fight this incurable, degenerative disease that can disable people, render them unemployable and leave entire families devastated by the sudden disruption of normal life,' he said as he adjusted his old, but clean and crisply ironed shirt.

From a job that involved being constantly on the move, to consciously taking each step with a walker, the journey had its share of anger, frustration and helpless moments. But Vikram was very religious and his faith in God gave him the strength to keep going and helped him develop a positive attitude. He did not give up; he was also too self-respecting to survive on charity. As he could not use his legs at all, he turned to his fingers and creativity for help.

Bikes had fascinated Vikram ever since he was a ten-year-old. After he was struck by MS, he started making, to scale, sport and street bike models. He collected pictures from magazines and then worked on making each model by hand. In time, his bikes adorned showcases and centre tables in France, USA, Germany and Delhi. His handcrafted models were made with raw materials that mostly comprised of scrap like cardboard, shoe polish boxes, broomsticks and wire. He also used metal wires, paper pins, Fevicol and coloured paper to give the glazed effect. Vikram had found a way to be happily and beneficially occupied. He remained as humble as ever. I learnt many lessons in humility from him.

I am not a bike fan but I found myself asking him to make one for me. Twenty days later, mine was ready complete with side panels, a tail lamp, mud guard, a seat, a silencer pipe, gear levers, disc brakes, speedometer, radium stickers on the tank and a number plate. The wheel rim and the inside of the headlights were pasted with silver foil from cigarette packets. The model also had a stand, a movable handle and an adjustable seat and the pencil cell battery, being connected to the brakes, made the wheels stop and the bulb glow.

My life got busier and I could not visit Vikram as often, but he never complained. As the next MS annual social evening approached, I received a call from the MSSI Pune chapter, inviting me to the event. I asked about Vikram and was told that he had been hospitalised. As I rushed to meet him, I found him lying in bed. MS had affected his entire spine; he could no longer sit up and he had lost more weight. But his eyes were shining. He was not only hopeful of recovering but was looking forward to completing the new bike he had recently started.

But it never was completed. Vikram expired a week later. That was in 2008.

At times when I feel depressed, I look at the little bike Vikram had gifted me. It inspires me not to give up. It reminds me of what an amazing human being Vikram was — a man who lived his life with dignity, hope and gratitude for life's blessings.

Sanaea Patel

Radha Bai

Radha Bai was my friend and our childhood neighbour. After her husband deserted her for a younger woman, she struggled hard to bring up her two teenage sons.

By the time they were settled in lucrative jobs and matrimony, Radha started suffering from degenerative arthritis and emphysema — a long-term, progressive disease of the lung causing shortness of breath and severe osteoporosis. She became fully confined to a wheelchair, and the severe spinal pain could not always be controlled, even with morphine. All the conditions were incurable, and it was very likely that the pain would increase over time. When the pain was at its worst she could not think or speak, and this could go on for hours, with no prospect of relief. Her family was unable to cope with her ailment or her suffering, and their only solution was to put her in an old age home.

Seventeen years ago she decided she could no longer face life. She wanted to die, and she even seriously attempted suicide several times. On one of these occasions she was taken to hospital and was treated against her will. I remember she was extremely angry with us, her friends, who had initiated life-saving treatment.

She went so far as thinking of going abroad to contact pro-euthanasia campaigners. But we dissuaded her; she could not qualify for euthanasia because she was not terminally ill, and loneliness and depression were not reasons enough for it.

It was then she agreed, albeit unwillingly, to join a project the old people's organisation had begun. It was a project to help disabled children. She agreed to become a part of it, little knowing that it would change her life forever.

I remember Radha saying to me, 'I felt no one loves me, but I do have friends and family. These babies are unwanted and unloved by their families. And it is a fact, they have not only saved my life, they've given it a meaning. Many of the children were so disabled they could barely manage to crawl in the dust. The first time I visited the children they called me "Mummy". They hugged and loved me, and as I was playing with them, I suddenly loved them all, overwhelmingly and fiercely, as if they really were my own. When we left, I thought I want to live. It was the first time I had such a thought in over ten years. My children have given me a reason to live. They love me overwhelmingly, just as I am. They too have incurable conditions, and many suffer much pain. But they can and do give and receive a tremendous love, which has transformed my life. Euthanasia or suicide would have robbed me of the last seventeen years of my life, and it would have robbed "my" children of the chance in life they now have. While people speak only of a right to "die with dignity" what lonely people like me really need is help and support to live with dignity until we die naturally.'

Till she passed away three years ago, Radha worked and lived for her newfound ever-growing family. Till the very end she strove to inculcate a sense of dignity in her children. Her motto was: Life presents many problems. Solutions are seldom easy but they always exist — if we are willing to look hard enough.

Gargi Chopra
(As told to Anita Jaswal)

Sheela Bua

Some people simply walk into our lives and leave their imprint all over it and we are never the same again. So it was with her, my loving Sheela Bua (my father's sister). She had come over to us in Jodhpur to join a government school as a teacher. A sister of my father's childhood friend, she was small, petite, fair and impish and she soon found a place in our hearts.

I must then have been around seven and my brother five. Our parents were stereotype parents of the 1960s. For us, Sheela Bua was a child's fantasy come true; she was so full of energy, mischief and spontaneity. In fact, the overall picture was so delightful that to us children the missing pieces of the puzzle did not matter. For instance, we never bothered to ask why she always wore a white sari.

My parents had a whole set of dos and don'ts and we were expected to toe the line. But no matter what sort of trouble we were in, we could always count on Sheela Bua to be our knight in shining armour.

Time spent with her was sheer bliss. She knew how to turn

every moment into fun, every activity into joy. Yet, as we grew older, we drifted into an absorbing world of our own. Like others who were once at the centre of our existence Sheela Bua, too, receded into the periphery — till that day when my best friend Medha came home in tears. She had broken up with her fiancé. She was furious, devastated and desperately in need of sympathy, which we knew Bua could offer.

Medha poured out her entire story, incoherently at first. Her fiancé was getting transferred to a remote town, which meant Medha would have to give up her job.

Strangely, Bua sat in silence, her eyes expressionless. I was extremely disappointed, almost annoyed by her insensitivity and told her so.

She looked at us in a way I had not seen her do before. 'You girls talk about love, relationships and commitments, but when it comes to living out anything in real life all your claims burst like bubbles.' She then went on to tell us about her own story, something I'd never heard before.

When she was in her late teens her father announced that he had arranged a match for her. The boy was studying law. He was the only son of wealthy landowners. His parents were no more but he lived in a joint family with his uncles and their families. They all came over one day and she was engaged. No questions were asked. She was supposed to comply, head bowed, but the imp in her had to do the unthinkable. She quietly sent a note to the boy saying that she must meet him alone. He obliged and they met in the ruins of the old temple, as suggested by her. An absolute baby at heart, she rattled off her list of demands, while the boy kept smiling tolerantly, amused at this delightful, chirpy little bundle of innocence.

After she was through with her monologue, she got up to leave. Suddenly she felt a tug; a firm hand had caught her arm. It was her fiancé looking at her intently. 'And what about my request?' he asked, in a grave, deep voice.

'Well! What do you want?' she asked impatiently.

He said, 'Give me your word that you will never leave me in this life.' For her, a child more than a woman, who had no inkling about love, longing and desire, this was the silliest thing anybody could have ever asked. She agreed dismissively, shook herself free and fled.

Soon after the engagement the boy's family left. The marriage was fixed for a year after. Destiny, however, had other plans. Hardly a few months had passed when an uncle arrived with the sad news that the boy had been detected with tuberculosis. The disease was in its terminal stage. In those days, a TB patient was a pariah, treated as an untouchable. He was therefore being sent to the TB sanatorium at Bhowali, in the hills. An old family servant would accompany him, to get him admitted and that would be the end of his association with the family. The uncle went on to say that for the sake of the girl, the boy's family was prepared to consider the engagement as null and void. It was evident that the relatives were happy at the prospect of becoming the sole beneficiaries of such huge properties at the death of the boy. When the uncle left, Bua's father announced that the chapter was closed as far as he was concerned and he would now find a better match for his daughter.

But suddenly there was a vehement protest from Bua. She who had been a docile, speechless little doll so far turned into a blazing fire. She announced categorically that she was already married to her fiancé by word and soul and any other ceremony would just have been a formality. She said that she would be going to Bhowali to be with her man and look after him for as long as he lived. It was as if in an instant the woman in her had woken up. Despite all requests, arguments, threats of banishments and the tearful pleas of her father, she packed her bags, calmly touched everyone's feet and left. There was an uproar among the boy's relatives who perceived her as a threat to their future wealth. They did not want her to go to Bhowali. Eventually, she signed a document stating that she had no claim to her husband's wealth.

She stayed with him for the next four months. He was a very sick man, a mere shadow of his earlier self, but she was by his bedside every minute of the day, nursing him, feeding him and cleaning him. Her presence was soothing and she cherished each moment as a blessing. He died in her lap. After he was gone she returned home a totally changed person, for she had now experienced love, the intimacy of caring, loss, anguish and pain and had gained in understanding. She now knew the value of a moment of true love, a moment of intimacy. She knew that in the journey of life there was no knowing how much time we had with a soul mate. But even to have shared some fleeting moments with one, was the truest celebration of life.

She honoured every word of her commitment to her man because that, according to her, was the path of love. When she finished her story, she raised her head. We could see tears streaming down her face. She whispered, 'Medha, I know how you feel right now. But then, such are the tests of love. Would you want to be a failure? Words of commitment may spring from our loving hearts but their roots must be deeper, in our very souls.'

I could see Medha's face lighting up. The lesson had been grasped. And Sheela Bua became even more perfect in my eyes.

Archana Pant

OSCAR-Worthy

It's amazing how the most ordinary people manage to do the most extraordinary things. A few weeks ago I was lucky to meet Ashok Rathod, a shy young man with a big clean heart. He uses football to engage and empower youngsters living in his slum, wean them away from drug abuse, and help them learn a skill. On seeing Ashok, I wondered how such a simple, no-fuss lad was able to come up with such a unique concept and pull it off with such vigour.

Ashok lives in Ambedkar Nagar, Colaba, Mumbai and hails from a lower middle class family. His father is a fisherman and if Ashok did not do what he does, he would probably be in the family business.

There is something very special about Ashok. Maybe it's his soft and polite manner of speech or his kind demeanour. One takes a liking to him instantly.

At first, he was shy to talk about his achievements. But upon my insistence he told me, speaking only in Hindi, how he noticed that most of the children in his slum dropped out of school and began to work as fishermen. Fishing earned them money, and while a part of this money would go to their families, the remainder was wasted on vices like smoking, gambling and drinking. When their families came to know of this, they would marry off the boys in the hope of steering them towards a better path. The situation actually worsened after they got married, because they continued to waste money on bad habits, and sometimes, in a drunken state, thrashed their wives and children.

A few years went by and Ashok noticed that the pattern was repeated in many families. He also became aware of other issues, such as child marriage, gender inequality, communal friction, lack of education and child labour that plagued the community.

Fortunately, Ashok had studied up to the twelfth standard and had the guiding force of his mentor Miss Bina Laskari Seth, founder of the Door Step School, who enrolled him in an NGO named Magic Bus. There, he developed his leadership skills. Fortunately, too, his parents did not force him to get married.

Mathew Stacy, who became Ashok's role model, runs Magic Bus. Mathew taught him how to teach football and rugby as a hobby for children who were going astray. Ashok worked with Magic Bus and credits Mathew for shaping his life and inspiring him to start his own venture to take up the cause of children in his slum. He realised that if nothing were done now to stem the social problems, the situation would only worsen.

At first, Ashok chose a group of eighteen boys, of whom twelve were dropouts and six were attending school, and offered to teach them football. It was something new for them, and the kids agreed excitedly. After one month of classes,

Ashok made a deal with these kids — they would have to go to school regularly for him to continue teaching them.

Initially, Ashok had to face a lot of resistance from the community and his own parents. For over a year, he hid his project from his family. When he mustered up the courage to tell them, they worried if he could pull it off and even if he could, how many children would he actually benefit. They were anxious about children getting injured. Another worry was Ashok's income; how would he earn a living?

After facing a lot of resistance, Ashok, at the young age of 21, managed to found OSCAR, (Organisation for Social Change, Awareness and Responsibility). He did so with the help of two NGOs, which continue to support him — Unlimited India and Parwah.

Ashok had to allay the fears of some parents who felt their children were loitering and 'only playing sports'; they were not helping with household responsibilities or fishing. Thus, Ashok started a give and take process with the parents. He advised them to use the football sessions as a means to get their children to help with household work. If the work were not done, they would not be allowed to attend sessions. Gradually, the feedback from the parents turned positive and OSCAR began to gain their trust.

As Ashok's understanding of the complexities of the situation increased, he started football sessions with younger children. Children being children, they became more interested in football than in their studies, so classes were started twice a week for the kids who attended football sessions. The parents were happy with this, as the children began to attend school regularly.

In the meanwhile, the OSCAR team had grown — Ashok, Ganpat and Suraj, now worked with the assistance of three volunteers. The two NGOs supporting OSCAR sponsored the children and helped Ashok earn a living.

It has been more than three years since Ashok's football sessions started and there are now more than a hundred children participating. The best players are given extra practice and represent OSCAR in tournaments. Football sessions are held three times a week and sports is used as a means to tackle community issues, impart life-skills such as the importance of education, decision-making and hygiene, and raise awareness about social issues.

Ashok has extended activities to include day trips, outdoor camps, dance classes and street plays. Now all the children contribute Rs 15 per month to the group so that equipment and travel costs are covered. The fee also gives them a sense of belonging and responsibility. The parents, pleased to observe a change in the behaviour of their children, have now agreed to pay rupees thirty per month.

Ashok's mission is not to make the children good footballers but good human beings. His efforts have inculcated a spirit of camaraderie and helped unite children of different castes and communities, creating a unique bond between them. He hopes, eventually, to invite girls to join OSCAR, too.

On asking Ashok about his personal plans for the future, he replies shyly, 'At the moment, nothing is more important than OSCAR. I have no time to waste on girlfriends, my children need me and I need them to move on!'

As told to Roma Kapadia

The Bigger Picture

What does it take for an abused housewife to become an award-winning photojournalist? Sarvesh's story says it all.

How much can a person bear before she realises that she has had enough? It took Sarvesh ten long years. At seventeen and barely an adult, Sarvesh, was married into a businessman's family. The decade she spent with her in-laws was abusive from the very first day. Raped by her husband on the first night, Sarvesh's hellish life was just unfolding. Mental and physical abuse became the order of the day for the tender teen. With in-laws as partners in crime demanding dowry, her parents, too, shut their doors on her. With nowhere to go she was forced to bear the spite and violence meted out to her. The abuse could be sparked off by things as minor as a household chore or clothes. Her tormentors had no dearth of excuses to torture her. The abuse got cruder when Sarvesh could not conceive. As days passed, the torture and physical demands by her husband also became intolerable.

The last straw was when her in-laws decided that Sarvesh's husband would marry for a second time, as there was no sign of her getting pregnant. In one of the altercations that followed, she just packed her bags and decided to leave. With no idea of what lay in store and without any qualifications, Sarvesh found a window of opportunity when she saw a poster about Saheli, a support group for women. She left her private hell and sought help from the NGO.

Learning to sew, she managed to earn a little money. Picking up the pieces of her life wasn't easy; she had no idea about the new challenges life would pose. But after a life of abuse, torture and insults, Sarvesh was soon filled with a sense of freedom.

However, she got a sense of her calling when one of her friends showed her a camera. It was love at first sight for Sarvesh and the beginning of a path of self-discovery and hope. Armed with a Pentax SLR K-1000, Sarvesh began to look at life differently. Her joy knew no bounds when a leading Hindi daily published her photograph. Surviving on a shoestring budget, Sarvesh skipped meals to save money to keep afloat. She also doubled up as a beautician to sustain her love for photography. Her efforts soon began to bear fruit. Accolades began pouring in over her work on the Uttarkashi earthquake in 1991, the Sitamarhi riots in 1992, Himalayan car rallies and the coalmines of Dhanbad and Jharia. In 1999, she covered the Kargil War, and the Ministry of Information and Broadcasting gave her an award for her coverage of the conflict. She has also been awarded by the Hindi academy and honoured by various NGOs.

'We need to stand on our own feet to explore our strength. It is ingrained in our system that women should be treated like slaves. Violence is the only means for a man to establish his power over a woman,' she says, looking back on her life. 'A surname is a burden. I don't want my husband's or my father's surname. I don't want to carry that baggage.'

Her experiences in life are reflected in her work as most of Sarvesh's photography revolves around celebrating the spirit of the women. Sarvesh's work was also showcased along with six other women photographers in 2005 as part of 'Fuji Films Super Six' photography exhibition in a special calendar. Her photograph, entitled 'Looking towards the future,' was featured and received rave reviews.

Her indomitable and never-say-die attitude are the main strengths in life; they help her to celebrate life and keep her chin up. Free as a bird, Sarvesh now revels in self-exploration and faces life on her own terms. Her spirits are kept flying by her monthly photographic assignments to the Himalayas and other places of natural beauty, which attracts her. Breaking the shackles of a life full of pain and suffering, she stands as an example of hope and struggle. 'I love my work and cherish my freedom. I have been through what many consider nightmare, but I have no complaints and am proud that I have faced challenges in my life,' she says, with a smile.

Preetha Nair

Standing on My Feet

The poet W.B. Yeats, had written, 'I shall arise and go now, and go to Innisfree' to live alone in peace in the 'bee-loud glade'.

By the immense grace of God, without 'arising and going', 'peace comes dropping slow' into my little haven in Kottayam, Kerala, where I live alone. I could not have gone anywhere in search of peace or fortune or anything else but mercifully God has sent his peace to me.

It is for the first time that I am yielding to pressure to write about myself. Some leading newspapers in Malayalam had approached me earlier for my life story. Journalists and feature writers very often tend to sensationalise otherwise ordinary events and lives and I did not want to run the risk of losing my privacy. I live an orderly quiet life. In *my* eyes there is nothing sensational, nothing special, in my life to be written about.

Dear reader, you might ask why, then, do I write now, when I am in my early sixties? Well, a close friend who understands me wanted me to open up. If she considers it worthwhile I must narrate my story.

In my infancy, one year and ten months to be precise, I had an attack of polio. From that time onwards, till the age of seven, my movements were on my fours, crawling. Treatment went on to improve my condition all the while. At the age of seven my parents took me to the Christian Medical College, Vellore, in Tamil Nadu. Till the age of twenty-two, I was in and out of that renowned institution. The doctors wanted me to stand up. Their eagerness to help me was enormous, I gratefully recall. There is one person I must particularly remember — Dr Paul Brand, my doctor and an Englishman. It was he who taught me to walk and to accept as well as to challenge life gracefully.

And my parents showed enormous patience. As far as I was concerned I was quite pleased with life. Of course, I was well aware that I was handicapped for life and, as I grew into a young adult, I knew that I would be single, going through life all alone. Somehow it did not bother me much. In all those years of operations and physiotherapy I often quipped: 'I should stand on my feet — though fitted with callipers.' My visits to Vellore had trained me to make light of my handicap. Vellore also made me stand on my feet — fitted with callipers — and I learnt to move with a walker. I have not been to either school or college. My parents and elder brother had wanted me to pursue my studies and arranged tuitions at home and I studied for their sake. I was more involved in the little games I invented or the rural, traditional ones that can be played at home — like the game children played with five or seven small pebbles. I was leading a happy carefree life.

My mother, a housewife, though full of affection, was a task master who disciplined me rather severely. She made me self-reliant. On looking back that has helped immensely — to keep to my schedules, to avoid being self-indulgent. However, slowly I was drawn towards literature — Malayalam as well as English. That is how I did my MA in English and eventually became a teacher of English. I taught for thirty-four years (1972-2006). I worked from 6.30 in the morning to 5.30 in the evening. Half the time was spent in the parallel college, Ninan's, and half at home, teaching. After nineteen years, I resigned from Ninan's and concentrated on work at home. When I built my own house I had the largest room in it furnished as a proper classroom. I could enter it from inside and the entry for students was from outside.

My house is fairly close to my 'tharavad' (a traditional ancestral house in Kerala) where I was born and brought up. The financial resources were in part what my parents gave, in part my savings, in part a housing loan. I have grown a garden in the yard with roses, jasmine and other flowers. When I open the windows of my bedroom in the morning the fragrance of 'karpura tulasi' (sacred basil) envelopes me. Even the small lotus pond in the garden is a delight.

As most people do, I have struggled. Somehow I do not consider it as a special achievement. To my mind I have been living a quiet and ordinary life, accepting whatever life offered me. In this I follow a golden rule I found in Ezhuthachan, the patriarch of Malayalam literature — there is no need either to chase enjoyments, or to reject the ones that come lawfully...

A prayer I came upon at the age of nineteen has since become a part of my daily worship and sums up the way I look at life:

'My father God, help me to expect Thee on the ordinary road of life! I do not ask for sensational happenings! Commune with me through ordinary work and duty. Be my companion when I take the common journey of life. Let my humble life be transfigured by Thy Presence!'

Elizabeth Koshy
(As told to O.V. Usha)

5
MATCHMAKING

I don't like to be labeled as lonely just because I am alone.

–Delta Burke

St. Joseph and the Spirit-Filled Husband

They cluck, they sigh, they grumble.
Between visits to match-makers,
They've even been known the occasional Novena to mumble.
I suppose mothers and aunts are entitled to,
Fret about the daughter, or niece, for whom
An ordinary Catholic boy, for a husband, just won't do.

But Oh! Woe is you!
Should you ever chance upon a stranger
Who wagers she knows a way
To send you dashing down the very aisle
You've successfully steered clear off
All this while.

On my way home from work one evening,
She leaped into my rickshaw-ride,
Without so much as a warning.
Of course, she was going my way
So how could I refuse to perform,
My good deed for the day?

MATCHMAKING

After a shrewd once-over
That included a surreptitious glance
At the bare ring finger on my left hand
She proceeded to enquire
About a boyfriend I might have left
On the back burner.

When I failed to provide the desired response
Repeat after me, she said sans pause
'St. Joseph, please send my way, a spirit-filled husband.'
And so I echoed as she commanded
The prayer that had trapped many a good woman,
In the shackles of conjugal martyrdom.

I suppose, if I had said it night and day,
As she prescribed
I might, by now, have been a merry bride.
Alas! This was not to be
For the free spirit in me,
Chose to take my chances with destiny.

Blessed are the kind, we're told.
So continuing in the conversational mould,
'What about your husband?' I asked with a smile.
'Is he as spirit-filled as you would like?'
'Of course,' she declared,
Without so much as a sense of the ironic
'He was truly spirit-filled. He was alcoholic.'

Averil Nunes

Being Single

My mother: 'When are you going to get married, beta?'
'I don't know, Mom.'
Pinky Aunty: 'Look, even your younger brothers have children now. What are you waiting for?'
Yes, the ultimate goal in my life is to produce children for my well-wishers or so-called well-wishers.
Kiran Bhabhi: 'Get married soon so that we can come to your wedding and have a good time.'
Okay, so for you to have a good time, I should shackle myself in the eternal bonds of holy matrimony with someone I don't even know.
Sheela Mami: 'Get married soon, you are getting older, all your hair will fall, and then no one will want to marry you!'
Yes, of course you are right. All bald people are bachelors, aren't they?
Welcome to my life. I am Shoumik, I am thirty and the most eligible bachelor in town. Okay, not the most eligible, but near about. I am a computer engineer by profession and I work in a reputed company. Now that makes me a commodity much

in demand with other desperate parents like my mother. She gets at least two marriage proposals for me in a week. She gets pictures of the girls and tries to force me to like them. But that's not the worst part; the worst part is when the parents arrange for me to meet the girl at a coffee shop. If I don't agree to go my mother tries emotional blackmail. 'Now that you're all grown up, why would you want to listen to me? You are earning well, so why should you care about your poor mother. If your Dad were here ... I feel so alone sometimes....' And all this interspersed with sobs.

Okay. Fine. So I go and meet her.

And the dreaded meetings follow a pattern, somewhat similar to this one. I sit and wait for the girl to arrive in one of the oldest coffee houses on Park Street, Kolkata. The girl's parents, of course, select the venue. I put on my headphones and start listening to music on my mobile while looking out of the window.

Okay, I have to admit that even though my attitude towards this meeting is negative there's always a bit of apprehension, a little excitement, a tiny butterfly in the stomach wondering if she's the one. What if she is my soul mate? Just then the glass doors open and a lady, maybe in her late forties, dressed in a striking red sari and struggling with her umbrella, enters the coffee shop. It's quite a scene. I can't stop smiling at her predicament. But my smile fades as she starts walking towards me. I thought she would slap me for smiling at her plight. However, she asks me, in Bengali, 'Are you Shoumik? The son of Mrs De, the nursing school principal?'

There are too many questions, and all at the same time. Stay calm, I tell myself. But there's only one simple answer. I admit meekly that I am.

'Good, I am Mrs Moonmoon Majumdar.' She stares hard at me, as if expecting an acknowledgment, or rather, applause. I get up quickly and touch her feet. A faint smile appears on her face.

As nervous as I am, I ask, 'But Ma'am, I thought I would be meeting your daughter?'

'Yes. Yes, she's here. Mrs Majumdar moves her gigantic body and from behind her there emerges a sweet looking girl, dressed in a salwar kameez, which looks like it was bought for this particular occasion. She is pleasantly plump, like most Bengali girls are. She has a round face and I can tell it's quite a simple one underneath the thick layer of make-up she has worn. She isn't particularly pretty but isn't that bad to look at, either. The problem with men is that even though we might look like Ron Howard or Kesto Mukherjee, we would expect the girl to be Aishwarya Rai. But I don't have any such problems.

'Pompa, this is Shoumik. Shoumik, this is my daughter Pompa.' (Pompa and Papai, how cute). The mother introduces us and adds, 'I will be sitting across at that table while you guys talk.' She points towards an empty table at the corner of the coffee shop.

After a pregnant pause, I offer the girl a chair and ask what she would like to have. She says, 'Nothing,' and keeps looking down. Our first conversation and her first words to me are 'nothing'. That's a start!

'Why not? Do have something. What about a coffee?'

'No. Thank you. I don't drink tea or coffee,' she says, looking at me for the first time.

Another pregnant silence.

Though I am a talkative person and have no problem striking up a conversation with anyone, this is a totally different situation. What should I talk about? Where do I begin? Perhaps by asking what she had for lunch today? Or what she likes eating most? What are her favourite movies? Does she like ice cream? There are so many questions and I just don't know where to start.

While I contemplate which question to ask first, she breaks the silence by asking a deep meaningful question herself — in a thick Bengali accent: 'What did you eat for lunch?' And without waiting for my response, she adds, 'I had chicken rice.'

I stare at her face in disbelief. I don't know what to say so I just say, 'Oh! So you like chicken?'

She says 'Yes. I just love chicken. You know every Sunday my Baba (father) brings a chicken from the market and Ma cooks it. You must come visit us some day. I'll ask Ma to cook for you.'

Oh! Wonderful! I am finally beginning to have a meaningful conversation about our future. At least now I know what Sundays would mean after getting married.

I begin wondering how to get out of this when she speaks again. 'What happened? Why are you so quiet?'

I say, 'No, I was imagining how good your mother's chicken might be.' She lets out a giggle. I smile. Please God, don't tell me that she will turn out to be my soul mate.

She sees the headphones and asks, 'Are you listening to music?'

Yes. I was, before you trampled on my pleasant life with that plate of chicken rice. 'Yes. I was,' I say with a smile.

Her eyes light up. 'Oh I love music! What were you listening to?'

'Pink Floyd.'

Her expression changes to a question mark. 'Who is that? Anyway I love Ricky Martin.'

Okay. That's it. I call for the bill and leave in a hurry, saying goodbye to Mrs Majumdar.

Back home, it was as I expected — my mother fervently defends the girl I just rejected. 'What's wrong with her? She is pretty, she is a graduate and she can cook. Just because she likes chicken rice and Ricky Martin is no reason to reject her.'

'Mom, you know it's not about chicken rice and Ricky Martin. It's about my soul mate, it's about connecting to a person at a mental level. I don't see her as my wife at all. She is not even close to what I imagine.'

'All your friends are married and have children by now and you are still imagining. Beta, come back to reality. No angel will come down from heaven for you.'

'Let it be, Mom. I don't mind, even if I don't get married my entire life, at least I won't have any unwanted clutter in my life. There is nothing common between us. In my social circle what will I introduce her as? Meet my wife Pompa, she loves chicken rice? If I won't be happy, would you be happy? And would she be happy? It doesn't make any sense to spoil two lives for the sake of social responsibility. So stop sacrificing innocent people at the altar of social responsibility. I will find the right girl at the right time, Mom, don't worry. Isn't being single better than marrying the wrong person and suffering?'

'Okay, fine, I get your point,' replies my mother.

I thank God for getting out of this, but just as I am about to leave my mother says, 'By the way I met Mrs Sinha at the market today. Her daughter is doing her MBA in Delhi. She is a pretty and very modern girl, just the kind you like. She gave me her daughter's photograph. Would you like to see it? Maybe she's the one for you?'

Shoumik De

The Perfect Match

Sighing with relief as she left her glass and steel office, Kriti joined Nafisa and strolled towards their coffee hangout. Dear Nafisa, soon to be married! How she would miss her. It was never the same afterwards, never, ever, and don't let anybody fool you into believing otherwise!

From her favourite corner she eyed the newcomer in their group. A friendly smile and a sense of humour too! Jaggu turned out to be a great conversationalist and she did so like a well-read, articulate man. Time sped by. She felt she had known him forever. Sparring amicably with him on the merits of the latest bestseller, she speculated idly if he was married. A dreamy look settled on her face. She wouldn't mind a quiet dinner for two!

'Easy does it,' whispered Nafisa, jerking her chin towards the well-built man who was standing expectantly near their table. Noting his gaze, she turned in surprise to see Jaggu blush and smile.

'Someone you know?' she asked him.

'My partner,' he mumbled as he said his goodbyes. Kriti

gaped while Nafisa gave an exaggerated sigh and grinned. So much for my little fantasies, thought Kriti. Why are some of the nicest men differently inclined? With a mental shrug, she settled down to an animated gossip session with her friends.

Later, driving home, she tried imagining her mother's reaction to Jaggu! Ma was orthodox and didn't like the natural order of her universe being disturbed. Since her stormy adolescence, Kriti had been at loggerheads with her on wide-ranging issues — fashion, careers, homosexuality and now her single status! Nothing would please the widowed Mrs Agarwal more than to see her only daughter settle down happily with a 'good boy', while Kriti, headstrong and independent, was determined never to fall into the trap of an arranged marriage.

Unlocking her door, Kriti called up home, a ritual she had followed since moving to Mumbai. It helped relieve some of Ma's anxieties as well as made her feel less alone as she entered her flat. She loved the freedom bestowed by independence, but in some respects, Ma had been right. It would be nice to have someone to share her life with, someone to walk with, hand in hand in the rain, or even to squabble over the TV remote! Definitely someone to help do the chores! Rapidly descending from the romantic to the mundane, Kriti looked with dismay at the overflowing sink she had ignored in the morning. Thank God, at least she didn't have to cook tonight!

Desultorily answering her mother's routine questions, Kriti suddenly jerked upright. 'What? Meet which boy? No Ma, you know I don't like all this,' she cried indignantly. There was agitated pleading from the other side. 'I don't care if Aunty will be angry! You shouldn't have encouraged her.'

But however much Kriti protested, she knew her mother would be very hurt if she didn't go to her aunt's home in Bandra and behave politely with the guests.

'I will not agree to this arranged marriage farce so don't you try to persuade me, Ma!' she ended vehemently.

Kriti was brimming with resentment the whole of the next day. Even Nafisa's sensible suggestion that merely meeting someone did not automatically mean marriage made little impression on her. In the evening, a reluctant Kriti, towed by an exhausted Nafisa, arrived at her aunt's residence.

Mrs Mittal, built like a battleship and with a temperament to match, sailed in, clucking disapprovingly at Kriti, 'Really Kriti, such a simple sari, didn't you have anything better to wear? Here, put this necklace on. You are a lucky girl you know. The Guptas are very well connected and Jagannath is a perfect match, so handsome and brilliant. Besides,' she said, as if clinching the issue, 'they are related to my sister-in-law.'

Turning to Nafisa, she cooed, 'Nafisa beti, how pretty you look and what a beautiful ring!'

With an apologetic grin, Nafisa soon left, fending off their appeals to stay for dinner. Silently reiterating that nobody could force her into this marriage, Kriti looked at herself in the mirror. She was not a classic beauty but she was petite and appealing.

A little later, seeing the guests come in, Kriti gasped in disbelief. Following the well-dressed couple in was Jaggu! Her head in a whirl, she went through the introductions. Jaggu, looking surprised and pleased, sat down next to her, and smiled his charming smile. Mrs Mittal, delighted that they knew each other, became even more expansive and gracious.

Kriti didn't know what to make of Jaggu. Surely she hadn't misread him yesterday? As she mouthed polite inanities, anger mounted. How dared he pretend to be what he was not!

An arch comment by his mother on how well they looked together seemed to finally galvanise him. Looking baffled, he haltingly explained that they had met just yesterday.

'There is plenty of time to get to know each other later on. After all, I met your father on our wedding day!' said his mother. Jaggu, puzzled, glanced at his father who gave him a faint, resigned smile.

Looking faint himself, Jaggu turned to Kriti and asked anxiously, 'What's going on?

She enlightened him, saying sardonically, 'We are supposed to get married.'

Under the cover of an animated discussion on family trees by the ladies, Jaggu whispered urgently, 'This is a real mix up! I'm sorry you have had to go through this but you know it's not possible.'

'I thought so! You haven't you told your people anything, have you?' she accused.

'No! I've been meaning to tell, but it's so difficult. I thought this was the usual social do.'

'Thank God! You had me really worried for a while. Let's just buy time till you can clear the air,' she suggested, greatly relieved that now even her indomitable aunt could not bulldoze her into marriage.

She heard the elders discussing auspicious dates. They can't be serious, she thought incredulously, laughter bubbling up. Jaggu, looking as though he had been hit by a freight train, glanced at her in apprehension.

'It is settled then,' said Jaggu's mother happily.

'What? No...I need to discuss some things!' he blurted out.

'We are not that old-fashioned, beta! The two of you must go out together and talk things over.'

'Yes, we will,' said Kriti, taking a hand as Jaggu seemed paralysed. After all, as Nafisa had said, a dinner date did not imply lifelong commitment. She winked at him as she continued, 'We need to know each other better before we can decide.'

'That's right,' Jaggu said, reviving, 'we need time.'

As they were leaving after dinner, Jaggu pressed her hand companionably.

'Thanks for being so understanding. I'll tackle the folks at home and close this chapter. You're a real pal.'

Kriti grinned mischievously. How she would enjoy telling her mother later about the perfect match they had found for her! Perhaps now they would let her be. Some day she knew she would find that elusive Mr Right, till then she was happy with her ever-growing circle of friends. Smiling at the irony of the situation, she turned over and slept peacefully.

Sarita Varma

Women, Journalism and Matrimony

Three years ago I got a phone call from my father about yet another marriage proposal. Nothing unusual about that; I was then a twenty-seven-year-old woman hailing from a south Indian Brahmin family and I was in the 'matrimonial market'. The first and only journalist in my family, I had broken away from the clan of engineers and scientists. My parents arranged a meeting with a boy who was a chartered accountant, working for a big company in Mumbai; he was young and good looking, though he did not wear a smile on his face.

As we sat together to have coffee, the first words that emerged from him were, 'How come you are wearing a salwar kameez?'

'Why do you ask?' I countered, quite put off by his question.

'I was expecting you to be wearing jeans and puffing at a cigarette,' he replied in an instant. I was outraged but managed to keep a cool exterior with some difficulty.

'Look, I have heard this from many people. My friends tell me that all journalists drink, smoke and are ultra modern.'

These were his words, and he seemed to have no remorse for having uttered them.

I hated him that moment. I could forgive a general perception about women journalists but how could any intelligent man jump to conclusions about a person's habits on the basis of their profession? What kind of man was he and how was he passing judgement on me without knowing me? I happened not to be among journalists who went to fashionable cocktail parties, drank or smoked. Did I have to clarify this to some man who came out of nowhere?

That was chapter one of my hunt for a groom. Talk about the woes of being single! I met many such men later who had their own judgements about my profession. They did not make an attempt to know who I was, what I wrote and what my life was about.

Women, journalism and matrimony! I have been trying to connect these three words ever since the topic of marriage was broached with great intent as I crossed the silver jubilee mark in my life. The time was ripe for me. I was on a right platform, rising to the next level of being a successful journalist, penning my thoughts on issues that stirred my soul.

I was proud to have a master's degree in economics from Mumbai University. But the family felt an MA does not fall under the 'professional' category. And a writer, no way! How was writing a profession?

The general opinion was that 'professional' pertained to science graduates. Only lousy, good-for-nothing people choose something as bland as economics. Being a journalist is often a stigma in the matrimonial market. Writing is not considered a profession and journalists are considered too audacious, dynamic, arrogant and stubborn. In short they fall into the category of those certified unfit for matrimony and family life.

I wonder who ever created such perceptions and why? Why is my ambition linked to my personal life? Who categorises professionals and non-professionals? The constant tussle I faced as a journalist in the matrimonial market was something, which haunted me for over five years. I was expected to give up my career. I was told that I should stop writing. I should leave my passions just to have a 'married' tag. Sometimes I wonder why being single isn't considered normal in our society.

Why can't a woman journalist be considered like any other professional? Why this prejudice? Why this judgemental attitude? Real life experiences made me feel that being single and enjoying my own company is far better than just having a married status, but living an unhappy life.

Once my father proudly took out a newspaper and showed it to a prospective groom, 'Look! My daughter has written this.' He did not even listen to my father or even look at the newspaper. Quit writing, he said. I am sorry, I cannot, I answered instantly and the conversation fizzled out in five minutes. These are the men who call themselves educated, work in foreign companies and make big money, but they seem to be wanting in basic intelligence. Often, even today, when it comes to marriage, a woman is expected to make a compromise and give up her career.

A beautiful relationship like marriage requires a lot of openness, communication and acceptance. Only when the other person genuinely wants to know you as you are, accepts you and your passions and respects your profession, can the foundation be created. A couple builds on this foundation, making marriage an enjoyable journey. At the end of the day, it is about an individual you want to live with and the values they possess and bring along which really matters!

I have to say, I feel happy. My single soul is a free spirit, penning thoughts as the mind pleases, travelling to exotic places, meeting new people and still hoping someone sensible exists out there!

Sharada Balasubramaniam

Oh! Are You Still Single?

'For the last time, Mom, I'm not going to the wedding with you!'

'And for the last time, you're coming, and I don't want any arguments!' she stormed. 'Wear the fawn and saffron tussar silk sari and the gold and tulsi beads. Now!'

Jeez! She forgets I'm more than twenty-five years old! I try again. 'But I'm exhausted, Ma. It was a very, very busy day at office. I had two interviews on the other side of Delhi. I'm totally pooped! Please!'

'Oh! You mean your father doesn't work in office?' she asks sarcastically. 'And what about all those other people attending the wedding after work? Are they useless idiots? Are you the only one in the world who works hard?'

I know when I'm defeated, and go to have a bath and deck myself out like a Christmas tree on display. It's no use telling her that when you are under thirty, female and single, it's a trial of nerves mingling with the extended family, especially on wedding-related occasions.

I realise that my attending these functions is as important to her as it is abhorrent to me. This incident took place about fifteen years ago, when a twenty-five-year-old single daughter was a social anathema. So, for Ma, such an occasion is an opportunity to prove to the world that if her daughter is unmarried at twenty-five, it isn't because she is ugly, or jobless or any such thing. Plus, there is also the unexpressed hope that someone in the family might pass on word of my 'eligibility' to an interested party!

And that is precisely why I shy away from all this. Relatives, especially old, female ones, have a tendency to peer at you, and wonder aloud in your presence: 'She's not bad looking … well educated, good family, and has a good job, too. Why isn't she married as yet?'

'Must be involved with someone,' some other gossipmonger would whisper in scandalised tones. And I would be barred by my upbringing from telling them that if I were involved with someone, I'm sure my parents would support me.

Suddenly remembering a cousin in a parallel situation, I ring her up quietly and ask: 'Are you coming to the wedding?'

'As if Mom would let me skip it,' she retorts, 'even though I utterly loathe all this, and I'm dead on my feet!'

'Same here,' I reply gloomily, 'but hey, it won't be so bad if you're there, too. We can always sneak away into a corner.' I hang up, somewhat cheered.

Duly presenting myself to Mom in said sari and jewellery, I'm instructed to 'hold myself up and smile pleasantly, for God's sake!'

Smile pleasantly! I'm not scowling or making faces, or anything, so why am I expected to simper? We reach the venue and are greeted with: 'Oh! Welcome! So glad you could come … and bitiya, too. Are you very tired?'

'No, Aunty,' I lie through gritted teeth. We move away.

'See? I told you to smile, but you have sworn never to listen to your mother.'

'Oh, for heaven's sake, Mom … look! I'm smiling! Okay?'

My eyes search frantically for my fellow sufferer. I finally spot her, trying to become invisible between a pedestal fan and a potted plant. I excuse myself and head for her, followed by Mom's instructions to 'mingle, and not hide myself in a corner.'

My cousin sees me and hails me with relief, and we thankfully slink away into a corner where there are two chairs and no relatives. Bliss!

'Did anyone comment on how tired you are looking?' I ask.

'What do you think? It's their stock-in-trade,' she replies. 'So many people here look more tired than us, but they'll pick on us because they want to imply that as independent career women heading towards spinsterhood, we must be fading blossoms, and that's why we look perpetually tired.'

'Hey, you're exaggerating! It's not as bad as that, it's just the way they are,' I say pacifically.

'Then tell me, why don't they comment on the exhausted looks of our male cousins?' she asks.

'Maybe they do?' I say. She laughs derisively.

And, as if on cue, my grandmother's sister and her daughter pass by: 'Ma, bhabhi's son looks really tired; he must have come straight from office … poor boy! And uncle's grandsons also look exhausted. Well, what can you expect on a weekday? The poor things have come directly from work and haven't had the time to freshen up.'

I give my cousin a meaningful look.

And then, in the next breath, 'Oh, Ma! Just look at Parul and that one there ... totally off-colour! Growing older by the day, and not married yet! Obviously the bloom of youth is on its way out! Poor things!'

'Let them be,' I sigh, holding my cousin back, as she starts to get up from her chair, presumably to tell them off. 'Just let them be.'

'You're right,' she says, calming down. 'Let's go eat. I saw some wonderful kulfi!'

Needless to say, both my cousin and I got married in due course (within a year of this incident, in fact). Today we are settled in our homes and jobs, walking the tightrope between housework and family, and trying to be as happy and contented as possible. But somewhere at the back of my heart and mind lies the memory of those single days, when a good kulfi was all one needed to assuage the irritation of parental pressures. For my mother, who was married at twenty-one, coping with a twenty-five-year-old single daughter was not easy. Now my daughter is ten. I hope I remember those days by the time she is of marriageable age!

Parul Gupta

Dog-Sense

I was twenty-one when my little dachshund Coco came into my life and we became best buddies. She understood my every mood and feeling and saw me through all the emotional ups and downs of my twenties. Coco had a mind of her own and never condescended to learn any tricks or to obey commands. Though she did more or less as she pleased, she was very sensitive to what any of us said to her, and never caused any real trouble. She loved all our friends and relatives and uninhibitedly expressed her joy when they visited us.

When I hit thirty still unattached, my cousin Sheila decided she should do something to push me in the direction of settling down. My parents and brother were not the type to 'arrange' a match for me, so Sheila and her husband Mahesh took the initiative and introduced me to Jayesh, the perfect guy. Not having anything against marriage per se, I went along with their efforts. I wasn't really thinking, just letting things happen, all very cool. Several of my friends had been through similar successful arrangements. Soon it was time for him to meet the parents, and he and his mother came over one day for tea. Sheila and Mahesh came along for moral support.

From the minute he entered our home, Coco began a barking marathon. I had to pick her up and keep her on my lap throughout the visit, and still, every time Jayesh moved or spoke she would start yapping in protest. At first I couldn't understand why she was behaving so crazy, and felt embarrassed. But suddenly I began to realise that I didn't really like Jayesh that much. Though he had all the conventional good qualities, I began noticing little things he was saying and doing that painted a picture of what life with him would be like, and the picture didn't please me. Though I managed to make all the socially correct small talk, and the visit ended cordially on both sides, I was relieved when it was over. After he left my mother's comment was, 'Coco doesn't seem to approve.' I gave Coco a big hug and she licked my face all over. My father shook his head at us, but his smile conveyed his silent agreement.

I told Sheila and Mahesh I didn't want to take things any further. They thought I was being irrational, but I was happy when I heard a few months later that Jayesh was settling down with someone else. It soon became clear to me that it wasn't just Jayesh; I wasn't cut out to have any kind of 'arranged' relationship. It had to be either total and spontaneous love and commitment, or nothing.

My little Coco died prematurely a few months later. Incidentally, I never succeeded in finding the right mate for her, either. Maybe she was too childish and self-willed to have made a good mother. But I'm ever grateful to her for loving me unconditionally and for teaching me never to do anything I don't wholeheartedly believe in.

Anonymous

Single Warriors

My friend Sachin is tall, smart, good-looking, successful, well-mannered and well-travelled. In short he scores high marks as an eligible bachelor and would make great husband material. The girls of marriageable age know this, their mothers know this and his family, too, is quite aware of his positive attributes. There is just one hitch in the situation — Sachin loves being single and has no intention of changing his status. So even as he deftly wards off mummies of betis (daughters) who are more than willing to cook delicious meals for him, and the betis themselves who seem to be treasure troves of talent, be it cooking, singing or housekeeping skills, Sachin is hounded.

'Have you seen how animals pounce on their prey? I feel like some sort of meat, the way the mothers will zero in on me at parties, at the temple or even on the road,' Sachin would groan to us, his buddies. He once had a family turn up with the priest in tow to conduct the marriage at his house. He was seeing the girl for the first time. Her mother had cornered Sachin at a community gathering and instead of brushing her off and hurting her sentiments, Sachin had politely said, 'Sure. Why not? Sounds good.' A week later they had appeared at his doorstep.

After learning his lesson, he is now more blunt and direct. His family has given up on him. 'Oh, when will I get a bahu? I am not growing younger, you know,' is his mother's pet complaint. But Sachin has become indifferent to her 'emotional drama' as he calls it.

He has even been caught off-guard while walking on the road when a mother saw him and crossed over to enquire about his single status. 'Still single, my son? It is because you have been waiting for my Mandeep? See her photo. How pretty she looks,' and out came an album from her huge purse. Mandeep had got a special marriage portfolio shot and Sachin had to restrain himself from laughing at some of the poses and images in the album.

There was one of Mandeep waving at nothing, as if seeing off her husband, one in which she was cooking, with a smile on her face, dressed in a full-sleeved salwar kameez, neatly-pinned dupatta, bangles covering her forearms and a big bindi on her forehead and another in which she sat day dreaming near the window. 'In today's world of multi-tasking, people don't have time to relax. Mandeep seems to be in a fairy-tale land,' said Sachin to us, later on.

When he did bump into Mandeep at a social event, she was dressed in a tight T-shirt with a mini skirt and solitaires. 'Don't ask. My mother made me dress that way and pose for the portfolio. It is silly, I know,' she replied when Sachin asked her what exactly was going on.

The two them are now friends and share each other's

'setting up' anecdotes. They even call themselves 'single warriors' because according to them, 'warding off potential matchmakers, aunties and uncles and their offspring is no less than embarking on a war.'

Xerses Irani

So Not Ready to Mingle!

'Is your friend gay?' I have heard this question so often in these last five years. Ever since my pal Rahul turned single yet again and refused to date.

He is young, intelligent, attractive, caring, fun and rich. The prize catch. Yet this adorable brat has decided to get off the dating game and seems to be much happier that way. What is amusing and exasperating are the reactions of people around him.

Like all of us, Rahul had the regular life, a great family, super job, lots of friends and a girlfriend he planned settling down with. Things didn't work out and he was upset when she left. Friends rallied around and within months he was seeing someone else. This time he was cautious. She seemed just right and the families got involved. Wedding plans were being made. Some strange family issues cropped up. He was ready to overlook them but she didn't think it made sense. They parted ways amicably. She found someone else soon but Rahul was hurting for a long time. After the next heartbreak he decided he was done.

He put all his energies into work and was soon heading the division and travelling across the globe. We were all so happy for him. Once he was back, Rahul was his usual chirpy self. Yet something had changed. He wasn't open to being set up by friends or to meet the girls his mother liked. He just asked everyone to back off.

Work, tennis, family and friends seemed to be his life. Soon his sister got married, his friends started getting married yet no one could get this dude to even think in that direction. He lost his cool with us when we started getting preachy and even got his mom to realise that this topic was not open to discussion.

He is close to forty now and on a roll. Besides the regular stuff, he also has a new sea-facing flat that he's done up brilliantly. He has two dogs he adores. Every weekend he spends time at an orphanage and dotes on the kids there. He does so much for them but never wants to talk about it.

Of course, people talk about him all the time. How come he's still single? Is he gay or involved with a married woman? Does he have some illness that he is hiding? None of that is true and as a very close pal I can vouch for that. He has a full, exciting life. He likes his space and is not willing to give it up...for now. He has his no-strings attached arrangements like most people in Mumbai do.

What is lovely is that he hasn't lost any of his sensitivity and continues to be the one giving us the sanest advice on marriage and relationships. Recently one night, when everyone was high and flying we cornered him. He confessed that he missed having a partner but wasn't paranoid about it. Made us all look around and see how many of us were in relationships that were driven by fear … the fear of being left alone.

It's amazing how Rahul can be so comfortable in his skin and not be afraid of missing the bus. Hope before any trace of bitterness sets in, a great woman can come along. Gosh, did I just sound like a smug married?

Shifa Maitra

Single and Fancy-Free?

In the late 1930s an Indian educated woman was still the exception rather than the rule and strictly confined to the upper classes. She was however, supposed to be humble, as though slightly ashamed of her adventurism and expected to conform to the ways of the modest, meek and obedient model dictated and cherished by patriarchy. And she might just have done all this if it had not been for those two pairs of bright black eyes that followed her wherever she went, the appeal in them growing more urgent by the day. A decision would have to be taken and soon...

But when the young lady in question, Shahana, fair, pretty, a graduate in psychology, daughter of an eminent naturalist, one of four daughters refused to get married, all hell broke loose, literally! The most vociferous was her grandfather, an eminent scholar himself, but a man who had clear-cut ideas about the role to be played by the 'second citizen'! He had, without qualm, told off Shahana's clever mother when she had dared to get a poem published in a widely circulated magazine with 'nationalist' tendencies, and although Shahana's father had tried his best to remonstrate, she had never 'ventured' again. The old man had not noticed the petite four-year-old Shahana, who had been listening and quietly forming her own opinions about the entire episode.

Much of Shahana's early years had been spent in the forests of northern India, as her father was a member of the Indian Forest Service. When schools were closed, he took his family along, placed them in a particular Dak-bungalow assigned to him and travelled all over his beat, mainly on foot, bicycle or elephant back. Very often Shahana and her younger sister accompanied him and roamed free in the villages or lurched along atop Chandmala, the service elephant, to distant locations. What struck her most was the contrast between the servile attitude of the villagers and the proud freedom of the animals. Her Dad had told her that animals operated on instinct and paid scant attention to advice or orders, even of their leaders. They did what the occasion demanded, whereas poor humans were completely shackled by 'dos and don'ts' and seldom had freedom of will. When a male leopard almost killed their Dad for trying to help his three cubs that were motherless, he lauded the animal's courage for taking on a man with a gun! None of this was wasted on Shahana. 'Remain your own master if you want freedom of thought and action.'

But if Shahana's grandfather was worse than dictatorial, his wife was no less. All of five feet tall, she walked two miles to the river Gomti at four every morning for a dip, feet firmly encased in tennis shoes and sari just below her knees, came back, made tea and woke up the household by six! The home was her domain and even her redoubtable husband seldom meddled in domestic matters. She had been married at eight, bitterly regretted her own truncated education, was sorry that her daughter-in-law's talents had not been recognised and determined that her granddaughters should be 'college educated'. She had also compelled her husband to allow her only grandson to cross the 'black waters' to be educated in England. She knew his 'Brahmanical purity' would suffer, but she would she would redeem his soul by feeding him some cowdung on his return! Conservative in most matters, she had the imagination to venture beyond, if she considered the cause worthy.

Which is why Shahana was sure that her grandmother would stand by her if worse came to worst, for just as she could not get 'the eyes' out of her mind, her grandmother was also obsessed by them, but in this one unique case the old lady had no idea how to solve the problem, and badly needed help. Another person Shahana managed to enlist on her team was the Head of the Psychology Department in her college. Single herself and a woman of formidable learning and repute, she would back Shahana to the hilt, if required.

Arranged marriages are an elaborate ritual: the initial step comprises of the exchange of photographs, caste details, family histories and horoscopes, and if these match, then round two begins. The groom's family members inspect the bride to be and if she has their approval then the couple is brought face to face in a room full of people to decide in a matter of minutes whether they will live with each other for the next half a century or more. And this practice continues in full measure even today, in the twenty-first century, seventy years and two World Wars after Shahana made her bid for freedom.

The day dawned bright and clear, and Shahana's mother chose to regard it as a good omen. She had her trepidations about her daughter who had protested vigorously to begin with, but tired of beating her head against an implacable wall of contemptuous silence, had suddenly surrendered and agreed to go through with round two. And now it appeared that the groom would also come without waiting for round three, so sure was his family that they would approve of Shahana. After all, the groom with a Tripos from Cambridge, had insisted on an educated girl for a life partner, and it would be challenging to find someone better than Shahana.

The groom was favourably impressed as soon as he entered the gateway for he was greeted by a jewel of a lawn and masses of roses so reminiscent of England, a country he had fallen in love with and almost decided to adopt. If it had not been for his mother, he would perhaps have never come back to his native land nor agreed to an arranged marriage, but now he felt that perhaps things were not so bad.

And he was not disappointed when he met the family — cultured and educated, they represented the best blend of East and West available in India, and surely their daughter would be even more modern in her approach and attitude?

When she walked into the room with her older sister, pretty as a picture in a pale peach sari that blended with her complexion, long plait draped over one shoulder, face innocent of make-up, he knew that his family had made the right choice. This would be the girl for him, surely?

She walked forward a trifle hesitantly it seemed, perhaps due to shyness? But she walked on, and suddenly collided with a chair, before her sister could stop her. She almost fell, but righting herself, announced with a dazzling smile: 'I am sorry, I wear very high-powered spectacles, but they told me not to wear them today, so I cannot see very well.'

Her sister, consternation writ large on her face, tried to guide her to a chair, but she limped forward determinedly and sat down in front of the would-be, flabbergasted groom and spoke loud and clear: 'I also wear special shoes because my left leg is shorter than my right, but today I am not allowed to wear them so I cannot walk properly. Sorry for the trouble and I do hope you don't mind too much?'

That was the first and last time the family tried to arrange a marriage for Shahana, for they realised she meant business. Also, her professor assured the family that Shahana was psychologically averse to losing her freedom and that tragedy would ensue if she were coerced in any way...

Today, she still lives in her father's house, retired, but Professor Emeritus and as sharp as ever. And those eyes are still trained on her although they have lost their limpidity, are now framed by wrinkles and their appeal has been replaced by pure concern, for her. The two little boys, three and five years old, who had lost their parents and power of speech in an accident and been thrown at the mercy of distant relatives, could communicate with no one but Shahana, and she knew that they would not survive her departure, a conviction shared strongly by her grandmother. Today they take care of her like the mother they have always thought her to be and to their family she is the presiding deity.

Still single but not fancy free!

Nonda Chatterjee

That Someone Special

'Being single isn't bad. What is bad is giving up hope on finding that someone special.'

In our society it is believed that if you are single, you are always ready to mingle. There was a similar perception regarding my brother Avinash, who was just thirty-two and, as my relatives would say, still single. He worked in Mumbai and had come to Kolkata for a short break. Apart from catching up with his old friends, my Mom along with her sister, Bina had set up meetings with prospective brides. My brother was reluctant and didn't approve of the idea of interviewing a girl the Indian way.

Moms are super smart and we always underestimate their determination. One afternoon over lunch, ours suddenly said, 'You know I think we should all go to Prema's wedding.'

'Who is Prema?' Avinash and I asked in chorus. The relationship my mother explained was more difficult than a dynastic family tree. What we could figure out was that Prema was some Arvind Uncle's daughter. But why we had never heard of Arvind Uncle still remained a mystery. Anyway, we both looked at each other and were quite sure that Mom would not take no for an answer, so we agreed to come along.

All three of us left for the wedding. Mom decked up as if it were my brother's wedding.

'Mom, it's not my wedding,' Avinash said before sitting in the car.

'You never know,' she said, with a big smile.

We arrived at the venue and soon Mom was surrounded by aunts and uncles. Suddenly from amidst the crowd Bina emerged and told my brother, 'You won't believe but the girl whom we had wanted you to meet is right here!'

My brother looked at Mom who stood behind her sister. She gave her typical 'I never knew' look, but it was evident it had all been planned in advance.

'But Mom, I don't want anybody to find a match for me and besides, I am not agreeable to getting married now,' Avinash said.

'Why not?' asked Bina. 'We all got married the same way — your mother, your sister (she meant me), so why not you?'

'Because I am already married,' said my brother, loudly.

I stared at my brother, who winked at me with a wicked smile on his face.

My mother nearly collapsed on her sister. 'See Bina, I told you something was wrong with him, otherwise why would anyone reject such a wonderful girl.' She started sobbing even as her sister tried to comfort her.

'I think we should leave now,' Mom said, wiping her tears. She was quiet all the way home. My brother switched on a heavy Indian song of the sixties, which only increased the tension.

When we reached home the first words we heard from Mom were, 'What's her name?'

'Whose?' my brother asked flinging off his blazer.

'The girl whom you married,' said Mom, starting to sob again.

'Oh, that! I'm still single, I said I was married just to get out of the situation you had put me into,' said my brother smiling.

I thought this would appease Mom; instead, it made her see red.

'You ruined my name in front of everybody,' she said as she picked up the phone and dialled Bina's number to give her the news before it was passed on to the entire family.

'Mom, if I am single, that doesn't mean I am ready for marriage. Please don't go around matchmaking. I want to marry someone special but only after knowing her well,' said Avinash, sitting next to Mom.

It's been a year now and Avinash still enjoys his single status, while my mother continues to hope that he finds his someone special soon.

Abhilasha Agarwal

6
STARTING AFRESH

Every new beginning comes from some other beginning's end.

–Seneca

The Single Marathon Runner

It's been eleven years since my divorce and I can't think of a single incident or event that affected me or changed me as deeply. No, it wasn't an ugly divorce! In fact, it was very cordial and amicable with both of us holding each other's hands. But yet it hurt so badly! It felt as if someone had pulled my heart out of my body or a lifelong drug addict had suddenly been turned in to rehab and gone cold turkey!

For the longest time I couldn't understand why. After all, we had been married for only seven months and had known each other for four months prior to that. Yes, it was an extremely intense relationship. Still, I decided to examine my pain. What was it about the relationship or about me that made me feel so much pain? I definitely did not want to go through that kind of pain ever again.

After some deliberation I figured, it hurt so much because I had always depended on someone else to 'complete me' and hence the pain when that person was gone.

Ever since I could remember I was either in a relationship or recovering from one. Yes, being in love made me feel 'complete'. But, was I so weak that my whole world would crumble just because a relationship didn't work? Couldn't I feel happy and fulfilled just being on my own?

What followed this introspection were long periods of forced isolation. I limited my interaction with people, including friends and family. I really wanted to experience what it meant to be alone and to feel complete by myself. I was never going to give the key to my happiness to someone else. I wanted to be invincible, master of my own destiny, with the key to my happiness firmly in my own hands.

I started by practicing silence for short periods of time. It was extremely difficult and painful in the beginning. I was living alone and dealing with a broken marriage and there was this constant need to reach out, to hear someone say, 'it is okay,' or 'don't worry, everything will work out,' or 'you are not alone,' just anything that could take me away from this pain. But I remained firm in my resolve. As time passed and with help from my friends and some counselling, I finally learnt to be on my own. Neither people nor circumstances affected me to the extent they used to, and if they did, I made sure to further strengthen my resolve to be self-sufficient or 'complete' as I defined it. This meant practicing silence even more strictly and for longer periods of time, watching all my urges and fears float in and out of my mind without acting upon them. Soon, I could be silent for days without missing anybody. I had succeeded! Or so I thought.

I became Mr Cool; nothing rattled or excited me. I could remain calm and unperturbed, regardless of the situation. Around this time I also started to shy away from people. I justified my unsociable behaviour by telling others and myself

'Hey, I'm an introvert and am perfectly okay being by myself, so why go out? Besides, I can't relate to most people, anyway.'

As time passed, my friends accepted me for what I was, or had become — a homebody, who was happy sitting at home, staring at the sea, reading some book on spirituality or philosophy. I was happy, or rather, peaceful.

Once, I was trying to figure out the meaning of happiness and came to the conclusion that it meant an absence of conflict between the mind, body and soul. But that also seemed to define the word 'peace'. So did that mean peace and happiness were one and the same? I left it at that; whatever I was, I was okay!

But actually, I was far from okay and nowhere close to being happy. Yes, I was peaceful because I had blocked out everything that could cause me any pain, detached myself from close relationships, even from the outcome of my work. In some ways, this detachment made me feel good about myself.

After all, I still had friends and my passion for work. I could have certainly done much better, but I wanted to be 'true' to myself. 'That's how God made me, and who am I to question God's ways,' I reasoned. God became and still is an integral part of my life. I was God's humble servant and tried to live with strength and dignity. It felt good and right! Even my friends secretly envied my convictions and my determination to adhere to those convictions, regardless of the outcome. I was strong, following the way of the Lord, so I thought once again.

In fact, I was weak and timid and far from happy. I had created these huge walls around myself and declared myself the king of the castle. I even justified my actions by giving it a larger, more profound meaning. Yes, like millions I abused spirituality. I used it as a refuge against pain. Instead of fighting my fears and daring to get hurt again, I convinced myself, and maybe some other people, too, how beautiful and pure it was inside this 'castle'. Secretly, I peeped through the windows and envied people playing the game of life. Not having enough courage or strength to break down the walls, I secretly prayed for deliverance.

Eventually, deliverance did come, after a lot of writing, reading and introspection. I finally found the meaning of happiness, and it is not absence of conflict or pain, but having the courage to get hurt once again, to be part of someone's life or something and letting that person or thing be a part of you. Happiness is not detachment, but having the strength to deal with the problems and pain that attachment brings. Where we are, is the present; it is heaven and hell, as we know it.

Those who have been fortunate enough not to face great difficulties or have been blessed with the abilities to deal with them, play the glorious game of life. The rest of us sit on the sidelines, watching and looking for a deeper meaning to this game. Or dismiss it as pointless because no one wins, no one loses and it comes to an end anyway.

As for me, I'm all geared up again — I've worn my sports shoes and am ready to run this race called life all over again.

Samir Soni
(As told to Roma Kapadia)

Suddenly Single

Like many women who have been married for several years, I occasionally indulge in a fantasy, wondering what my life would have been like if I was single instead of being married? I must confess that several times I had thought that life would have been more fun for a mature single woman.

Ah, I would think, if I were not married, I would not be bogged down by the humdrum of domesticity. Where was the romance in picking up soiled clothes, texting reminders for groceries? I would have been out flirting with intelligent, successful, handsome men who would woo me with charming solicitude. I would have had my pick of hot hunks. Dearly as I loved my husband, at times I envied the carefree existence of my single friends.

Reality hit hard and heavy when several months after my husband passed away suddenly from a heart attack, I summoned up the strength to sortie out into society. The last thing on my mind was interest in men and I was startled that I did get quite a bit of attention. All of it from a few much-married men: old acquaintances who were quite eager to invite me to drinks, dinner, and to cosy vacations.

Though I longed to splash my drink on their faces or knee them in the groin, my years of observing society cautioned me that if I were to object publicly, it would boomerang on me: a) the wives would firmly support their dear husbands, refusing to admit their errant ways; b) the men would make up false stories about my wickedness. Either way, my reputation would be shot. I would lose the friendship of a few good women and end up being a social recluse. I chose to engage in diplomacy not confrontation. I learnt to extricate myself skilfully from such offers.

As I brooded on my less-than-enjoyable state, I found that I seemed to have become a chick magnet. I am not homophobic but I am simply not geared for a same-sex relationship. Repeated 'passes' had me questioning my close friends if I was unknowingly giving off some gay vibes. Then came the delicate task of saying no without upsetting genuinely nice women whose friendship I treasured but whom I could not see as lovers.

In between all this, when I had given up the slightest hope of ever meeting someone with whom I could have an uncomplicated normal relationship, I met a presentable, single man. Our meeting was sheer coincidence, we seemed to have a few things in common and both of us found it pleasant to spend time together.

It was too good to last, though. The very first proper meeting or 'date' had set the tone. All he had done was talk about his ex-wife. Constantly, incessantly and ceaselessly. I tried to talk sense into him, tried to make him realise his divorce was final and that he ought to look at the future. I must have done my job of pepping up his bruised ego only too well, as he announced that he wanted to get married. He would start meeting many different women, he said, as the more women he dated the easier it would be to meet the woman of his dreams. His decision upset me. While I didn't want to marry him in the least, I didn't like being treated like a convenient stopgap. Obviously then, it was time to stop meeting him. Getting him out of my head though, was easier said than done.

It seemed to me that a few weeks were far too short a time for me to become so used to his presence. It took a little introspection to figure out why I had become dependent on a relationship that devalued me. When I met him, for the first time in many months, I had a companion to hang out with — to see movies, go on random drives, chat idly. I was beginning to feel happy about not waiting like a charity case for an afterthought of a phone call from family or friends who would call to include me in their plans. In my loneliness, I had grasped at this man's presence, without examining if we were compatible at all.

Once I figured it out, the solution has been simple. Having accepted that one person can clearly never fill the gap in my life, I now nurture an active social life with a network of friends. Instead of clinging to one person or one group, I have a particular set of friends with whom I watch plays, one set with whom I watch movies, another set with whom I check out new restaurants and so on. Besides, I have my sweet son, my caring Dad and my sisters and their families to celebrate special days.

I have joined hobby classes, I meet new people and I use social networking sites to stay connected with friends and family across the world. I have been fortunate enough to find true friends among old acquaintances and new ones whose unselfish words of encouragement keep me going. I would never have the support of these lovely people if I had closed my heart to the world.

Being suddenly single in my forties has forced me to rediscover my true self. To look within and find the girl who viewed the world as an exciting discovery. I have learnt to take myself, and life, less seriously. I still suffer acute pangs of guilt during which I castigate myself for wanting to enjoy myself when Allen's life was cut so cruelly short. But it's slowly easing as I make a conscious effort to celebrate the good times we had shared, to accept that I have to put myself first again.

As for romance, que sera sera, I had one good innings and if a repeat never happens, I have learnt also not to be greedy. And if I were to be fortunate enough to find love again, I hope I will be able to welcome it with gratitude and cherish each moment.

Sandhya Mendonca

Towards the Sky

In the aftermath of my divorce, I have been inspired to live life on my own terms. Through my work and travel, I have met people who are not afraid to live in strikingly unconventional ways. By doing so, they forge enriching, fulfilling lives. Such people expand my horizons and give me the confidence to shape my reality.

For instance, this morning, I visited the Blanco Estate. Brightly coloured birds wander through Blanco's charmed garden. Deep fuchsias and flaming oranges stand out against the verdant green palm and terraced paddy fields that frame the estate. Antonio Blanco lived his life passionately, revelling in the beauty and sensuality that surrounded him. Originally from Spain, he came to Bali in the 1950s and set up his studio in Ubud. Like the playful, sensual figures in his paintings that extend boldly beyond each whimsical frame, Blanco refused to be constrained by the social mores of his time. Instead, he created a magical world of his own and brought his fantasies to life.

Hours after leaving Blanco's world, I am still enchanted, drawn to his spirit. His paintings, on display in the Blanco

Renaissance Museum, are set against a backdrop of jewel-coloured walls, gilded flower trellising, soaring Corinthian pillars, red and gold Balinese woodcarving, and deep green marble floors. His last architectural project, Blanco's monumental museum overwhelms the senses with a thrilling fusion of Eastern and Western aesthetic sensibilities.

Blanco died ten years ago, shortly after his museum was finished. Around the time of his death, my twenty-three-year-old marriage came to a crashing end. After a harrowing year trying to understand why my husband wanted to end our marriage, I found an email from my husband's lover. His betrayal, his deception, made it possible for me to leave decisively. I knew he was no longer worthy of my love, trust and respect. Like an amputation, which causes searing then numbing pain, I ruthlessly severed myself from the world we had built together.

Although on a very different plane from Blanco, I too have created a sensually rich and intellectually vibrant world. I express myself ... my warmth, creativity and passion for life through my intimate relationships, my love for art, my abiding delight in reading and writing and my commitment to feminist struggles for rights, dignity and justice.

I do not take my present life for granted. I recognise that my freedom has been hard won by generations of women's rights advocates. Despite our commitment to women's empowerment, many women still do not have the economic means or the social freedom to assert control over their lives. Whereas Blanco was a remarkable man by any standards, he enjoyed many privileges due to his status as a European man who chose to live in the East. On arriving in

Bali, the reigning king gifted him land to pursue his artistic endeavours. Blanco fell in love with a Balinese woman and had the freedom to marry her. He had the resources and the social approval to build a rich cultural and emotional life for himself and his family.

I, too, have moved East, recreating my world and myself. After living for thirty years in the United States, I have returned to Kolkata to be closer to dear friends, live in the apartment where I grew up, and enjoy the artistic and intellectual vibrancy of the city. I open my home to my friends from many walks of life. They visit and fill my home with diverse rhythms. While my home is modest, like Blanco's Estate it houses my dreams. My home reflects my sensibilities and speaks of the places I visit, the lessons I learn, and the people I love and admire.

I spend moments in wonderment, recalling the days when I had fled my married home in anguish, leaving my whole world behind me. Who knew that my deepest trauma would rekindle my spirit? Rebuilding my life, I have taken risks, worked harder, travelled farther, loved more passionately and found my inner core. I spend my time with my two daughters and my many women friends. They have been with me for the good times and through the very hard moments on my life's journey.

In my bright, open apartment, the art I have collected from many parts of the world converges. Striking self-portraits by Frida Kahlo sit beside Buddha deep in meditation. Masked spirits from West Africa commune silently with painted tribal figures of India. These pieces expand and enliven my spirit. In the home I have created, I dance with abandon to Bob Marley and quietly savour the sculptures that project special moments in my life on my mind screen. Perched on my high mahogany bed, I look out over the mango tree in front of my window and upwards towards the sky.

Jael Silliman

Bless this Mess!

She stretched out her arms, yawned as she sat up in bed and forced herself awake. It was another day, another week. She started to make mental notes about the immediate tasks at hand: prepare breakfast, pack his lunch box and get ready to go to work. A routine she now seemed to mechanically follow with every sunrise.

As she dragged herself out of bed, she heard the shower running in the bathroom. 'He is getting ready early to go to the office,' she thought to herself. He was the CEO of a software company based in Hyderabad, which he had started after returning from the USA with a Masters degree in Computer Science tucked in his pocket. His proud and affluent father, who lived in Delhi, had very lovingly financed the set-up three years before they were married and could not but be happy with the rising profit of the company.

Today was their fifth wedding anniversary and by now she had trained her heart and mind not to expect any affection or acknowledgement of any special days in their lives. As she stood brushing her teeth in front of the mirror in the guest bathroom, she recollected how a common family friend had arranged this alliance, the happy days of the first year of their marriage and how slowly but steadily those happy times had now diminished to … zilch! Sharing physical space also seemed like a drag, the way mental and emotional space did.

On this blue Monday morning, her well-lit kitchen with bright tiles and white cabinets seemed welcoming, also because of how hard she worked every evening to keep it spotlessly clean. She put the kettle on the boil and kept the bread ready to toast as soon as she heard the shower stop. Racking her brains about what to make for lunch, she mechanically reached for the flour and started to knead some dough. After chopping okra, she squeezed some fresh orange juice. The shower stopped running and she immediately switched on the toaster. He had never taken kindly to cold food. Even his lunch was packed in thermos boxes and later, heated and served by the office boy. What luxury!

She started to roll out rotis and made three by which time he had sauntered into the kitchen and sat at the breakfast table with a crisp 'Good morning'. He ate his buttered toast and sipped orange juice while reading the newspaper, which she placed on the table every morning. She packed his lunch and saw him off without a hug, without even a word. It had been this way for a few months now.

She jumped into the shower and quickly got dressed as she hated being late for work. She worked as a journalist in a local newspaper and did the weekly column on Page 3. This job was her gateway to sanity. She grabbed a quick bite on her way out and remembered to pack some lunch, though her appointments rarely allowed her to eat peacefully. Her aim was to get done with work on time and get home before he did, to fulfil the conditions he had laid before she took up this job. To him, her job was only a means of keeping her busy; he had never thought much of it.

She got home after a day's hard work only to continue doing some more. It was time to spruce up the house — a lovely three-bedroom house, designed by a well-known local architect, with a spacious, landscaped backyard, which helped alleviate the tension. She put away the laundry and cooked dinner. Impatience had become his forte; he would lose his temper if dinner were not served the minute he walked in through the door.

Looking at the clock, she realised she still had time to soothe her tense muscles with a refreshing cup of tea, which she took out into the garden. Walking barefoot on the grass and sipping her tea, she started to mull over the turn her life had taken. Invariably, tears rolled down her cheeks as she questioned her presence in this house and in his life. It may as well have been a maid in her place and one would not be able to tell the difference. It broke her heart.

After the first months of romance, fun and frolic, which followed their wedding, things had changed steadily. He had become increasingly irritable and intolerant. Nothing could be out of place. He had started to compare her with other women they knew, women who apparently had succeeded in balancing their careers with their responsibilities at home. Of course, it was not his fault that medically he could not father a child! This was something they had discovered two years into their marriage when they decided to start a family. It was a turning point but committed as she was, her sensitive, emotional and loving self drove her to pamper and cajole him, lest he felt deficient in any way.

But at the end of five years, she realised they had drifted apart and were living like parallel walls in the same house. He had stopped taking her to social events with him in the last couple of months and preferred to go alone. He would come home in the evenings and quietly retire to his study after dinner or would scream his head off for apparently no significant reason ... maybe something was not exactly to his liking or she had forgotten to run an errand he had asked her to. She felt like a punching bag and doormat, rolled into one. She felt she was being destroyed by all that verbal and mental abuse.

'Aastha! Aastha! Wake up! What's wrong? You are crying in your sleep!' She finally opened her eyes and saw me hovering over her. She had been my best friend for the last fifteen years and we shared a lot. It had hurt me to see her suffering in the last couple of years and I had been deeply concerned. Aastha realised she had been dreaming all along. But every scene was still vivid in her memory as she narrated every detail of the hard times she had faced. But now her mind was uncluttered and her thoughts were crystal clear. She felt she could finally see the horizon. She had moved in with me yesterday, exactly a week after her divorce and the room was still messy with only half the unpacking done. She got up from the bed, her eyes swiftly taking in the scene and came across to hug me tightly, saying, 'Bless this mess!'

Amisha Shah

A New Sunrise

Just as every little girl cultivates her secret world in which she weaves a million dreams about growing up to be beautiful, happily married, I nurtured mine, too. I was a weaver of dreams.

Years ago, when I would see my older friends and cousins get married, I would start to envision the exciting married life I would live some day. Having experienced my share of relationships and break-ups, I set out to create a new life at twenty-five. This meant forgetting the hurts of the past and starting out afresh with the intent of marriage, a union that would last a lifetime. I was not the kind who could ever easily accept the idea of an arranged marriage, not because it was a conventional Indian rule that needed to be changed by the young but because I was awfully sceptical about arranged marriages culminating in the permanent and happy co-existence of two people. Nonetheless, I bought into the idea and finally met someone I thought was my Mr Right, just as he reckoned I was his soul mate.

We fostered a great relationship within a span of six months from a distance of thousands of miles and eventually tied the knot. I uprooted from India and flew to his home country — the United States. We both promised each other eternal happiness and lasting companionship. I was weaving more dreams and higher hopes and with every step of our togetherness, I was happy, truly happy.

But a year and a half into what I thought was a happy alliance I had to struggle with the challenges that life unexpectedly threw at me. What ensued was a painful and distressing parting. We separated and eventually divorced.

I was 'single' again. I moved back to my home in India carrying my wounds and leaving behind a successful career, unfulfilled dreams and unmet aspirations. I felt my life was falling apart. As if this were not enough, the anticipation of what I'd face from traditional Indian society was already taking a toll on me. I was right! The dream weaver had to become a warrior.

There were even more challenges related to the present and the future that pushed me further into an abyss. Every morning I'd wake up tearful, and in addition I'd have to discreetly handle questions from people around. It was as though society were destroying my very identity. I wanted to survive and kept battling, though I was rapidly sinking.

Some of us think that the society has changed. It has! But the change is limited to a superficial acceptance of a divorced woman. In truth, she is rejected when it comes to making her a part of one's space. In traditional India, divorced women were rejected outright and their options were fearfully limited. Today, they are accepted in society but with some suspicion and contempt. Prejudice is still prevalent! I was fortunate because my parents shielded me while trying their best to keep me happy.

However, I am pleased to say I rose above my despair to try to live one more time and I made a beautiful success of it!

I pledged to never give up but face all challenges with courage and determination and to create a better life for my family and myself. I told myself day in and day out that tomorrow would be a new day and a new sunrise. I turned inward, engaged in meditation, did a great deal of soul searching and had conversations with God. This gave me far more realistic reasons to move on. I held the pursuit of my career in the highest esteem. Also, I started to understand that the respect we expect and receive from the world is proportionate to the respect we give ourselves.

The first step towards rising above my situation was to regain my lost identity. It was critical for me to accept myself as much a woman as I was since the day I was born. One fortunate afternoon I promised myself it was the last time I would cry over the debris of my past life. Moving ahead relentlessly in search of a job that would justify my MBA and career quest, I secured a position that changed my life, for good.

I'd work all day but my sleep was restive, with disturbing dreams. I longed for a peaceful sleep and that called for forgiving my ex-husband. I began practicing Buddhism and learnt about the law of karma and forgiveness. That's when, along with the continued support of my parents, fellow members and Mother Sai, I started to get my strength back. I was determined never to look back.

The second step was to overcome my depression completely and accept the emotional support extended by my parents and friends. This not only healed me but healed them, too. My bitter divorce had caused collective emotional damage. We all needed each other and we needed collective healing. I spent more time with my family and we shared and cared much more than we had earlier.

The third and most significant step was to regain hope. It only takes a ray of light to break through the darkness. I immersed myself in work and held on to my family's love more firmly than ever. I received successive promotions at work, found deep appreciation, great co-workers, and good friends who continued to bolster my hope and confidence. People began to look upon me as a strong, tough, happy and independent woman, as I was indeed becoming, a woman who turned her life from gloom to glory. I reached out to women who were abused in marriage, separated, divorced, widowed or lost in life and turned into a source of strength for them.

But I did not stop at that. It is women like us who need to bring about a change in our society's perception of broken marriages. Society must be made to see that broken marriages are often the result of difficult choices that people make or are forced to make. Rather than indulging in self-pity, I plunged into self-development. I was able to see I had the freedom to move towards a better future. All it took for me was that one potent realisation that we get only one life and there shall always be a new sunrise.

Vishakha Rana

Rainbow in Your Heart

'You are so beautiful ... your eyes are deeper than the ocean ... your smile dazzles me and lights up my life....' The voices played over and over in her head as Ayesha sat on the swing in the garden of her parents' lavish bungalow in suburban Delhi. The garden with its terraced landscape was complete with a Jacuzzi and gazebo. But the corner at the far end of the garden was Ayesha's favourite spot. This was where the large swing hung from carved wooden posts, in the shade of mango trees. The peace and quiet of this space was disturbed now and then by a squirrel or birds flying by. The swing creaked just a little as Ayesha lay down, just as she had done every afternoon for the last few months.

She stared into the blue sky while her mind travelled back in time to those exciting years in art school. Though it now seemed to belong to a previous lifetime, it was only eight years ago that she had graduated in Fine Arts from a reputed institute in the city. She had been one of the most talented and attractive girls in the college during her three-year course in painting and sculpture. She had been sought after by a lot of boys, some of whom had even proposed marriage!

But Ayesha always knew that her parents would only settle for an arranged marriage to a boy of their choice. So she consciously kept her admirers at bay. Within the first year and a half after graduation, she had a couple of highly successful painting and sculpture exhibitions in reputed galleries in the city, Then her parents decided it was time for her to get married. So the search began for a suitable groom. She was introduced to a few apparently eligible bachelors but none interested her; she couldn't see herself spending her entire life with any of them. But she was much sought after; her tall slender frame, fair skin, wavy brown tresses and million-watt smile left many weak at the knees.

A flock of sparrows flew by her as she recollected the day Rahul had walked in with his parents. Rahul was an MBA from IIM Ahemdabad but had moved back to Delhi to live with his parents. He had recently got a job in a multinational firm. He was tall, well-built and had a commanding and alluring personality that Ayesha found very attractive. She felt herself drawn to him in a manner that she had not experienced before. The positive vibes the two shared when they met the first time seemed to have unknowingly sealed their fate! The same evening, Rahul had asked her out for a cup of coffee and she had accepted, much to the delight of her parents.

Ayesha was thrilled at the comfort level that she and Rahul seemed to share as they chatted over coffee. Rahul didn't hide his interest in getting married to her; she came across as such an attractive, confident and practical person. Three months later, they were married and they moved into an apartment close to Rahul's workplace.

As Ayesha sat up, placed her feet on the manicured lawn and pushed the swing back and forth, her heart fluttered at the thought of the first few months of their marriage — all those little love notes they wrote each other, the flowers he brought her, the gifts he showered her with, the romantic trips and much more. After the first year, Ayesha felt the urge to go out and get a job and put her creative skills to use. But to her surprise and dismay, Rahul was not happy about her decision to take up a job. He wanted them to have a child, while she wanted to wait another year before taking the big step. They argued for a few weeks and eventually Ayesha yielded and was pregnant by the end of their second year of marriage.

Unfortunately, as fate would have it, Ayesha had a miscarriage and they lost the baby. They were both devastated. The families did their best to lend the couple as much moral and emotional support as they could. But it was evident that Ayesha was miserable and was slowly slipping into depression. She barely ate, didn't say much and the smile had vanished from her face. Both sets of parents coaxed Rahul to set aside his own sorrow and take care of Ayesha, as she needed him more now than ever before. 'You both are still young and healthy and can have a child in the future; but now is the time to help Ayesha through this difficult period,' advised his mother. So did her parents.

But something had snapped. Rahul and Ayesha seemed to have grown apart. Any amount of visits to the psychiatrist, counselling sessions and medication did not seem to help. A deathly silence now pervaded their marriage. Life had come to a standstill for Ayesha; she stopped taking an interest in herself and let herself slip away. She started to gain a lot of weight. Rahul had gradually refrained from any display of affection, which hurt Ayesha even more, and eventually she got trapped in her own web of misery.

Days would pass by and not a word would be exchanged between the two. Rumours of an affair between Rahul and a colleague didn't help matters. By now, Ayesha had eaten her way into depression and was twice her original size. She blamed Rahul and his disinterest in her for her current state. After heated exchanges between the two families, divorce seemed like the only solution to protect Ayesha from being completely destroyed. That was a year ago, since when Ayesha's parents and friends had been lovingly and patiently nursing her back to health.

Here she was, on her favourite swing, breathing in the fresh afternoon air and noticing for the first time in weeks how beautiful the garden was this time of the year. And she smiled, finally!

Tomorrow was going to be her first day as professor in the art college and she was very excited! She got up from the swing with a spring in her step, feeling light at heart. She had regained an interest in herself after shedding a few kilos, which gave her back most of her lost confidence.

As she walked across the lawn towards the house, Ayesha felt that the colours had finally filled the rainbow in her heart. Never ever was she going to give up on herself or on life for anyone!

Amisha Shah

Fruit Plate

Grandpa had died three days ago. I knew it for certain because I was holding him in my hands — ash and bone fragments in an earthen pot, with a municipality label that said 'SY Raman, deceased 28 February 2009.' I was in a car with Dad, my aunt and Grandma, speeding towards Nasik, where the ashes would be cast into the waters of the Godavari.

Grandma had kept a stoic silence these three days. Grandpa had died while taking his afternoon nap. He was ninety-three. When I rushed home from office, he was there on the floor, legs tied together, nose plugged with cotton wool. The whole family had gathered — aunts, uncles, cousins and grandchildren, four whole generations. Some people were sobbing, but Grandma was sitting quietly by Dad. She said nothing that day, except remarking to my father that she felt betrayed. She seemed miffed that Grandpa had departed before her, though he'd promised her he wouldn't leave her alone. But she seemed to have accepted it, even expected it. When a man reached ninety-three, the only thing you expect him to do is die.

We cremated him in the night and the next day was spent in all manner of rituals for his departed soul. Grandma just sat by, saying nothing. I thought it was a bit strange. I thought she'd break down any minute and start sobbing, but she never did. In the afternoon we collected the ashes and made plans to go to Nasik for the last rites.

On 2 March, we set out before dawn. We hoped to reach Nasik and get on with the ceremony before the auspicious hour passed. We were quite far out of Mumbai city, the sun was high in the sky, and we were all hungry. We came across a dhaba and our hunger pangs intensified. There was no need to ask anyone, all of us knew instinctively that we had to stop.

We trooped into the dhaba and began looking into the menu for options. Idli, dosa, poha, shira, puri-bhaji.... Then Grandma indicated she wanted something. For a moment we carried on as if nothing happened. Then we all froze.

Grandma wanted to order something.

Grandma, the orthodox matriarch of the family. Who had never, ever eaten anything not home-cooked, not even a glass of bottled water. Whose observance of every ancient custom would often irk us. Who was an awkward presence when we went to a restaurant and we had to let her tag along because she could not be left alone at home. The same Grandma wanted to order something.

It wasn't as if we hadn't brought anything for her to eat. But she didn't want any of that. The rest of us were ordering stuff, and she wanted to order something, too. It was a novel experience for all of us. We squirmed. We felt awkward. We were uncomfortable. But she had a look of eagerness in her face.

So my aunt went over the menu with her since it was in English, and Grandma could not read. No idli-dosa, no puri-bhaji. Nothing fried, roasted, boiled or cooked in any other way. She wasn't ready yet for stuff cooked by folk she'd never seen. Then she noticed a counter where a man with gloved hands was cutting fruit.

She asked for a fruit plate.

Our orders came, we set about eating with our fingers or cutlery, as we saw fit. There she was with all of us, eating her fruit pieces with the tiny plastic disposable fork. The fruit seemed fresh, and all the ones she approved of — banana, papaya, apple, grapes and watermelon. When she finished it, I thought I saw a tiny flicker of a smile on her face. It barely lasted, but I'm sure it did. It was gone before I could tell Dad.

I spent the rest of the journey to Nasik speculating what had made her break her orthodoxy? That too after all these years? She had been the more rigid of the two; I knew Grandpa was a habitual offender, happily visiting Udupi restaurants and ordering masala dosas when Grandma wasn't with him. And what did that smile signify?

Perhaps it was her way to enjoy, how so ever briefly, her newfound freedom. There was no domineering husband to be waited on hand and foot, anymore. She didn't have to bother about the orthodox customs that demanded sacrifices of her to ensure a long life for her husband. She had followed them, without once erring, from the age of thirteen when she had entered our house as a child bride.

Now it was time to do her own thing. She didn't have to live out the daily pretences expected of a family matriarch; her eldest daughter-in-law could now act out that drama. The orthodox slavery was behind her. Perhaps the fruit plate was a way of beginning to live her life.

No one asks her out to restaurants now. They take her to temples, ashrams and holy rivers. Nor has she ever asked to be taken to a restaurant. But I'm sure she would relish the chance of a fruit plate again.

Raamesh Gowri Raghavan

Life is Beautiful

Two years had passed since Susan and Hari decided to part ways. Looking back, she found that the enormity of the situation had taken time to sink in — twenty-one days, to be precise. In a way she felt relieved. This meant an end to the fights, which had assumed a routine nature for the past four years. The day would always start off with a sulk or a frown, a residue from the previous evening and would simmer through clipped conversations into a boiling rage. It is not as if they hated each other but the magic of marriage had lost its charm somewhere and it was irretrievable.

When they first got to know each other, seven years back, life seemed like a pretty picture. Susan had resigned from her monotonous teaching job in a college in Kerala and come to Bangalore to do something 'exciting'. At twenty-four, teaching was not something that she dreamt of pursuing. The job was safe and right for a 'good Catholic girl,' is what her family kept reassuring her. She was not convinced and wanted to come out of the protective environment lovingly built around her. Bangalore had always been a dream city and writing was her dream career. She always associated the two for a reason that was unknown to her. Passionate about the language and perceptive about her environment and circumstances, she felt that she could tell the world a lot that it was missing. Once she was in her dream city, the link to writing was to follow.

Contrary to what she expected, her first exposure to a big city did not petrify her. She felt at home, despite the initial struggle. She lived with a bunch of twelve girls in a room that was half the size of her bathroom at home. All she ate was sambaar and rice but that did not worry her strictly non-vegetarian palate. After weeks of knocking at doors of advertising agencies for a copy-writing job ('It is the perfect launch pad for an aspiring writer,' she was told) she finally found her mark in one of the not-so-renowned agencies, but that was a good start. After long days at work, she would hang around the most frequented coffee shops in the garden city. There she would sit alone with a mug of latte, watching people, observing the interesting ones closely and making mental notes.

It was during one such evening that she saw Hari. He was sitting with a bunch of friends, smiling a half-dazed smile that told her he was somewhere far away. A couple of evenings of telescopic observations later, Susan found Hari at her table. What made him join her at her table that evening still remains a mystery, but he was there and after that, life changed.

Hari was heading the interactive division of an IT firm in Bangalore when Susan first met him. Though tagged a 'Mallu' as Malayalees are generally referred to by others, he preferred to call himself a 'global citizen'. There was plenty to talk about and Susan was all ears. There was something very clean and warm about her and that appealed to him. For Susan he opened the doors to a brand new world. Their camaraderie blossomed. There was much that they liked in each other and after six months of courtship, they got married.

Laughter kept them going, but with passing of years it found itself a very small corner. Once they got married, Hari got caught in his struggle to create a plush lifestyle for his family. He stopped talking about his dreams. The only thing that mattered to him was money. An adorable daughter happened along the way, but busy in his pursuit, Hari missed out on the precious moments, which marked her growth. Susan took up the roles of both parents and that left her edgy and unapproachable at the end of the day. She gave up her passion for writing and focused on being the perfect homemaker.

It was difficult for both Hari and Susan to let go of their cherished dreams. Gone was the laughter; in came arguments and harsh words. They decided to call it quits when the little one began to get affected.

To move on after a separation requires immense effort and a strong and focused mind to begin with. There were moments when Susan thought she could go no further. In a society where single mothers are still looked upon with mixed feelings, she felt alone and helpless. But her little one pushed her along; slowly and steadily with her tiny little hands. Soon Susan found her feet again and from thereon, they walked together. A couple of months after the separation, Susan was going out to parties and to meet friends with little Eva in tow. People found them a happy pair, with no traces of an upheaval upon them. Eva had a lot of friends and was much sought after by all of them. Susan began to realise that life was about to begin for her too, a second time over. She locked up all the skeletons in her closet and set out to make her life interesting. Today, two years and four months later, Susan is getting her first stories published. Her little one, a chirpy seven-year-old, with a wisdom that is beyond her years, enjoys the best of both her parents.

Asha Francis

Gini

She was sixteen when she was swept off her feet and married a man twice her age. At thirty she was left a widow with three children to raise. Her life had been a happy, breathless whirl of good living, with never a care in the world. The family thought her a social butterfly, a woman of little substance. She had chosen to get married rather than finish school; she was not equipped to face the world on her own. This was India in the 1950s where women were not expected to exercise their independence, especially if they came from a privileged background.

When her husband died, her father wanted her to pack up her belongings, gather her children and go back home with him, and family and friends also thought that was the thing to do.

But Gini refused to give in to circumstance. She stayed on in her own home and taught herself shorthand and typing. She then moved to Kolkata and got herself a job. She who had lived in the lap of luxury all her young life started working. Life was hard but she was able to keep body and soul together and take care of her children. She created a career for herself, neither seeking nor receiving help from anyone. Gone were the gossamer wings of the butterfly. The family treated her with awe and respect.

When life was at its peak, her husband had built three large, beautiful houses in Patna. Then the dreaded kala azar, or blackwater fever, put an end to all their dreams. As the disease sucked the life force out of him, his business began to fail. By the time he passed away, his affairs were in a hopeless state. Gini had already lost two of the houses to financial and legal tangles. She decided to sell the third. It would make life more comfortable. She could perhaps even buy a place of her own when she moved to Kolkata.

But life had not equipped her to deal with the murkiness of the marketplace. Gautam, her eldest son, had gone off to work in the tea gardens. Neena and Deepak were still in school and not much help in these matters. Her father was crippled with diabetes. There was no one she could turn to, so when an old friend said he would help her out, she jumped at the offer.

But it was not so easy. The friend looked at the papers and told her that the house could not be sold because there were some legal problems. This was an unexpected turn of events. Was he absolutely sure? Yes, he said, there was no doubt at all in his mind that it was not a saleable property. Gini accepted his verdict; how could she doubt him? He was a friend, after all. But, as a long-time friend he offered to do a deal. He would buy the house from her, obviously at a nominal sum. At a later date she could buy it back from him at the same price. Gini had no choice. She agreed to his proposal.

A few years later, Gini went back to Patna. She had saved

enough to reclaim her property. Armed with her chequebook, she was happy and optimistic as she arrived at the house, which she had 'temporarily' sold. So imagine her shock when the gentleman smiled his best avuncular smile and said she must be mistaken. He did not recollect making any such arrangement. There was no question of selling the house back to her. Gini was stunned. Choking back her tears of disappointment she got up to leave. He called her back. There was a way out, he said. She could have the house back, without paying a paisa. All that she had to do was agree to her son Gautam marrying his niece, and he would give them the house as a wedding present.

Gini wept. Not out of self-pity, but with rage and frustration. She, who had always forged her own path and prized her independence above all else, could not and would not tell her children who they should marry. She walked out of the house forever. She had lost all hope of ever having a home of her own. But her son got to marry the woman he chose.

Rajyashree Dutt

A Second Chance

The glass chamber of illusions came crashing down when they decided to call it quits. A marriage that seemed would last forever was destroyed, right in front of her eyes. She could just not believe it. Maybe, because she was raised in an orthodox family, which believed in the dictum that marriages are forever; a dictum, which had been passed down for generations, never to be questioned. As she sat numb in front of her TV, unable to listen, to feel or hear anything, she recalled the events of the past eight years.

'It's over, darling, and you need to move on.' The oft-repeated words of advice from her cherished family and friends seemed clichéd. But in the end, she did move on. How did that happen? The loving hands and hearts around her pushed her back to life, slowly but steadily. She found herself laughing again at the silliest of jokes with her crazy friends and crying over mushy movies she watched with her sister. Her life with Vinay had plenty of beautiful moments. With the passing of time, she learnt to cherish them without missing them, and learnt to bury the unpleasant memories safely in the farthest corner of her being. It would take still more time to forget him totally but till then, this worked well for her. She was finally on her own.

The invitation to attend the International Film Festival in Jaipur came as a surprise to her. She considered herself an ardent lover of movies and a sensible critic, too, but the invite caught her off guard. It came via the mailing list of a friend's friend. Talk about chance! Any other day or time, she would have deleted such an email but this time she paused. The dates looked good to her; she could afford to take three days off from work. And the venue was an added attraction. She had always wanted to visit Jaipur. So she packed her bags and left. Jaipur, so rich in history and architecture, fascinated her.

Popular names and familiar faces thronged the festival. There were people from all walks of life, discussing art and films. She moved around, alone in the crowd, trying to take it all in. A man with a friendly face caught her attention. His small eyes almost disappeared when he smiled. Now that's a true smile, she thought.

Without offering any elaborate introduction, he took it upon himself to settle her down and introduce her to some of the known names and faces. Lina felt like a school kid on an excursion with her best friend. They joked and talked non-stop for three days. The camaraderie between the two had an adolescent flavour to it. Three days flew by and it was time for them to say goodbye, with promises to keep in touch. She was sceptical: there was nothing special between them, she thought. Being good-natured, he would easily help strangers. Anyway, she would wait and see.

Surprisingly, he did remain a part of her world, through phone calls and text messages. There was a charm in the way he communicated and she was able to sense it. He was surely amongst the last breed of gentlemen, but was that enough for her? He was fiercely loyal, but did she need more? Past experience had made her cautious; there was no room for being impulsive. Should she succumb to her emotions or should she wait and watch? She needed time; she could not rush in to something like this.

'How much more time?' was the persistent question from the other end of the phone? She could not answer him. She was still scarred and scared and did not want him to wait for her. That would not be fair to him; he had been waiting for so long for his special partner, and to start a family. After ten months they decided to meet in Jaipur again. She told him she could not commit herself just yet. He needed to move on and realise his dreams. He pleaded with her, promised her everything she would ever want in her life. She knew that he would move mountains to keep her happy but that was not enough for her.

Finally, she understood what was missing. She was not in love with him.

Months later, there was yet another invite in her mailbox: Vinod weds Shreya, it said. She smiled as she saw it. She was filled with joy for her dear friend and with a renewed hope that she, too, would find love once again.

Asha Francis

The Woman with Two Birthdays

I first met Priyanka in 2002. She was doing a dipstick survey for a research project and I was one of the respondents. In her form, she wrote two dates against date of birth: 23 November 1973 and 26 April 1993. I asked why, and this is what she told me:

I was a nineteen-year-old student of Sophia College, Mumbai, when, on 26 April 1993, the Indian Airlines flight on which I was travelling crashed outside Aurangabad airport. Of the one hundred and eighteen persons on board, sixty-three survived. I was among the fortunate ones.

I had felt the plane break behind me and the heat of the flames, as the fire spread. I fought with my seatbelt, the metal buckle of which was unbearably hot, freed myself and leapt out of the rear end onto the runway. Other shocked and injured, terror-struck and screaming passengers who had also escaped were running away across the field with no thought but to flee the burning wreckage. Dazed, I ran with them. Fuel was aflame on the runway and we had to get through a ring of fire to reach safety. I remember two things — an old man running next to me, urging me to keep going, and that as I approached the ring of fire, I lost hope and wanted to give up. It was at this point I heard God's voice telling me I had to live. I crossed the ring of fire and ran some more until I dropped.

I was very badly burnt.

I have random memories of my recovery. My elbows had got fused. It was as if someone had folded and bound them. I couldn't move them at all. The bones had melted and were further made stiff by calcification. It was terribly painful. And the physiotherapist was trying to make it right.

About the people ... I remember so many. My father was always there, never complaining. I couldn't sleep until he put his hand on my forehead and chanted some mantras. I have had close to eighty surgeries, but I never went without my father wheeling me into the operation theatre. After some time I had to take painful baths every day, baths to dress my wounds. The procedure was done under anaesthesia. But I was getting addicted to anaesthesia, so they started using water instead, pouring it till the bandages came out. It was incredibly painful. My mother couldn't bear to see me yelling so she'd leave and my dad, along with my nurse and aunt, both crying, would bathe me.

My sister Mini and I were never like friends. Never. But I remember being in the hospital, lying under the protective cage and feeling most happy when my sister was coming. I believe I kept asking for her. I don't think she left the hospital for the next six months. When we were going home, she went to the Oberoi and bought a smart bag for all my medicines, one in which the bottles would remain standing. Oh, the details she went into for me, like scrutinising movies for violence, fires and accidents before I saw them....

Before the crash I had a boyfriend, but he could not handle my condition and we parted. More than a decade after the crash I fell in love and, over a span of five years, built a relationship with a man who is now my husband. But till then, I had coped on my own. My parents taught me to love myself and be proud of my scars and I want to continue that way. I don't want to forget ... I want to be proud of my battle to recover and my scars, both physical and emotional. My scars are a part of my history and who I am.

Once, on Rakshabandhan, we were watching old videos with my family and some relatives from Jodhpur, who wore that "poor thing, look at her scars" expression. The screen went blank for a second, familiar voices were singing "Happy Birthday", and then, suddenly, a visual, followed by silence. It was the first visual I had ever seen of myself in hospital. And I looked young, clean, fully bandaged and tired, with dark circles under my eyes ... and very strange. I connect with this person, yet I don't feel it's me. I am trying to sit up straight but my body feels too weak. But I look okay, not at all scared.

This video was taken four months after the crash. I can't imagine how I must have looked just after it happened — and how my family took it. The people with me in the hospital all look happy: my sister serving cake, my little cousins, my parents, doctors and nurses, all happy and smiling.

Today it really seems like a miracle, and I'm proud and amazed by the journey. So much has been achieved since that day. I cannot place in any order the people who have helped me get well, the list is long, so here goes.

The man who put five of us who were seriously injured in his jeep and sped us to the hospital at Aurangabad with one hand pressed to the horn, yelling his lungs out to clear the traffic.

The man who called his family from a movie hall where news of the crash was flashed during the film ... the family sat by my side, as I lay alone in the hospital.

The reporter who took down my father's number and called him to inform him that I was alive.

The nurse who bandaged me up even though she could have lost her job, as she needed a senior's prior approval for removing all the jewellery I was wearing before bandaging me.

The aunt and uncle who flew down immediately to Aurangabad and got me back to Mumbai, although, I'm sure they were afraid to fly over the crash site and take the same route.

The airhostess who sat on the floor of the aircraft next to my stretcher when I was being flown to Mumbai, even though it was against regulations, holding my hand, keeping me calm.

The ambulances and motorcycle pilots who made sure that I reached the hospital in a hurry.

The doctors and nurses waited for me at that late hour and pacified me, saying that all would be well.

My nurse, Bula, who was with me during the critical month in the ICU, taking care of me, pushing me harder and harder to recover, to overcome the pain, chiding me when I didn't follow doctors orders, forcing me to eat ten eggs a day and being my friend when I needed to talk.

The uncle who read out the *Economic Times* to me every day, even though I didn't understand a word ... and another who read me Khushwant Singh's jokes.

My friend got a hairdresser to disentangle my singed hair and tie it up with red ribbons. My friends from college never failed to visit at four in the evening, always brought cheer.

My teachers who promised to keep my seat in college and reassured me that I'd be able to get back in no time.

The physiotherapist worked with me continuously, even when I cried out in pain, refused to follow her instructions and hated her with all my heart. She never gave up.

My family stayed by me for months, taking turns, not leaving me alone even a moment. Encouraging me every minute to go on, making me feel nothing tragic had happened to me.

My cousin, all of twelve, who stayed with me for a month, who sat next to me with her hand on my forehead while I cried.

Sometimes, when I look back, I feel like it is someone else's story.

But I really did go through it all, and don't want to be so caught up in the usual business of living — relationships, marriage, in-laws, domestic quarrels — as to forget the courage and determination I needed to emerge from that crash.

There is a reason I survived and I now have to understand that reason….

As told to Shikha Aleya

Single by Choice

Roma — intelligent, imaginative and very pretty — had a rather materialistic, soul-less and unforgiving father who could not see beyond marriage as her future, even though she excelled at academics and had serious ambitions. The father wanted her 'settled' before he retired in two years and though her mother did try to intervene, she proved ineffective as her husband controlled the household, courtesy the purse strings. So when they found a boy who worked as a political journalist with a reputed newspaper in Delhi, Roma agreed. He was the only son of well-to-do working parents, and Roma thought she might be allowed to study further and ultimately become an economic journalist herself.

However, the reality proved very different. The in-laws expected her to bear children. She did produce a boy and a girl in quick succession and, along with her parents-in-law, became wholly absorbed in them. So, while her husband's assignments took him further afield, she stayed home and happily took care of her babies and their grandparents. Even when she had the opportunity to live with her husband and children on a foreign assignment, she made him cut it short so she could return to her settled existence.

In any case, the kids needed to go to school and soon their activities and studies began to take up more of her time and attention. Besides, their grandparents too were not getting younger. Very often, when her husband returned late he would find her asleep over a book, his dinner thoughtfully placed in the microwave. So he would gently put away her book and allow her to sleep on, for she looked exhausted.

But he did miss her attention, and perhaps as a result, his own attention began to stray. And it strayed no further than the proverbial girl next door. She was very fetching, smiled sweetly at him, flattered him and commiserated with his loneliness. They were known to be just good friends, nothing more.

But his mother warned Roma: 'Don't trust a man so much; he is young and attractive and you give him no companionship. Look out!'

Roma laughed their fears away and deliberately turned her back on the entire episode. However, the young girl next door was herself lonely. Her father was a misogynist, who had never forgiven his wife for saddling him with a daughter and then dying on him. The future looked bleak to him.

For the daughter, who desperately sought a better life, and when all the single boys in her circle had turned away from her mainly due to her father's attitude, she clung all the more desperately to Roma's husband, appealing to his chivalrous instincts till he capitulated. Then it was a case of pure blackmail by the father who had been just waiting for an opportunity to foist his daughter on someone without any trouble or expense to himself.

'You have to make an honest woman of her, or I will go to your employers,' is what he told Roma's husband.

The husband did consider doing the right thing by throwing himself at his parents' and Roma's mercy, but he lacked the courage. Eventually, one night, like a coward, he left with the girl, aided and abetted by her father.

While the parents mourned, commiserated and considered legal action, Roma got herself a job with an advertising firm, editing copy. The salary was not great, but enough to cover her children's needs. She told the children that their father had gone on an important assignment and insisted her parents-in-law do the same. This took care of prying neighbours, immediate and virulent gossip. In a year's time it became clear the situation was permanent — a fact accepted by all, including the children who were now old enough to understand that their father would not return. The divorce went through quietly, without fuss and Roma's husband married a second time.

Now, twelve years later, Roma is a big name in the world of advertising. Her parents-in-law have come to look upon her as their only child. Her son has got a scholarship to study economics in the US and the daughter is planning to follow suit. The once-pitying neighbours respect her more than they ever did her husband and the 'girl's father' has moved away from the neighbourhood.

It was only when Roma's ex-husband made a tentative move to return to the fold, pleading that 'he missed the children' did she react sharply: 'He should contact the children directly; I have no opinion on the matter.'

The children refused, indignantly, and that was that.

It was only after this incident that Roma realised that while she had always wanted children, she had never really wanted a spouse, never wanted anyone to share her progeny and domain, which is why she had turned a blind eye to her husband's peccadilloes and faced adversity with such courage and equanimity.

Today she has everything she ever wanted and her children, most of all, look upon her as a heroine. But no one knew that she was single by choice.

Nonda Chatterjee

The Gift of Life

I am a survivor of loss and pain. In days gone by, I would probably have been ostracised by the community, maybe even stoned, driven away to eke out my existence in an ashram far away, my worldly goods confiscated, my very shadow shunned for bringing bad luck to the family. In today's slightly more humane, modern urban India, I am merely looked at with pity or politely ignored.

I lost my husband of twenty-five years to a sudden heart attack. His death robbed me of a loving companion. Exactly hundred days later, my son died in a freak accident — my only child, just stepping into manhood.

How does one cope with such tragedy? I do not know. There were no easy answers then and there are none now. There were no comforting platitudes or reassurances that could penetrate the thick fog that enshrouded me then. There was an unbearable emptiness inside me, an aching void; it felt as if a vital part of my body had been extricated.

Later that year I was diagnosed with lymphatic cancer. Could things get any worse? *Annus Horribilis* just about summed it up. So what next, I wondered dully. The nauseating grind of chemotherapy, the multiple pills I popped daily, strangely enough seemed to help me cope. The immediate danger took over completely, as I distanced myself from all other realities.

It's been ten years now since that traumatic year, ten long years since I have discovered that life has to be lived, no matter what happens. The world will keep on moving, night follows day. The demands of the body can be tyrannical, imposing some basic routine, some discipline into life. Bills have to be paid, deadlines have to be met, and the world does not wait at your convenience. I know now that life is a gift, not to be wasted or spurned.

My work as a volunteer at the local children's cancer care centre has saved me from drowning in self-pity. Ever so slowly, I have clawed back to life, scarred but healing, revelling in the brightness and laughter, and rejoicing in the zest for life that I see every day at the cancer care centre. My heart overflows with love and admiration at the courage of young innocent children, smilingly, stoically accepting the raw deal life has dealt them. If they can face such challenges and still hope for the future, why can't I?

Once the centre of a warm circle of friends, I now watch from the periphery. As a single woman, I am an awkward number; maybe also a threat to some married women, all too conscious of the roving eyes of their errant husbands. I no longer figure in the invitation list of many friends. Why do I still call them that?

My true friends and my family have stood by me, ready to listen, to talk, to share, to scold and prod when needed. Yes, there are still times when I wake up in the middle of the night, drenched in fear and carry an unimaginably heavy heart the following day. Yes, there are still times when a song on the radio triggers a moment of intense longing and sorrow and I weep. Perhaps such moments will always be there. But there are also times when I sit with my friends and family over a pot luck dinner and laugh over shared memories, when I pore over old albums and smile in remembrance, when I excitedly plan my day ahead and step out in happy anticipation, ready to face life.

I have learnt to be gentle with the past, to let it go.

I have learnt to live each moment to its fullest and to cherish the good times — to laugh out loud, to savour good food, enjoy good music and feast my eyes on the beauty that surrounds.

I will be forever grateful for all the love that has illumined my life and the second chance I have been offered. I treasure my blessings, for who knows what tomorrow may bring!

As told to Sarita Varma

Resurrected

She had the same dream every bride had. She kept looking at the glass bangles and the black beads of the necklace that her mother had kept in a box under her bed. Her mother, who worked as a maid, had taken two months' wages in advance from me. Taking out the small, cracked mirror, she looked at herself. Her lustrous eyes looked too big in her thin face. She did not like her nose. It was too small and her lips too thick. She rubbed some lipstick on her palms and coloured her cheeks. Her yellow zari sari clung to her small frame. Tomorrow she would go to her husband's home.

No, she would not be married the next day. She had already been married two months ago to a man from her village. He was the youngest son of a farmer. Her brother-in-law, who was married to her father's sister, had arranged the alliance. Tomorrow was her gauna, the formal departure of the bride from her father's house to her in-laws. In Uttar Pradesh, there is a custom in the rural areas, of the bride returning to the parental home four days after her marriage, where she would then stay for a couple of months or years, as decided by the elders until her gauna. So she had been living with her mother in the servant quarters of my house. I had seen her as a pig-tailed kid, tagging along behind her mother and I blessed her with all my heart for the new life she was about to begin.

Two months later, she was back. Her husband, it seemed, was of unsound mind. She would spend all day looking after the family, cooking dozens of chapattis on an earthen stove for the men who would come back ravenous, after a hard day's work at the farm. She would clean out the cow-shed, wash the two buffaloes and massage hot oil on her mother-in-law's feet. And every night, he would bolt the door and beat her up black and blue. Her screams went unheard, her scars unnoticed, in a family where this was the norm.

Though she came from a family that earned money by working in other people's homes, she had been brought up with care by her mother. Moreover, she was used to city ways and loved watching TV or dressing up like the daughters of the houses where her mother worked. She was used to wearing hand-me-downs, which had been tailored in boutiques.

She did not go back to her husband. Fights ensued as her in-laws threatened and cried foul. But she remained firm. She was not willing to tell her mother anything, nor was she thinking of a legal separation.

It was a bride's tale gone awry. Slowly, she resurrected her life. Perhaps, the child she was expecting helped her to find those reserves of strength from the recesses of her soul, to bear everything with a smile even in the closeted social stratum to which she belonged.

Today, she is working in eight houses, dusting, cleaning, cooking and washing. Her child is studying in an English medium school and she herself has completed her graduation. She is contemplating joining a computer course run by the government. Of course, her family has stood by her in a rock-hard stance, but it was she who dared to take the plunge and be different.

One day, when I asked her where she got her strength of purpose from, her answer was simple: 'I don't know. I didn't think about whether I could or could not do something. I just moved forward and grasped at the possibilities that came my way.'

Perhaps, that's how life should be lived; perhaps one should move ahead without philosophising or trying to base one's actions on preconceived notions.

Monika Pant

I Look Forward

The little plans I tried to carry
have failed
Oh! dear God.
But I will not sorrow
I will pause a little while
and try again tomorrow.

After a few tiring days of meetings and phone calls, I sat quietly in the departure lounge, waiting to board the flight back home. My eye caught the date flashing on the cell phone's screen: 11 July 2010.

Six years ago, on this very date, I had lost my serenity and my hope. I could recall how my voice became inaudible to my own ears, how my eyelids had drooped with the enormous dose of sleeping pills, how everything else had faded into the darkness that engulfed my spirits. Gradually I had slipped into the realms of oblivion. Only the chaste and radiant face of my daughter had floated through my unconscious mind.

Now, when I reflect on that episode of my life, I can only conclude it was an act of cowardice. I cannot understand how

I could ever have subjected myself to such a drastic act. What was I running away from?

The emotional trauma I had been undergoing had created such turmoil within me as to imbue everything with darkness. Perhaps it is normal to feel this way when the man you loved cheats you. It compelled me to attempt suicide; I thought it was the best solution to the crisis, even for those around me.

But at the eleventh hour, I was saved. I owe my survival to my family and friends. I realised that I was blessed with such loved ones; so what if my marriage turned out to be unhappy. I had to go through unpalatable legal battles and trying emotional ones, alone. I was scared of these battles and had wanted to avoid them. But finally it all ended, relieving me of a decade of depression, agony and insecurity. A relationship, which I had always imagined being made in heaven, ended up in the murkiest manner, on a piece of paper. Once again I had to start from a blank page.

I resolved to never again turn my back on my then two-year-old daughter, whose eyes constantly searched for me, who cried in her sleep for my touch, who depended on me. I finally realised the long-term consequences of my knee-jerk reaction. I could not escape the desire born with motherhood — the desire to nurture and care for the tender and loving baby I had brought to the world. I promised myself to be an example to her. I wanted her to believe that her mother is strong and always put up a brave face. She kept my spirits buoyed at times when I lived on a wing and prayer.

And my life started again, a new birth, a new beginning. More beautiful and well defined. The storm had left me stronger, giving me clarity of thought. I understood relationships better.

I learnt to listen to my inner voice. Once again, I turned to those activities I loved: singing, painting and writing. I learnt to express my emotions, both positive and negative, and learnt to accept them. I explored new dimensions within myself and in my career. I discovered happiness with my daughter, and gave happiness a definition. I grew spiritually. I learnt to deal with the rough patches of life and still remain focused. I learnt not to latch onto people for emotional comfort and I learnt that expectations reduce the joys of life.

Yes, my divorce taught me the best lessons of my life. I discovered my hidden potential. I regained my shattered confidence.

The last call to board my flight interrupted my reverie. I stood up and headed towards the aircraft. I smiled, as I set out to fly to newer and greater heights this time.

Anushree Karnani

Mamma's Boy

'Hi! Hemant? Guess who?' asked an excited voice at the other end of the phone. The accent seemed vaguely familiar but the tone was not. And then the person laughed.

At that moment I knew exactly who it was. 'Ajay? It is you, right?' I asked. He had a peculiar way of laughing. It was a giggle that grew into a loud, full-throated roar. Ajay was thrilled that I recognised him, even after two years. He was my old neighbour. I confess he was not one of my favourite friends and I had nicknamed him PKP or 'pallu ke peche' (tied to mother's apron strings) simply because Ajay was such a mamma's boy. Yes, I know all of us men are mamma's boys but Ajay took the term to a whole new level.

Even though he was in his late twenties his mother would make his bed, decide what he wore and pack his bag when he came with us for the odd overnight trip. He would call her and narrate, word by word, each incident that had taken place during the trip and we would wonder if Ajay was twenty-eight or ten. He never took any decisions on his own; his mother took them for him. Though he was handsome, his shoulders drooped and he lacked confidence when talking to people. He was shy, an introvert and had very few friends. His father worked on a ship and provided well for his family.

Ajay did nothing for a living. He was well aware that we didn't approve of his lifestyle or his reluctance to move out of his protective shell. When we would explain to him that he needed to grow up, take responsibility and be a man he would shrug off our suggestions and change the subject. So when I came to know that Ajay had taken up an assignment as a voluntary teacher in a school for the underprivileged, it was a pleasant surprise. Further, the job was in a different city. I wondered if Ajay would be able to cope with the challenges. Would he be able to deal with the emotional, mental and social pressures of living on his own? Or would he return home in no time at all? We learnt later that an attempt had been made to arrange his marriage but the girl had rejected him because of his lifestyle. That became the trigger for his leaving home.

And now two years later, I am meeting him at our favourite restaurant. As I was waiting for him to come, a confident man dressed in a kurta and jeans walked into the restaurant, I couldn't help but notice him. It was Ajay! There was something pleasingly different about him. He looked fulfilled, like a man who knew his life's purpose. I couldn't stop myself from saying, 'You look good! What happened when you were single and alone in a new city?'

Ajay laughed his signature laugh and replied, 'I grew up. I learnt to think for myself, take my own decisions and bear the consequences. And so far I have no regrets!'

As we settled into a conversation over a cup of coffee, Ajay spoke more about the changes that had taken place in his life.

'I was living such a wasteful life before,' he said. 'When I teach the kids who are grateful for small blessings of life, I realise my potential as a human being to make a positive difference in their lives. I owe it to myself to explore my talents,' he said matter-of-factly. I never imagined that I would hear Ajay speak so wisely. As he took the menu card and decided what he wanted, I felt as if I were in the company of a whole new Ajay, a more mature, sensible and responsible one.

'I remember you used to call me PKP. I am proud to tell you that it is no longer the case,' he said as his mobile rang. One of his students had called to ask his assistance on a personal matter. I watched Ajay logically go about explaining the right course of action to the child at the other end. The 'protected' had blossomed to become the 'protector'.

Seeing my stunned expression Ajay smiled and said, 'When you stay on your own in a new city, your coping mechanism kicks in. For me it was a new beginning. At first, it was very difficult but I kept going and now am quite adept at managing situations. Quitting or escaping from reality was just not an option for me anymore. I had done it my whole life, and it got me nowhere. I thank the girl who refused to marry me. She sowed the seeds for my new, productive life,' he said.

As we left the restaurant, I began to think of a new nickname for Ajay. 'Champion' is what came to mind.

Hemant Patil

The Chanting Room

Sunaina settled into a comfortable position and took a deep breath. The sonorous strains of Tibetan chanting echoed in the room, lulling her into a meditative trance. Faint smoke from the joss sticks curled around the room, niggling worries flickered and faded away as a serene peace permeated her being.

She knew that, this is what has kept her alive and functioning. This is what has helped her face each unmerciful morning, each day she has looked at herself in the mirror and wondered, 'Was it my fault?'

Rahul, who had such zest for life, who used to be the life and soul of a party, who every morning would clasp her waist and twirl her around before demanding his breakfast. Rahul had gone so far away that even God was helpless.

Long before the company takeover, long before the failure of his marketing venture, the cracks had begun to appear. In retrospect, his laughter had seemed forced, his bonhomie exaggerated, his plans even more grandiose. Why hadn't she paid more attention to his mood swings? Why hadn't she questioned him more closely about his long absences? Had she been guilty of seeing only what she wanted to see? Had she been too busy? Too preoccupied?

The children, as always, had provided the excuse. They were all consuming in their demands on her time and she had been their willing slave, so full of love and concern that she had failed to see Rahul's need for her, until it was too late.

Could she ever forget that night? As the news had spread, neighbours had come rushing, friends had called and held her hand, and the entire family had rallied around, wrapping her in a protective cocoon. Her sister had taken time off to take care of the children; her father had patiently gone through all Rahul's papers and investments, trying to pick up the tangled strands.

The most difficult part had been telling the children. She could do nothing more than to gather them in her arms and say over and over again, 'It's alright, we have each other.' Natasha, on the threshold of adolescence had gazed at her with troubled eyes. Neeraj, much younger, had unquestioningly hugged her back and then innocently asked, 'Then I don't have to go to school today?'

Slowly, she learnt how to sleep without downing pills. Trying to get her life back on an even keel, working at a travel agency, helping indecisive customers finalise their itinerary, the haunting memories would surface and her heart would ache. The journey back to a semblance of normalcy had taken time. Time when she would rage in private, envying the bright, normal lives everyone around her seemed to enjoy. There were times when she would be filled with anger and haunted by the question, 'Why me?'

She has come a long way since then. Slowly, very slowly, life ceased to be a burden … the normal tasks of everyday life didn't weigh her down as before. Gradually, she started reaching out to her friends again, the few who had stood by her. Funny how it took a tragedy to find out who her real friends were. All those centuries ago, the Bard had been right when he extolled the virtues of adversity! She learnt to smile again, laugh at a joke, and enjoy a movie with friends. The healing was like the first hesitant steps of a newborn, every stage a milestone to be noted.

Trying to be both father and mother to two lively children had taken all her ingenuity and patience. The children had their own challenges to overcome. Life had taught them a harsh lesson very early on. Neeraj could not understand why his classmates whispered behind his back. Natasha developed a rebellious streak and Sunaina had worried for a time that she was drifting away. She herself found that she could not bear the pitying looks that people often gave her.

Change of job and location proved a lifesaver. A course in counselling done years back in college provided the perfect means of getting away, of starting all over again. The residential public school, high up in the foothills of the Himalayas, which she had joined as a crafts teacher and student counsellor had not only helped provide a free education for the children, but had also let her establish herself as Sunaina, not just 'poor Rahul's wife.' Like a phoenix rising from the ashes, she thought wryly, of herself.

The school proved a good training ground for both the children, allowing them to develop their talents and grow, making her a very proud mother indeed. The packed schedule and the academic environment were therapeutic and for some years they were completely caught up in its comforting embrace.

Life, however, had more in store for her. A chance reading of a book on meditation and the power of chanting took her in a new direction, opened her to new possibilities, and helped her cope with her private nightmares. Joining a circle of enthusiasts, she got trained under the best teachers, and soon found herself invited to hold sessions independently. She counselled not just confused teens in school, but also the stressed employees of multinational companies. From there to meditation therapy and Buddhist chanting, it had been a long, fulfilling journey, one she looks back on with a sense of achievement. Like a late blooming flower, Sunaina had blossomed ....

The room glowed softly in the golden light cast by candles in intricate metal holders, designed by Neeraj during his first year at the Institute of Design. The chanting faded and deep silence settled in the room. The participants sighed, shifted positions and gathered their belongings. The session was over for the day. Natasha, slim and impeccably groomed, a legacy of her training as an airhostess, slipped a companionable arm around her mother. Sunaina quietly wished everyone goodbye and turned back to the room. The same room where she had rushed in one fateful night after hearing a loud crash, had seen her world flicker and die. The same room where she had looked at Rahul's body swinging from the fan, the same room where she had instinctively picked up the chair he had kicked away.

Sarita Varma

Single and Sane

'What's a pretty woman like you doing alone?' She's heard that line at least once a week in the past year. She has a crazy quip ready most times. As a close pal, today I can confidently say that 'singledom' is the best thing that could have happened to Kanika.

We became pals in college when this firebrand walked into my hostel room ... and life — never to leave! It's been over fifteen years and the bond has only got stronger. For a long time, most people thought and continue to think Kanika has the most charmed life. Pretty and perky, intelligent and witty — that describes Kanika. Coming from a privileged background, Kanika was rather sorted I thought, and not as much a brat as she could have been. Her mother had brought her up as her father had moved away. She went to the best hostels in the country and when she expressed a desire to study English in the big city, arrangements were made.

For the first time she was on her own and loving the attention and freedom. Those were really crazy times, heady and intoxicating. Discovering a new world from

Milan Kundera to Mrinal Sen. Smiling at fruit sellers to give discounts and realising how overrated virginity was. Four years at college was bliss. Alcohol and other highs made it a blissful blur, I guess.

When real life beckoned, Kanika and I decided to share a flat. Both of us had just got jobs and were discovering independence. What I found surprising was how she was getting all clingy with Debu, her poet boyfriend from college. We had all moved on to greener pastures, yet she wasn't able to.

Then began a series of bad relationships. The better she did in her advertising job, the worse she seemed to get in her choice of men. It was amazing how someone who had the best men dancing to her tune didn't want them. All she seemed to want were losers whom she could set right. Sure, all of us make mistakes, but Kanika got her high from them. Her drinking was getting out of hand, but luckily better sense prevailed in the form of a sensible boss she respected.

She fell ill and her mom came to nurse her. You could instantly see from whom she inherited her beauty and her insecurities.

We explained to her that she was better off than her mother and her life did not have to pan out the way her mother's had. She always agreed. She was sensible and in control in every other sphere of life. She was winning awards and getting noticed at work.

One Sunday she walked in late at a lazy lunch with pals. With her was Debu, the Delhi loser. He was in Bombay trying his hand at being a film director. Kanika was beaming as she announced they were getting married that day.

Without trying to sound cynical, Kanika really messed it up. She hated Debu as much as she loved him. We felt sorry for the guy who was a pet project that caught her fancy at times and at other times irritated her. Yet she paid for his upkeep and used all her contacts to get him work. She was in denial and we all tried to reach out to her but she wasn't willing to listen.

Being a lovely person, she was genuinely happy for all of us as we moved into normal stable relationships. I remember telling her once how it didn't feel right for me to move on and not be there for her as much. She was genuinely surprised and said she actually didn't think of herself as a problem child.

Debu began cheating on her. She was devastated and landed up in hospital with a nervous breakdown. I begged her to stay away from men for some time. She promised and promptly got into an affair with her married boss. Kanika started hiding things from us and it came to a point where she began avoiding us.

The man knew how good she was at her work and so the two of them started their own ad agency. We watched from the sidelines and could see that she was putting her heart and soul into the project. She even asked her dysfunctional father for a loan. As the company got bigger, so did her problems. Her partner suddenly wanted to sideline her and things got messy. She was thrown out of her own company. But she emerged stronger and started from scratch again.

One more relationship with an alcoholic was her next adventure and this time when she came looking for help everyone was angry. She moved into my household and seemed to be healing. She still met the guy occasionally till, one night, in a drunken state, he beat her up. That was the real jolt, the wake-up call. She did not press charges but decided to put her life in order.

Kanika got rid of her alcoholic friends and triggers. Finally she decided to build a relationship with herself. It was tough and liberating, for her and the people close to her. It's a Herculean task for her to spend time by herself. That's true of a lot of people. I have often seen her get tempted to lean on a man's shoulder and then refrain from doing so. It is working; she has realised how capable she is. She always was, but she never believed it.

Yoga and trekking, learning the sitar, brushing up her dancing — she is discovering different sides of her by herself every day. She is a new person. She is learning how it's not so difficult to walk into a party alone, how it's not the end of the world if you don't have a date on Valentine's Day. This Valentine weekend, she took her mother and had a super time.

She sees a therapist and now believes that she does not need a man to validate her. She can choose to lead a full life without clinging on to some man. Sure, she has a way with men and she knows it. It's just that the player is taking a break!

In my friend Kanika, I have seen a living example of someone who took fifteen years to discover oneself. And I know she is not going to give up her exploration easily.

Shifa Maitra

Starting Anew

Anu smiled as she coached the eager marketing trainees. How young, enthusiastic and naïve they were, confidence oozing from every pore, sure of their sales pitch, sure of making big bucks and very sure that once they become rich, they would be happy! But they lacked her passion and commitment. What was for most a second profession, a source of extra income, was for her, independence and liberation. No longer did she have to kowtow to bosses or compromise on her values to ascend the ladder of success.

Born into an orthodox, middle-class family from Assam, she was the first of her generation to break the shackles of feminine conventionality. Highly ambitious and clever, she had rejected the very idea of an arranged marriage, fearing it would clip her wings, as it had done to both her elder sisters. With a much younger brother still in school, she had been determined to be the 'son' to her aging parents. A job as a high-flying legal finance executive with a reputed company in Delhi had brought with it the much longed-for financial security.

It seemed that all her dreams came true. She had flung herself into her career with zeal and energy, steadily making a name for herself in the industry. Confident and self-sufficient, she was proud that she could make her parents' retirement years comfortable and secure. Generous to a fault, she lavished gifts on her many nieces and nephews, bestowing upon them all her suppressed maternal love.

She had imagined, with all the innocence and optimism of youth, that one day she would meet her perfect man, the one who would truly complement her. Romance for Anu had followed a pattern. The roller-coaster ride of heady love and laughter, wine and roses was followed by betrayal and a terrifying plunge into the dark lows of doubt, disbelief and depression. Ajay, who had seemed genuinely fond of her, finally married the girl of his parent's choice. Later, a chance meeting with an IT engineer, Ramesh, turned into a long, drawn out affair. The much-promised divorce from his wife did not come through, leaving her with the feeling of having been used.

Sadder but wiser, she now asks ruefully, 'Why do I attract the wrong kind of man into my life? Why can't I see beyond their charm to the selfishness hidden there? Will I never learn?' The confident, incisive Anu, who smartly juggled numbers and unerringly pierced the layers of obtuse jargon, hidden traps, and deliberate falsifications so common in her profession, was like a babe in the woods when it came to personal relationships. Her sense of judgment erred and her emotional insecurity left her vulnerable.

As she grew older, the pitfalls had become apparent. There were very few eligible bachelors who could match her financial and social status. Anu missed out on some of the simplest pleasures in life. 'Not much fun dining at a fancy restaurant alone or even munching popcorn in a movie hall all by myself!' Being a single girl also meant having to cope with the usual, especially the late evenings. While married friends would occasionally include her in their jaunts, many evenings were spent simply watching TV, and many weekends she would paint her heart out on a canvas with vivid colours. Wary about crossing any social boundaries and jeopardising her ties of friendship, she usually worked late at office.

Most of Anu's colleagues were male and 'happily' married. She was friendly with many of them, becoming a favourite aunt to their children, and trusted confidante to their wives. But there were also some who merely wanted a fling on the side. Office romances, though discouraged by company policy, were an open secret. Intent on avoiding such overtures and the embarrassment they led to, she had developed a cheery bonhomie with her colleagues. It was not a very successful tactic. As time went by, it had become awkward to attend corporate social events alone as some wives, intimidated by her poise, viewed her as a threat to their marital security.

Slowly growing disenchanted with the whole corporate culture, she had mulled over her options. The turning point came when her new boss, with all the finesse of an elephant, hinted that the path to a directorial position lay through his bedroom. Numb with shock, she had walked out of the room. She knew then that she no longer had a future in the firm. In the rarefied atmosphere of her profession, she also knew that the chances of her getting an equally good job elsewhere were dim. Such news always travels fast, and there would be too many queries about the reasons for her hasty exit from a coveted position. Not wanting to become the object of unsavoury speculation, and yearning for a break from the 'rat race,' she resigned, citing health reasons and returned to her parents' home.

Her mother always maintained that whatever happens is for the best. Now, many years later, Anu is a successful business woman and looks back on her journey with pride. It has not been an easy one, certainly not one she could have managed without her family's unstinting support. They had provided a safe haven, where she could let down her guard, cry her heart out and give vent to her anger and pain. Her father offered her sage advice, reminding her of half-formulated business plans she had conceived a while ago. With help from her brother, she took up the venture as a challenge. Her many friends provided the vital contacts, pulling strings to get her lucrative orders. It was payback time for all the goodwill she had invested during her career. Slowly but surely, she settled into the new role of an entrepreneur.

Anu is now immersed in her business. Her single status does not matter, as her associates know that behind that pretty face is a razor-sharp brain. As her own boss, she dictates her own terms to the men in her life. The framed photo of herself and her ex-boyfriend, which she had kept on her bedside, has long since been dispatched to the wastepaper basket. It's time to move on.

She has vowed never again to bare her heart and become a puppet in unscrupulous hands, never to feel 'left-out' at social gatherings, but to carefully nurture her true friendships. Nestled in a comfort zone with her parents and extended family, Anu is that rare woman, content and secure, willing to let destiny play itself out.

'Perhaps one day I will meet my perfect match, my soul mate. Or perhaps not ...'

Sarita Varma

Bait of Hate

'You have got to be out of your mind — don't be a lunatic!' Jeanette gasped.

Evidently something very out of the ordinary was taking place. In the twenty-two years of their friendship, never had Jeanette used that tone with Tina, or such piercing words.

However, looking at Tina, Jeanette realised her words were falling on deaf ears, for Tina's mind was made up. She was opening her home to Mona and her twin sons. Sure, Mona was Tina's younger sister. But Mona was also the woman who had destroyed Tina's marriage and run off with Tina's husband.

Tina and Geoff had been a fairly happy and well-placed couple with two lovely daughters, Jennifer and Joan. It was a story book marriage: Geoff was a successful stockbroker, and Tina was vice-president in a multinational, a job that involved a considerable amount of global travel. Blessings seemed to be pouring in from every side and it was with generosity of heart that they had received that crucial letter from Tina's mother. Mrs Wood had written from the small town Tina had grown up in, and asked Tina if she would mind accommodating her younger sister Mona for a few weeks 'until Mona can go through a training that will equip her with marketplace skills, get a job and find a place of her own,' was how she had put it.

The couple readily accepted. Tina had been like a second mother to her baby sister during the happy childhood they had shared; after all, Mona was just a few years older than her own daughter, Jennifer. It worked out well. Mona enrolled for a computer course and helped out with the children. Not much helping out was needed, since they had a very efficient nanny and all the required domestic staff.

The problem happened after a year. Problem? It was catastrophe of the worst kind. Tina returned from an extended global assignment to find the daughters watching TV with the nanny. There was no sign of Geoff and Mona. But there was a long letter from Geoff propped on Tina's pillow. The gist of it was that he and Mona had fallen in love; they had tried hard to resist it, but they could not help themselves. They had discussed it and debated it threadbare but now they felt it was in the best interests of all concerned if they just 'disappeared from the scene.' He apologised again and again, 'Darling, I really am sorry, I did not mean for this to happen, but it has. Forgive me if you can.'

They were divorced a year later. The shock killed Mrs Wood who blamed herself for having sent Mona into their home. To avoid the ill feeling towards them from the rest of the family and the community, Geoff and Mona migrated to Australia. Several months later, Geoff wrote once again to Tina, apologising and asking her forgiveness. He missed his daughters a lot, but said he and Mona had settled down well.

The daughters were desperate for their father. Their grades had gone down and so had their spirits. 'When will Daddy come back?' they often asked their mother. One day, she sat them down and dealt with the issue at length; told them facts with minimal attack or pain.

Jennifer said, 'Just because Daddy does not love us, does it mean we are not allowed to love him?' That sentence got to Tina's heart. It also prompted her to write to Geoff and ask him to keep in touch, for the sake of his daughters.

He wrote infrequently, once or twice a year. Then, five years later, came the shocker, 'Dear Tina, I am dying. I have an inoperable tumour in my brain and the doctor says it is just a matter of weeks. I don't know if I mentioned it but Mona and I were blessed with twin sons last year. We have no savings. It has been difficult starting life again from scratch. As you know, Mona never completed her computer course and has not worked for a single day. I know you will consider this audacity but I am desperate and short of time. After I go, will it be possible for you to send Mona and the boys some money each month to help them tide by until Mona can stand on her own feet?'

For several nights, Tina sat with that letter. She dealt with every emotion wrought by the request. She prayed like never before: 'To You, O Lord, I lift up this situation. Help me to do what is right in your eyes.'

The next day, she wrote to Geoff, 'Well, to be honest, by the time I pay all the bills and the children's tuition fees, there is not much left over. What you can do, however, is tell Mona she can come home to me.'

It was when Jeanette heard of this decision that she had

expressed incredible disbelief — even as she knew that once Tina made up her mind about something, God and no one else would be able to change it!

Three months later, Tina stood at the Mumbai international airport waiting to receive Mona and the twins. Geoff had died a month earlier; Tina and the girls had wept with grief and regret.

Mona walked out of the terminal, aided by an airhostess who helped her push the strollers. Tina saw her sister first. She later told Jeanette: 'As I saw the young boys, who both look so much like Geoff, I went into shock for a moment. A surge of hatred rushed up and caused a red mist before my eyes and for a split second I understood what makes people want to kill.'

But, Tina bowed her head and simply prayed, 'Jesus, help me. I cannot do this without You, Lord.'

At that moment, Mona looked up and saw Tina with fear and uncertainty in her eyes. Tina smiled and held out her hands.

The grace of God took over and saw to everything else.

Ingrid Albuquerque-Solomon

Awakening

Rashmi Anand has such an amiable personality that it is hard to believe she has gone through immense suffering. Hers is a story of pain, struggle, grit, hope and success. The horrors she endured for ten years in a violent marriage could easily break a person, physically and emotionally but the forty-four-year-old chose to fight and has emerged victorious.

Born into a well-to-do family and pampered by her parents, Rashmi enjoyed a comfortable existence at her Kolkata home. Her life took a dramatic turn eighteen years ago, when she shifted to Delhi after her marriage. Her husband made endless demands for dowry and his needs were insatiable. He would become violent, and at first, a bout of violence was followed by profuse apologies. But soon, he would become violent again. And it wasn't only the husband; Rashmi's mother-in-law was also an accomplice, which added to her miseries. Physically and emotionally abused, Rashmi was forced to wear high-collared and full-sleeved clothes even in summer to hide her injury marks.

Violence became the order of the day and Rashmi had

to put up with the torture and remain silent, as she was pregnant. But that didn't stop her husband from beating her up. She was thrown down the staircase when she was four months pregnant.

The shame of speaking out against the torture forced her to bear the abuse heaped upon her. To make matters worse, her husband stopped giving her money towards household expenses. Rashmi began freelancing from home to support herself and the baby. But soon things took an uglier turn. During her second pregnancy, she was hospitalised twice — once after her husband smashed her face and again, after being battered over some trivial issue. She somehow managed to hold herself together to deliver her second child.

It wasn't easy for Rashmi to muster the courage to go to a police station and file a complaint against her abusive husband. Social ridicule and peer pressure didn't matter much when her five-year-old son stopped talking and her nine-year-old daughter turned into a recluse. After all, they were witness to the daily routine of torture that their mother went through. 'For years, I'd forgotten who I was,' said Rashmi. 'I was suppressed, harassed and violated in every way, physically, mentally and emotionally.'

But one morning, after suffering for ten years, she decided it was time to put a stop to a life of ignominy. 'At some point, the awakening has to come. One says enough, no more. I walked out of a miserable, constricting, violent world and into my own,' she said.

With the help of the police and a few NGOs, Rashmi got a divorce and the custody of her children. The divorce marked the beginning of her journey of self-discovery. At thirty-five, she published her first collection of poems, 'Woman of Elements'. The educationist Abha Adams, Lok Sabha Speaker Meira Kumar, well-known retired cop Kiran Bedi and environmentalist Vandana Shiva wrote forewords and the book was released by the All India Women's Conference.

Rashmi's book soon turned into a source of inspiration for many. Her new born freedom translated into a collection of inspirational stories, *A Heart that Honours*. It was published in 2007 and in this book, Rashmi writes about love, destiny, hope, the courage of conviction, willpower, justice, roots and gratitude. This was followed by *Journey of the Goddess*, a work on the soul's eternal quest for truth. She has also written a book for children and is currently working on what she calls a book 'on death'.

Laurels and recognition followed. Rashmi became the face of Delhi Police's 2010 calendar, which was based on her book and her life.

'I died many times. Now I want to live and I'm enjoying every moment of it. I do not see myself as a victim. I am a woman who has come through, and the first step towards coming through was having faith in myself. I believe in joy, in honouring, treasuring and cherishing every moment and in truly living out every facet of life. I do all that my heart tells me to, and all that my conscience allows. I have been through a lot in life, but I do not believe that pain is unique to me — all of us suffer in different ways, it is just that my problems are more obvious than those of others. And this is all the more reason for each one of us to find joy wherever and as often as we can,' said Rashmi.

But what keeps her going is a reminder of what she went

through in life. 'I don't want to forget anything — not even for a moment. Only then will I feel the pain of the woman in front of me.'

For now she sits in Room No. 103, Nanakpura Police Station, the very place she went to as a victim, battered and bruised, seeking justice. She counsels women in the dedicated crime cell for women. Incidentally, Rashmi will be soon publishing her new book *Room No. 103, Nanakpura Police Station*, which chronicles the stories of several women she has counselled. It is as if justice has come full circle to inspire thousands who can only dream of a better tomorrow. Rashmi stands as a symbol of hope and an icon of courage in a world where freedom is often just a seven-letter word.

Preetha Nair

Who's Listening?

How could she have done this to me? I'm feeling knocked out and emotionless!

I want to talk to somebody, 'Lord, and I know You are listening.'

I may be single but I am not alone. Not since that night when you stopped me from doing something very foolish. My husband had just abandoned me; I was left to fend for our young children; overwhelmed with dread, pain and emptiness, I was on the way to end my life. The plan was to walk into the sea and to keep walking. From a point ironically called 'Land's End'.

Then it happened. I don't know whether I found You or You found me. You were there; You held my hand and led me out of the deep waters, both physically and metaphorically.

I was born again.

You said to me, 'Fear not, I am with you.' I could hear You but I could not believe You. You continued, 'I will never leave you, nor will I forsake you.'

It took months to actually fathom the depths of Your love,

and to believe You. I have been on a roll ever since. Twenty years have gone by. I've never felt alone for a single minute.

Today is one of those days, Lord, when I need to talk. I want to talk to somebody, Lord, and I know You are listening. A friend has betrayed my trust and I don't know how to deal with it. I'd felt the need of a mentor, and somehow I imagined and wanted to believe that You had sent her my way. She befriended me, came regularly to pray with me, she appeared to be so loving and caring.

I was filled with delight at the friendship and wanted to run into the streets proclaiming, 'Stop, world, and listen. I have finally found the perfect friend.' I was so blinded by my delight that I wanted to respond to her friendship in word and deed. In my slavish gratitude, I became a sitting duck for what followed.

She exploited my vulnerability for her own needs. She began to use my skills to fulfil her dreams. I was almost completely exploited.

Then it happened. Once again, I do not know how it happened but You were there. My eyes opened. I realised what was happening. I walked out of her project. Just in time to save my soul.

My soul saved, my skills and energy too. But that did not stop me from staggering under the piercing aftermath of betrayal.

I want to understand this today. Why do people betray?

I cannot discuss this with my children or other friends. Everyone is either busy or concealed behind walls.

Walls that are self-made, walls of work, walls of silence, even walls of words.

Thank God that with You there are no walls. You understand my emotions, You are privy to my thoughts, You sort them out.

You are making me see, Lord, that I've acted like a fool; I have brought this problem upon myself. Of course, we need to be open to friendship and relationship. You want us to love one another. You would always want us to be kind and generous with the gifts and skills that You have bestowed upon us. But above all, You want us to be wise. To know where to draw the line, to function within boundaries that protect our vulnerability and preserve our souls.

We single women sometimes tend to forget that.

Starved of affection, when the slightest glimpse of appreciation comes our way, we turn crazy. 'Someone actually loves the unworthy me!' We lose our balance. We give more than we should. We give without being asked. We give everything that we have. Then suddenly we discover we are spiritually bankrupt.

My heart is filled with hostilities. I feel hurt, disappointed, dismayed, let down. I feel buffeted and bruised and knocked almost witless.

Now who's going to pick up the pieces?

You, Lord. As always.

You do it with such style. First, by showing me how I brought all this mess upon myself. Then, You bless me, by helping me, by giving me the courage to face up to my own mistakes. You help me to face the truth about myself, however bitter the truth may be. You stop me from being overpowered by the gravity of my faults.

It's not an easy process. It plunges me into the depths of remorse. There I wash myself clean. You erase the hostilities and help me to approach the day with peace in my heart. I learn once more not to put my trust in people, but in You.

Thank you for sorting me out Lord, for unwinding me, for unlocking me. I am no longer angry or sad, or frozen with the pain of betrayal. I feel so free, flowing joyfully, softly, gently, into Your healing rest.

And the biggest miracle of all!

I am able to still love my friend. The forgiveness is so complete, without reservation and with a more mature affection. I am able to see how vulnerable and needy she is, too.

I pray You will bless her as You have blessed me.

Ingrid Albuquerque-Solomon

The Divine Touch

When I got married in my teens it was against the wishes of my family. Except for my mother, others severed relations with me forever. But to my relief, they did give me five cents of land, on which my husband and I built a small thatched hut. Later, my mother came to live in my house when my son was born.

My husband was a driver of heavy vehicles and was often away from home on long trips. When he was at home, he did not share any responsibilities and worse still, spent most of what he earned on alcohol. A common story! Let me cut out the details — we were fast drifting apart.

By the time my baby was a year old we were in really bad shape. I couldn't work, as my mother did not have the energy to attend to an infant on her own. No one would hire a twenty-six-year-old woman with a small baby as a housemaid, either. Occasionally, my aged mother earned a paltry sum from plaiting coconut fronds for thatching roofs. We could barely afford one proper meal a day and were often starving.

One day, an old lady, whom we called Varkala Amma, dropped in. My son was crying incessantly. When she asked, out of genuine concern, what the matter was, I told her the truth: 'He is just hungry!'

Varkala Amma was upset when she heard there were no provisions in the house and gave me fifty paisa to buy something immediately. I took the money gratefully and got some food. After a while Varkala Amma said, 'I shall take you to a place where you can have a satisfying meal.' She said it was a house of prayer and it would be really nice if I could somehow make a small offering — say, a packet of joss sticks. There was absolutely no money in the house that day. I searched for something that could be sold or pawned and eventually found my steel tiffin box from my school days. I pawned it with a neighbour who gave me ten rupees.

Varkala Amma paid my bus fare. We started out next morning and travelled some thirty kilometres to a place near Pothencode in Thiruvananthapuram district. We had to cover the last kilometre or so by foot, and finally reached an ashram named Santhigiri.

We did not have to wait for long to see the founder of the ashram, Navajyothi Sree Karunakara Guru. The moment the guru set his eyes on me, he said, 'Take this woman to the dining hall and give her food immediately.' We were fed delicious rice-gruel and tapioca. I couldn't even remember when my son and I had last eaten to our heart's content.

We were then summoned to the guru's presence. After being told about me, he gave us some toffees: 'Eat and see if it tastes good.'

I took a toffee from its wrapper and put it in my mouth, 'Yes!'

'Is there anything special?' the guru asked.

'It tastes like a toffee,' I said, puzzled by his question. He smiled and sent us away, asking me to visit now and then.

And that is what I did in the days that followed. I would set aside a few paisas from my mother's erratic earnings for those visits. Sometimes, he himself would give me money even if I had my bus fare with me.

Soon I was possessed by a desire to make offerings to the guru. When I had nothing else to offer, I picked beautiful wild flowers and he accepted them graciously. Gradually, prayer and devotion became a small but vital part of my life.

Somewhere within me a strength was being awakened and I soon had the courage to make it clear to my husband that it was better for us to part ways.

I got a job as a cook in the nurses' hostel in Thiruvananthapuram. Though I was not trained for such a task I took up the challenge, leaving my son in my mother's care. My salary of forty-five rupees was a great relief to us. In addition, the nurses gave me generous tips. The superintendent even gave my son a uniform and school bag. In the midst of all this I was able to visit the ashram from time to time.

My mother died after three years. I could not manage my son and the job, so I asked the guru what I must do. He gave me a handful of currency without counting them, and said: 'Leave the hospital and do something on your own. Do whatever you like ...'

What he gave was a lot of money for me at the time. I still treasure a part of it in the room where I worship. After much consideration I chose to be a vendor of vegetables and fish in my locality. Over a period I got a number of regular customers and did well for myself. Once a week I would deliver fresh vegetables to the guru's kitchen. I was able to start saving small amounts of money. I bought a calf and named her Shanti Mol or 'my daughter Shanti'. She was only a few days old and had to be bottle-fed. She grew up to be a beautiful, loving cow but calved only once. The calf was given in godaan (the ritual gift of a cow) to the guru on one of the special occasions in the ashram.

My son completed his schooling and joined the Ayurveda pharmaceuticals in the ashram. He seldom stayed with me after that. He is a father now, and lives independently with his family. I have always lived in Karikkakom, near a small river called Parvati Puthanar. In place of my old hut, I now have a proper house with a fairly comfortable cowshed for twenty-seven-year-old Shanti Mol. I gave up selling vegetables in my locality some years ago. Now I am a wholesaler for limited items and need to spend only a few hours in the Chalai market.

The awareness that the Creator provides for all creatures unseen has grown into a conviction. In my mind, the guru has come to represent that Abstract Absolute in its kindest aspect. It is a mystery how guidance came unsought, to a poor woman on the solitary path of her bitter struggles!

It is a mystery how His Grace descended unsought to redeem and strengthen that rash woman who made a mess of her life, defying her family in her teens.

Vanaja
(*As told to O.V. Usha*)

More Chicken Soup?

Share your heart with the rest of the world. If you have a story, poem or article (your own or someone else's) that you feel belongs in a future volume of Chicken Soup for the Indian Soul, please email us at cs.indiansoul@westland-tata.com or send it to:

Westland Ltd
S-35A, 3rd Floor
Green Park Main Market
New Delhi 110 016

We will make sure that you and the author are credited for the contribution. Thank you!

Contributors

Abhilasha Agarwal works in Kolkata with Kritagya, an organisation that cares for the aged. She also writes poetry and fiction, which has been published in leading newspapers and on vcherish.com. She has written an e-book, *Vibrant Palette* and her poetry was part of Transportraits, organised by Jagori at the India Habitat Centre. Contact: abcal37@yahoo.co.in.

Aditya Sondhi practices and teaches law in Bangalore. He writes when time permits, which is seldom. Aditya has authored a work of non-fiction titled *Unfinished Symphony* for Penguin (India) and has ranked among the top-three winners of the Deccan Herald Short Story Competition, 2010. He can be reached at: aditya.sondhi@gmail.com.

Ambika Pillai is a diverse personality. Married young, her life revolves around her daughter, Kavitha. Ambika's profession as a make-up artiste and hair stylist, which started as a necessity, became a rocking success much to her (though not others') surprise. Her latest passion is jotting down her life's events.

Amisha Shah, an architect, lives in California with her husband and son. She has worked as an architect and interior designer in Mumbai and then as Principal Correspondent for *BuildoTech,* a magazine for sustainable building technologies. Her hobbies include Bharatnatyam, reading, art appreciation and playing the violin. Contact: shah_ami@hotmail.com.

Anita Jaswal is married to an army officer. She spent eleven years teaching pre-primary classes and now does freelance editing and content writing. She enjoys working with animals and children, and would love to teach the latter about nature and wildlife. Contact: neetujaswal22@gmail.com.

Anuradha Gupta, a US-based writer, earlier worked in the corporate field and now volunteers in the non-profit sector. She is glad to be back to writing which is her first love and also helps her support causes that matter to her, like sustainable development. Contact: anusharma86@yahoo.com.

Anuradha Nalapat is a professional artist and has exhibited her paintings throughout India. Her poetry has been published by Writers' Workshop, Unisun, the Sahitya Akademi and other journals. Her short stories have been translated into Malayalam by Poorna Publishers. See her work at www.anunalapat.com.

Anushree Karnani is a business developer with a fashion house in Kolkata and mother to her ten-year-old daughter. She has been writing since childhood. She has written for *Chicken Soup for Indian Soul at Work*, as well. Contact: anushree76@gmail.com.

Archna Pant has worked as an advertising professional. She was in charge of Corporate Communications for Kelvinator, prior to which she was with *The Indian Express*. A management graduate, she passionately believes that words are the bridge through which we can reach many lives, many souls. Reach her at archna22@hotmail.com.

Arjun K. Bose is a businessman settled in Kolkata. He has a keen interest in literature, fine arts, films and music — in short, all things creative, in spite of being a commerce student. He can be contacted at basuarjun@gmail.com.

Asha Francis has always been fascinated by the written word. After working as a lecturer and German language trainer, she is now a training lead at Hewlett Packard. Read her work at ashreflections.blogspot.com and in *Ripples*, an anthology of short stories by Indian women writers.

Averil Gomes is a lawyer, who loves tramping across the Himalayas (backpack on someone else's back), while she explores and writes about

CONTRIBUTORS

the people in her head who stomp around screaming for attention. She also makes little clay men and hopes to create a clay woman or two, should they choose to venture out.

Averil Nunes is currently researching truth, meaning, love, faith and beauty in the laboratory of life. Maybe one day she'll figure it all out and write and illustrate a book about her experiments. In the meantime, you can exchange a word or two with her at averil.nunes@gmail.com.

Bharati Mirchandani freelances as a graphic designer and writer. She has diverse interests, which include a passion for India, people, spirituality, education and values, health, ecology and sustainable development, which she explores through travelling, writing, drawing, photography and just being. Email: 2manavi@gmail.com.

Bhawana Somayya has been a film critic for thirty years, contributing to several leading newspapers. She was the editor of *Screen* and has authored nine books. She is currently on the Advisory Panel of the Censor Board of Film Certificate. She is also a film expert for 92.7 Big FM, does film reviews for the BBC and is working on three more books on cinema. She can be reached at: contact@bhawanasomaaya.com.

Eva Bell is a gynaecologist and also a freelance writer. Her articles, short stories and children's stories have been published in magazines, newspapers, on the net, and in several anthologies. She is a published author of three novels, two children's books, and three e-books. Website: www.evabell.net, blog: http://muddyloafers.blogspot.com

Hemant Patil is a Pune-based lifestyle and architectural photographer. His work has featured in leading design magazines of India. A versatile and experienced photographer, he has worked with several advertising agencies and business houses. Contact: exposureone@gmail.com.

Ingrid Albuquerque-Solomon has been associated with mainstream media for thirty-nine years. She has been the editor of several national publications including *Stardust, Savvy* and *Bangalore Times*. She has launched a publishing company and authored several books. Currently, she works for Haggai Institute International, a leadership institute which trains Christian professionals. Contact: ingridalbuquerque@yahoo.com.

Jael Silliman has extensive work experience in the field of women's rights and was an Associate Professor of Women's Studies. She has been a donor, writer and activist in the transnational feminist movement. Her books include *Jewish Portraits, Indian Frames: Women's Narratives From A Diaspora of Hope*. She has two daughters and lives in Kolkata.

Joie Bose Chatterjee has degrees in Literature from St. Xavier's College, Kolkata and JNU, New Delhi. Previously a freelance journalist and educator, her creative endeavours have been published in newspapers and anthologies. Settled in Kolkata, she is working on her collection of short stories and can be contacted at joiebose@gmail.com.

Khursheed Dinshaw is a Pune-based freelance writer with more than six hundred twenty published articles in major Indian newspapers and magazines. An avid traveller, she writes on lifestyle, travel, health, food, trends, people and culture. She has also undertaken editing for publications and can be reached at khursheeddinshaw@hotmail.com.

Monika Pant is an English language teacher. She has authored several English textbooks and her short stories have been published in various collections. She is currently writing a couple of novels based on her experiences with students and as a cancer survivor. She can be reached at mpant65@gmail.com.

Mumukshu Mohanty writes because her day job demands it and sometimes, simply, because there is a story to be told. Either way, she believes in writing with honesty and simplicity. She can be reached at mumukshum@gmail.com.

Namratha A. Kumar is a freelance writer, staying in Bandra, Mumbai. She roots for the underdog, and devours fantasy and graphic novels. Contact: namratha2006@yahoo.co.in.

Nandita D'Souza is a developmental and behavioural paediatrician, whose *raison d'etre* is children and all who care for them. Her 'arrested development' is an asset, she believes. She prefers to write in her head, though on rare occasions guilt propels her to pen down her thoughts.

Nina Irani is a homemaker who doubles as an agony aunt for her daughters' friends. She has travelled extensively and can be contacted at irani.nina@gmail.com.

Nonda Chatterjee was earlier the Principal at Calcutta International School and is currently the Principal of Cambridge School, Kolkata. She is the only Indian to receive 'The Cambridge Inspirational Teacher Award'. Her stories and articles have appeared in leading journals and newspapers. *The Strawberry Patch*, a collection of short stories, was published in 2004 and her first novel, *Half A Face*, in 2010.

Parul Gupta is an alumnus of DSE and a former journalist with *The Observer* group. She is currently writing stories for the Chicken Soup for the Soul series, newspapers and magazines, and executing research analysis projects in the social sector with various NGOs. Contact: parulmudita@hotmail.com; Website: www.wordsandmore.in.

Preetha Nair is a journalist by profession and considers gender issues crucial to any meaningful change. Her ideals are reflected in her work in some of the leading dailies in India. What really fascinates her are the small joys that people often experience doing some of the most ordinary things in life.

Raamesh Gowri Raghavan moonlights as a copywriter by day, though his real profession is 'budding novelist'. He believes his chief talent is in inventing really funny jokes though sadly most of his friends do not share that sentiment. He lives in Thane, near Mumbai, and hopes to be remembered with 'tears' centuries from now. Contact: azhvan@yahoo.co.in.

Radhika Chandiramani, a clinical psychologist, is the Executive Director of TARSHI, an NGO in New Delhi. She works on issues of sexuality and rights. She has written *Good Times for Everyone: Sexuality Questions, Feminist Answers* (Women Unlimited, 2008) and co-edited *Sexuality, Gender and Rights: Exploring Theory and Practice in South and South East Asia* (Sage, 2005).

Radhika Singh has done her MPhil thesis on the textile industry from Jawaharlal Nehru University. She started Delhi's first photo agency, Fotomedia, and since 1987 has produced audio-visuals, worked as a consultant photo editor and been the curator for photo exhibitions in India and abroad. Her first book, *The Fabric of our Lives: The Story of Fab India* was published by Penguin in 2010.

Rajyashree Dutt is a writer, editor and publisher, working primarily in the development sector (www.write-arm.com). She also runs an art gallery in Bangalore (www.right-lines.com). She loves acting, bird watching, travelling, her dachshund, and writing. Contact: mamadutt@gmail.com.

Ranjan Pal always wanted to write but the demands of making a living sidetracked him into preparing professional macroeconomic reports for investors. This was in his role as Chief Economist for Jardine Fleming, the leading investment bank in Asia during the roaring nineties. Now he revels in the luxury of writing for himself.

Reema Moudgil is the author of *Perfect Eight*, editor of *Chicken Soup for the Indian Woman's Soul*, occasional RJ, compulsive painter and a full-time mom to a son and two cats. She has been a journalist since 1994 and has written for leading newspapers, assorted magazines and is toying with the idea of starting a website for writers.

Ritika Chawla is a post-graduate in HR Management and is currently working with an organisation called 'Teach for India'. She teaches standard two children in a municipal school in Mumbai. A 'people's person', she loves reading, blogging and travelling. She also loves figuring out directions and sleeping!

Roma Kapadia is a freelance writer. Her work has appeared in numerous international and Indian publications. She has also contributed to *Chicken Soup for the Soul: Indian Women*. She is an avid reader and her varied interests include fashion designing, skin care, cooking, singing, music and dancing. Contact: roma.kapadia@hotmail.com.

Saadiya Kochar is a photographer. At the age of twenty-four, she published a book titled *Being*. Her exhibitions on Sufism, nudes and on female stereotypes are an expression of her intrinsic journey. She is currently working on two books: one on the natural beauty of Kashmir and the other on the lives of Kashmiri women.

Sanaea Patel is an avid travel writer who loves travelling, listening to music and reading non-fiction. Contact: sanaea.patel@hotmail.com.

Sandhya Mendonca is a journalist turned media entrepreneur who co-founded Raintree Media with her husband Allen Mendonca, a columnist and writer. After his untimely death, she initiated 'Under the Raintree', a not-for-profit forum for creative exchanges in literature and arts 'to keep the conversation going'. Contact: sandhyamendonca@gmail.com.

Sarita Varma is a freelance writer and has written inspirational short stories for *Plan India* and articles for websites and magazines on history, travel and health. She is a volunteer with the Pune Chapter of the Multiple Sclerosis Society of India and has represented them at national and international conferences. Contact: saritas56@gmail.com.

Shalini Saran has been a freelance writer, photographer and editor for more than twenty-five years. Her work has been widely published and she has held exhibitions of both her photographs and digital drawings. She lives in Gurgaon.

Shaphali Jain lives in Florida, with her husband and two children. She is a writer in every spare moment and has edited and published a South Asian print publication. She has recently finished her first work of fiction, *The Cracked Paperweight*. Contact: shaphalijain@gmail.com.

Sharada Balasubramaniam is a journalist. Her articles have appeared in publications like *Tehelka*, *The Hindu Business Line* and *Outlook*. Sharada also loves creative writing and her short story was published in an anthology, *Ripples*, with twenty-five other women writers from India. Know more about her on www.sharadawrites.com.

Shifa Maitra is a full-time media professional and a part-time writer. She is currently creative director at UTV Bindass. She has written TV shows, live events, title tracks and songs for a feature film. She has also written for *Chicken Soup for the Romantic Indian Soul*, *Chicken Soup for the Soul: Indian Mothers* and *Chicken Soup for the Soul: Indian Fathers*. Contact: shifamaitra@gmail.com.

Shikha Aleya wanders regularly between writing, research and working with people and animals, and on themes that matter to her. She is focusing on creating spaces and support systems for caregivers. She often carries her laptop during pet sitting sessions and balances reading and writing with feeding the cat and walking the dog.

Shoumik De is an IT Engineer by profession and a writer by choice. One winter afternoon in Gurgaon, he decided to quit the cantankerous corporate world and pursue his passion. Writing came naturally to him. Shoumik is a voracious reader, loves to travel and is a photographer. Contact: shoumikde@gmail.com.

Srinath Girish practices law in Kochi and Calicut. His articles have appeared in the *Indian Express* and his short stories have been published by Penguin India (BlogPrint2008) and Westland (*Chicken Soup for the Soul: Indian Fathers*). He blogs at www.sulekha.com. He lives in Calicut with his mother, wife Rathna and son. Contact: srinathgirish@gmail.com.

Dr Sruti Mohapatra fights for the rights and dignities of the differently-abled from her wheelchair. She is a teacher by profession and disability activist by passion. She has written a collection of poems, *Echoes*, as well as two books on disability. She is the founder and chief executive of Swabhiman, a disability information and resource centre, and is the recipient of several awards, the most recent being the CNN-IBN Real Hero Award 2010.

Tanya Mendonsa is a poet and a painter. After nineteen years running a language school in Paris, she returned to India. Harper Collins published her first book of poetry, *The Dreaming House* in 2009. She is currently working on her second book, *All The Answer I Shall Ever Get*.

O.V. Usha has worked as an editor with Tata McGraw-Hill and Vikas, in Delhi. Later, she became Director of Publishing, M.G. University, Kerala and is now Associate Editor, Santhigiri Research Foundation. She is a well-known Malayalam writer and has published four collections of poems, a novel and five collections of non-fiction. She lives in Santhigiri Ashram, Trivandrum.

Vaishali Shroff is a part-time consultant, full-time writer, and an overtime mother. She believes short stories have the power to transform lives. Amongst her other work, 'Raindrops' is her first story to have appeared in *Chicken Soup for the Soul: Indian Women* and she continues writing stories, poems and a dream book. Contact: vaishali.shroff@gmail.com.

Varun Todi is twenty-four years old, an ex-advertising guy and co-founder of 'Oye Happy', a venture specialising in creating surprises. When not surprising people, he's happiest writing short stories in a corner of his 168 sq. ft. room in Bangalore. He can be reached at varun@oyehappy.com.

Vishakha Rana is an avid reader, inspirational writer and an animal lover. As a management professional, she continues to pursue her career in the fields of writing, consulting and research. Vishakha is associated with development programmes for blind children. She also loves travelling and dancing, high-energy workouts and long drives.

Xerses Irani is fond of listening to music and communicating with Danny, his pet dog. In between, he experiments with his mechanical mind. He can be contacted at xersesglb@hotmail.com.

Permissions

A Perfect Life. Reprinted by permission of Arjun Bose. © 2011 Arjun Bose.

Mother, Not Martyr. Reprinted by permission of Ingrid Albuquerque-Solomon. © 2011 Ingrid Albuquerque-Solomon.

Vermilion at Amber Light. Reprinted by permission of Anuradha Nalapat. © 2011 Anuradha Nalapat.

God, Why Me? Reprinted by permission of Ambika Pillai. © 2011 Ambika Pillai.

Shaped by Nature. Reprinted by permission of O.V. Usha. © 2011 O.V. Usha.

A Dream and a Mojo. Reprinted by permission of Vaishali Shroff. © 2011 Vaishali Shroff.

The Little Girl's Town. Reprinted by permission of Shifa Maitra. © 2011 Shifa Maitra.

Amma. Reprinted by permission of Radhika Singh. © 2011 Radhika Singh.

How I Found My Inner Dog. Reprinted by permission of Tanya Mendonsa. © 2011 Tanya Mendonsa.

Holding Out for an Elusive Hero. Reprinted by permission of Namratha Kumar. © 2011 Namratha Kumar.

Strange and Lovely Things Happen. Reprinted by permission of Radhika Chandiramani. © 2011 Radhika Chandiramani.

Awaiting a Wedding. Reprinted by permission of Bharati Mirchandani. © 2011 Bharati Mirchandani.

Married, Yet Single! Reprinted by permission of Roma Kapadia. © 2011 Roma Kapadia.

Status? Umm ... Single. Reprinted by permission of Mumukshu Mohanty. © 2011 Mumukshu Mohanty.

Till Death Do Us Part. Reprinted by permission of Anuradha Gupta. © 2011 Anuradha Gupta.

Escapade. Reprinted by permission of Joie Bose. © 2011 Joie Bose.

Find Yourself. Reprinted by permission of Ritika Chawla. © 2011 Ritika Chawla.

Single at Forty. Reprinted by permission of Reema Moudgil. © 2011 Reema Moudgil.

Window to the Soul. Reprinted by permission of Saadiya Kochar. © 2011 Saadiya Kochar.

It's Only Fair. Reprinted by permission of Shifa Maitra. © 2011 Shifa Maitra.

The Single Soul. Reprinted by permission of Bhawana Somaaya. © 2011 Bhawana Somaaya.

Following the Tambourine Man. Reprinted by permission of Tanya Mendonsa. © 2011 Tanya Mendonsa.

The Singles' Club. Reprinted by permission of Shifa Maitra. © 2011 Shifa Maitra.

Love in Licatuc. Reprinted by permission of Srinath Girish. © 2011 Srinath Girish.

Single in India. Reprinted by permission of Sandhya Mendonca. © 2011 Sandhya Mendonca.

One Last Sip of Sap. Reprinted by permission of Tanya Mendonsa. © 2011 Tanya Mendonsa.

Single Belle, Single Belle, Single All the Way. Reprinted by permission of Ingrid Albuquerque-Solomon. © 2011 Ingrid Albuquerque-Solomon.

Twice Married. Reprinted by permission of Khursheed Dinshaw. © 2011 Khursheed Dinshaw.

My Story. Reprinted by permission of Varun Todi. © 2011 Varun Todi.

Free as a Bird. Reprinted by permission of Sarita Varma. © 2011 Sarita Varma.

Culinary Adventures. Reprinted by permission of Hemant Patil. © 2011 Hemant Patil.

My Nomadic Daughter. Reprinted by permission of Nina Irani. © 2011 Nina Irani.

Sister Lavinia. Reprinted by permission of Eva Bell. © 2011 Eva Bell.

Ann's Date-o-logy. Reprinted by permission of Khursheed Dinshaw. © 2011 Khursheed Dinshaw.

Rocking K. Reprinted by permission of Hemant Patil. © 2011 Hemant Patil.

Family in Court. Reprinted by permission of Ingrid Albuquerque-Solomon. © 2011 Ingrid Albuquerque-Solomon.

Jacob's Joy. Reprinted by permission of Nina Irani. © 2011 Nina Irani.

Sisters-in-Arms. Reprinted by permission of Nandita D'Souza. © 2011 Nandita D'Souza.

Remembering My Father. Reprinted by permission of Ranjan Pal. © 2011 Ranjan Pal.

A Debt for Life. Reprinted by permission of Roma Kapadia. © 2011 Roma Kapadia.

An Army Couple. Reprinted by permission of Anuradha Gupta. © 2011 Anuradha Gupta.

My Dad, Superman. Reprinted by permission of Sanaea Patel. © 2011 Sanaea Patel.

Oh, Alisha! Reprinted by permission of Preetha Nair. © 2011 Preetha Nair.

Pop Tate, Take a Bow. Reprinted by permission of Aditya Sondhi. © 2011 Aditya Sondhi.

No Child's Play. Reprinted by permission of Preetha Nair. © 2011 Preetha Nair.

Dreams are Forever. Reprinted by permission of Sruti Mohapatra. © 2011 Sruti Mohapatra.

PERMISSIONS

A Turn of Events. Reprinted by permission of O.V. Usha. © 2011 O.V. Usha.

Arunchandra, My Teacher. Reprinted by permission of Khursheed Dinshaw. © 2011 Khursheed Dinshaw.

The Caregiver. Reprinted by permission of Bharati Mirchandani. © 2011 Bharati Mirchandani.

Against All Odds. Reprinted by permission of Roma Kapadia. © 2011 Roma Kapadia.

A Count of Blessings. Reprinted by permission of Shaphali Jain. © 2011 Shaphali Jain.

Amazing Grace. Reprinted by permission of Shalini Saran. © 2011 Shalini Saran.

Nobody's Single in a Community. Reprinted by permission of Anuradha Gupta. © 2011 Anuradha Gupta.

Cooking and Singing. Reprinted by permission of Nina Irani. © 2011 Nina Irani.

In Quiet Confidence. Reprinted by permission of Eva Bell. © 2011 Eva Bell.

A Giver to the End. Reprinted by permission of Monika Pant. © 2011 Monika Pant.

Vikram, My Inspiration. Reprinted by permission of Sanaea Patel. © 2011 Sanaea Patel.

Radha Bai. Reprinted by permission of Anita Jaswal. © 2011 Anita Jaswal.

Sheela Bua. Reprinted by permission of Archana Pant. © 2011 Archana Pant.

OSCAR-Worthy. Reprinted by permission of Roma Kapadia. © 2011 Roma Kapadia.

The Bigger Picture. Reprinted by permission of Preetha Nair. © 2011 Preetha Nair.

Standing on My Feet. Reprinted by permission of O.V. Usha. © 2011 O.V. Usha.

St. Joseph and the Spirit-Filled Husband. Reprinted by permission of Averil Nunes. © 2011 Averil Nunes.

Being Single. Reprinted by permission of Shoumik De. © 2011 Shoumik De.

The Perfect Match. Reprinted by permission of Sarita Varma. © 2011 Sarita Varma.

Women, Journalism and Matrimony. Reprinted by permission of Sharada Balasubramaniam. © 2011 Sharada Balasubramaniam.

Oh! Are You Still Single? Reprinted by permission of Parul Gupta. © 2011 Parul Gupta.

Single Warriors. Reprinted by permission of Xerses Irani. © 2011 Xerses Irani.

So Not ready to Mingle. Reprinted by permission of Shifa Maitra. © 2011 Shifa Maitra.

Single and Fancy-Free. Reprinted by permission of Nonda Chatterjee. © 2011 Nonda Chatterjee.

That Someone Special. Reprinted by permission of Abhilasha Agarwal. © 2011 Abhilasha Agarwal.

The Single Marathon Runner. Reprinted by permission of Roma Kapadia. © 2011 Roma Kapadia.

Suddenly Single. Reprinted by permission of Sandhya Mendonca. © 2011 Sandhya Mendonca.

Towards the Sky. Reprinted by permission of Jael Silliman. © 2011 Towards the Sky.

Bless this Mess! Reprinted by permission of Amisha Shah. © 2011 Amisha Shah.

A New Sunrise. Reprinted by permission of Vishakha Rana. © 2011 Vishakha Rana.

Rainbow in Your Heart. Reprinted by permission of Amisha Shah. © 2011 Amisha Shah.

Fruit Plate. Reprinted by permission of Raamesh Gowri Raghavan. © 2011 Raamesh Gowri Raghavan.

Life is Beautiful. Reprinted by permission of Asha Francis. © 2011 Asha Francis.

Gini. Reprinted by permission of Rajyashree Dutt. © 2011 Rajyashree Dutt.

A Second Chance. Reprinted by permission of Asha Francis. © 2011 Asha Francis.

The Woman with Two Birthdays. Reprinted by permission of Shikha Aleya. © 2011 Shikha Aleya.

Single by Choice. Reprinted by permission of Nonda Chatterjee. © 2011 Nonda Chatterjee.

The Gift of Life. Reprinted by permission of Sarita Varma. © 2011 Sarita Varma.

Resurrected. Reprinted by permission of Monika Pant. © 2011 Monika Pant.

I Look Forward. Reprinted by permission of Anushree Karnani. © 2011 Anushree Karnani.

Mamma's Boy. Reprinted by permission of Hemant Patil. © 2011 Hemant Patil.

The Chanting Room. Reprinted by permission of Sarita Varma. © 2011 Sarita Varma.

Single and Sane. Reprinted by permission of Shifa Maitra. © 2011 Shifa Maitra.

Starting Anew. Reprinted by permission of Sarita Varma. © 2011 Sarita Varma.

Bait of Hate. Reprinted by permission of Ingrid Albuquerque-Solomon. © 2011 Ingrid Albuquerque-Solomon.

Awakening. Reprinted by permission of Preetha Nair. © 2011 Preetha Nair.

Who's Listening? Reprinted by permission of Ingrid Albuquerque-Solomon. © 2011 Ingrid Albuquerque-Solomon.

The Divine Touch. Reprinted by permission of O.V. Usha. © 2011 O.V. Usha.